EXPLODING THE DOOMSDAY MONEY MYTHS

EXPLODING THE DOOMSDAY MONEY MYTHS

Why It's _Not_ Time to Panic

SHERMAN S. SMITH, Ph.D.

THOMAS NELSON PUBLISHERS
Nashville

Published in Nashville, Tennessee, by Thomas Nelson, Inc., Publishers, and distributed in Canada by Word Communications, Ltd., Richmond, British Columbia, and in the United Kingdom by Word (UK), Ltd., Milton Keynes, England.

Scripture quotations are from The Holy Bible, KING JAMES VERSION.

Charts on pages 80 and 88 are reprinted by permission of FORBES magazine. © Forbes Inc., 1993.

Library of Congress Cataloging-in-Publication Data

Smith, Sherman.
    Exploding the doomsday money myths / Sherman Smith.
      p. cm.
    Includes bibliographical references.
    ISBN 0-7852-8182-7
    1. United States—Economic conditions—1981– 2. Economic forecasting—United States. 3. Finance, Personal—United States. 4. Stewardship. Christian. I. Title.
HC106.8.S65 1994
332.024—dc20   93–40959
                                         CIP

Printed in the United States of America
1 2 3 4 5 6 7 — 00 99 98 97 96 95 94

Dedicated to:

Napa Valley Baptist Church
My Family
Alex Colovos
Megan Sue

CONTENTS

. . . .

ACKNOWLEDGMENTS

. . . .

I wish to thank Dr. Rudy Holland, who put my financial ministry on the map and has worked, for the past few years, helping me to get positioned to help others.

I wish to thank my agent, Joyce Hart, who put her reputation on the line, found the publisher, and convinced them to take a look at this book.

I wish to thank my editor, Val Cindric, who believed in this project and worked tenaciously to see it through. Without her commitment, this project could not have been done.

I wish to thank my new friend, Duncan Jaenicke, former senior acquisition editor at Thomas Nelson Publishers, who persuaded his company that this book was worth the risk of capital and who made tremendous input into the project to make it successful.

I wish to thank one of my best friends, Dr. Demas Brubacher, who plodded from library to library, doing research and looking up facts for my doctoral dissertation while I wrote this book. The result of his hard work enabled me to formulate some of those facts into the book you are about to read.

I wish to thank my associate pastors at church, Paul Newell, Roy Williams, Dr. Ray Owen, and especially our executive pastor, Jim Counihan, who took the everyday work load off me so I could attend to this work.

I wish to thank my associates, George McCuen CFP, Tom Gillons, Tom Remboldt, Scott Smith, and Shawn Smith, who encouraged me by taking care of a lot of my financial business while I was traveling or working out of the office during the writing and promotion of this book.

I wish to thank Marilynn Robinson, my longtime personal secretary, whose untiring loyalty and devotion have made it possible for me to jump more than one hurdle through the years.

FOREWORD

. . . .

Americans are obsessed with gloomy prognostications about the future. George Orwell's *1984*, Don Meadow's *Limits to Growth*, Larry Burkett's *Coming Economic Earthquake*, Paul Ehrlich's *The Population Bomb*, and Harry Figgie Jr.'s *Bankruptcy 1995* are examples of such doomsday forecasts. Sherm Smith's book is an antidote to all of this. This book could change your thinking. At the very least, it will cheer you up.

Doomsdayers for centuries have argued that we are about to run out of vital resources—trees, oil, coal, minerals, fertile soil, etc. In sixteenth-century England fears were flamed about the impending wood shortage and the lives that would be lost because people had no wood to warm their homes. Hindsight revealed that the price of wood rose, which led to wood conservation *and* to the development of coal as an alternative heat source. The "wood crisis" was over.

In the 1850s dire predictions were made that the world was running out of whales and hence whale oil, the primary source of artificial lighting. Again, prices were allowed to rise, bringing with them the search for good alternatives. Sure enough, that led to the burning of kerosene for light, and thus ended the whale oil crisis.

Later, as Sherman tells it in this book, doomsday predictions were made about the "oil crisis." In 1914 the Bureau of Mines estimated that only six million barrels of oil remained in the U.S. Then we discovered more. But again in 1926 the Federal Oil Conservation Board told us we had only a seven-year supply of oil. But then we discovered more. Two decades later, the Secretary of the Interior forecast a five-year supply of oil remaining. But rising prices kept leading to finding more oil—and doomsday was extended another year or two. By the 1970s the end-of-the-worlders got really sophisticated. Using computers, the MIT geniuses published their Club of Rome studies, which told us of diminishing resources and the upcoming environmental calamity. And if all that wasn't enough, they predicted that sometime late in the twenty-first century, the population crisis would have us standing shoulder to shoulder.

All of these predictions have been proven wrong.

Three main factors almost always derail such gloomy thinking: political policies change, technology changes, and markets self-correct.

Doomsday forecasters have the inexcusable habit of failing to recognize that prices change people's behavior. Higher costs also exert pressures that lead to policy changes. Private ownership provides people with a strong incentive to conserve as well as to search for substitutes. As relative prices change, producers, innovators, engineers, and entrepreneurs have an incentive to find or invent new substitutes or to conserve—both of which can and will make dim forecasts turn into rosy results.

A strong case could be made for America's upcoming Indian Summer of economic growth. Global expansion, higher savings rates, seventy-five million baby boomers coming into the most productive stages of their lives, manufacturing productivity rising to number one in the world, and many more reasons tell me that the best is yet to come. Sherm does us all a favor by debunking the myths of catastrophe and conspiracy. His book is a most refreshing view of where we have been and where we are going.

—David P. Clarke, Vice President
of a major securities firm

FOREWORD

. . . .

Americans are obsessed with gloomy prognostications about the future. George Orwell's *1984*, Don Meadow's *Limits to Growth*, Larry Burkett's *Coming Economic Earthquake*, Paul Ehrlich's *The Population Bomb*, and Harry Figgie Jr.'s *Bankruptcy 1995* are examples of such doomsday forecasts. Sherm Smith's book is an antidote to all of this. This book could change your thinking. At the very least, it will cheer you up.

Doomsdayers for centuries have argued that we are about to run out of vital resources—trees, oil, coal, minerals, fertile soil, etc. In sixteenth-century England fears were flamed about the impending wood shortage and the lives that would be lost because people had no wood to warm their homes. Hindsight revealed that the price of wood rose, which led to wood conservation *and* to the development of coal as an alternative heat source. The "wood crisis" was over.

In the 1850s dire predictions were made that the world was running out of whales and hence whale oil, the primary source of artificial lighting. Again, prices were allowed to rise, bringing with them the search for good alternatives. Sure enough, that led to the burning of kerosene for light, and thus ended the whale oil crisis.

Later, as Sherman tells it in this book, doomsday predictions were made about the "oil crisis." In 1914 the Bureau of Mines estimated that only six million barrels of oil remained in the U.S. Then we discovered more. But again in 1926 the Federal Oil Conservation Board told us we had only a seven-year supply of oil. But then we discovered more. Two decades later, the Secretary of the Interior forecast a five-year supply of oil remaining. But rising prices kept leading

. . . .

to finding more oil—and doomsday was extended another year or two. By the 1970s the end-of-the-worlders got really sophisticated. Using computers, the MIT geniuses published their Club of Rome studies, which told us of diminishing resources and the upcoming environmental calamity. And if all that wasn't enough, they predicted that sometime late in the twenty-first century, the population crisis would have us standing shoulder to shoulder.

All of these predictions have been proven wrong.

Three main factors almost always derail such gloomy thinking: political policies change, technology changes, and markets self-correct.

Doomsday forecasters have the inexcusable habit of failing to recognize that prices change people's behavior. Higher costs also exert pressures that lead to policy changes. Private ownership provides people with a strong incentive to conserve as well as to search for substitutes. As relative prices change, producers, innovators, engineers, and entrepreneurs have an incentive to find or invent new substitutes or to conserve—both of which can and will make dim forecasts turn into rosy results.

A strong case could be made for America's upcoming Indian Summer of economic growth. Global expansion, higher savings rates, seventy-five million baby boomers coming into the most productive stages of their lives, manufacturing productivity rising to number one in the world, and many more reasons tell me that the best is yet to come. Sherm does us all a favor by debunking the myths of catastrophe and conspiracy. His book is a most refreshing view of where we have been and where we are going.

—David P. Clarke, Vice President
of a major securities firm

PART 1

EXPLODING
THE MYTHS

Not long ago a pastor called my brokerage office to tell me about a recent transaction.

"I cashed out my retirement fund early," he explained. "Of course, I had to pay a 10 percent penalty for early withdrawal [in some cases 20 percent is withheld] and take a tax bite on the added income. It seemed like the right thing to do at the time. Now I'm not so sure."

"Why would you even consider cashing out your retirement?" I asked incredulously.

"I wanted to pay off the mortgage on my house and a few other debts I had," he replied.

"What for?" I quizzed, still trying to understand why he would take such drastic action.

"I read about the 'coming economic earthquake' and thought I'd better get completely out of debt before the final crash," he explained sheepishly. "I didn't want to lose everything and have no place to live. Besides, I figured if these are the last days, like everybody says, I won't need my retirement anyway."

He paused, and I could hear a long sigh on the other end of the line. "At least that's what some people are saying," he said in a low tone.

My gut reaction was to reprimand him for his foolishness, but the distress in his voice made clear that he was already heartsick over his mistake. Besides, he was not to blame. That dear pastor had only followed the advice of popular financial experts whose theories are blindly accepted by many people as the final word on money management.

THE OTHER SIDE OF THE COIN

Since that phone call, I have advised a host of confused Christians who are reacting to the doomsday jargon floating around today. Although it was too late to help that pastor, who now has almost no money for retirement, I have since rescued other clients. Usually cautious, these people were suddenly considering making long-term financial decisions based on man's predictions about the future—predictions that reflect more personal theology than economic principle.

I searched the Christian bookstores, looking for a book to recommend to my clients. *Surely someone has written a rebuttal to these doomsday economic theories,* I thought. Unfortunately, I couldn't find even one. That's when I decided it was time for an author with bona fide financial credentials and who is a qualified Christian minister to step forward and give an opinion on the other side of this economic struggle. That's the reason for this book.

My ministry centers around two intertwining professions. I am first and foremost a full-time Baptist pastor with a love for my church and a passion for the ministry. At the same time, I am also a Registered Principal with the National Association of Securities Dealers and Financial Advisor active in a unique brokerage ministry.

Within the past few years, I have established a securities brokerage business staffed by qualified Christian men and women who desire to use their expertise as financial professionals to serve the Lord. In an effort to bring to the Christian community a sound approach to financial theory, my associates and I provide financial advice and manage investment securities for Christian (and secular) clients, churches, pastors, and missionaries across the United States and around the world.

Once every five weeks I am out of my pulpit to minister in a host church where I present my seminar, "How to Double Your Church's Financial Base." Developed from my experience as a businessman, a pastor, and a financial adviser, this "mini course in business management," as some have called it, focuses on the principles I have learned from Scripture and the education I have received while studying for my M.B.A. and Ph.D. in Business Management.

During the periods of open discussion with the pastors, laypeople, and businesspeople who attend my seminars, one question comes up repeatedly: "Is an economic earthquake imminent?" Wherever I go, people ask me: "Are we headed for the worst financial crash in history?"

During my appearances on Christian television and radio talk shows, listeners call in with questions about the latest economic theories sweeping Christendom. Whenever I mention an opposing opinion to the one espoused in Larry Burkett's books *The Coming Economic Earthquake* and *Investing for the Future,* the phone lines light up.

Although I do believe Larry Burkett provides—in his other books—excellent biblical principles on personal money management for practical, everyday living, I cannot agree with his advice on investments or his predictions for the future of the American economy. By presenting his personal economic theory as a nearly factual forecast, he is, I have to reluctantly say, overstepping his bounds and treading on dangerous ground.

Don't get me wrong. Although Larry Burkett and I may disagree on several points, I respect him as a brother in the Lord. His contributions in the area of personal financial management are practically without parallel in the Christian world. But the field of macroeconomics (the study of national economies) is a different ballgame altogether. For the sake of readers everywhere, I feel constrained to offer another viewpoint on this complex subject. In fact, I'm sure even Larry would admit that there is room among Christian brothers for a second opinion on these controversial and difficult to understand topics.

WHY I DON'T PREDICT THE FUTURE

At our brokerage offices in Napa, California, we receive calls almost daily from people wanting to know what to do with their money in light of the "fact" that the end is near. Many Christians—influenced by economic doomsday books—are afraid to plan for life beyond the year 2000. That's where the danger lies.

The works of several secular economists, such as Harry Figgie's *Bankruptcy 1995* and Joel Kurtzman's *The Death of Money*, are also flooding the market and ending up on the bestsellers' list. All the while, however, they are creating a paranoia in the American public at large. Although the doom and gloom economists say they aren't predicting the future, they use emotional words such as "global depression," "the coming crash," "bankrupt," and "greatest economic calamity of the millennium." No wonder people are scared!

Economic downturns in a free market economy are inevitable. Every economist knows that. Still, whenever we hit a recession, doomsayers come out of the woodwork and predict the worst. Even the most knowledgeable economists in America can't predict what the economy will do from one day to the next—much less what will happen in the next seven years.

I spend most of my time studying the economy, dealing with the markets, and trying to do what is best for my clients, but I don't try to predict the future. My philosophy has always been "Live like Jesus could return at any moment, but plan like He never will." (Of course, Jesus *will* return, but I hope you see my point in this expression: We need to live responsibly each day, as if it might be another thousand years before He comes back.)

My purpose is to show the other side of this unpredictable economic phenomenon we call capitalism. I realize that my ideas will be controversial, but I ask the reader to digest the information with an open mind.

Do I have all the answers? Of course not. I can, however, logically refute some of the money myths being perpetrated in the Christian and secular communities today. In so doing, I hope to dispel fear and keep my readers from making mistakes that will affect both them and their children for years to come.

An instance that embodies the reason I've written this book occurred just a week before my final deadline for this book: One of my biggest customers called and told me to sell all his assets—regardless of the loss—and "put them in gold." Shocked, I probed his reasons and found that he was in the grip of the paranoia of an impending crash. After only twenty minutes discussing this book's material, he was so relieved that he wrote me the following in a thank-you note: "Thanks so much for your advice this morning about my not needing to pull the plug and take my money and run for the hills. You're a lifesaver."

In the chapters to follow, my goal is to paint a realistic picture of the present state of our economy and what could happen in the future. As we look back at history and ahead to the end of this decade, I hope the principles discussed will benefit you—and future generations—no matter what the economic climate.

MYTH ONE:

The End
Is Near!

O ctober 19, 1987, began quietly as I sat at my desk in the offices of Thompson/McKinnon Securities. Suddenly, my Quotron machine indicated a flurry of activity taking place on the New York Stock Exchange.

Before I could react, the market fell 42 points, then 82. My concern turned to shock as numbers on the screen plummeted more than a hundred points and finally ended with the most incredible decline in history—more than 500 points!

Phones rang furiously in every broker's office as news of a market crash shocked clients and the rest of the country on—what we call today—Black Monday.

ENTER THE DOOMSAYERS

Secular doomsday writer Ravi Batra wasted no time in taking advantage of what appeared to be the beginning of the end. His book *The Great Depression of 1990* predicted that the '87 crash would usher in the depression we had all been fearing. Batra's sequel, *Surviving the Great Depression of 1990*, was a feeble attempt to capitalize on the fleeting success of the first best-seller.

Most people have never heard of Ravi Batra or his two books. Why? Because there was no depression in 1990.

Books that predict a future holocaust, however, have long captured the attention of the American public, especially those who feed on disasters and are captivated by tragedies. That's why media reporters, movie producers, and book authors compete to satisfy this insatiable appetite.

Throughout the centuries, doomsayers who have trumpeted, "The end is near!" have always had an audience. The books heralding the fall of our nation are too numerous to mention. From Nostradamus's *Centuries* to George Orwell's *1984*, prediction after prediction has pronounced the death of life as we know it.

But George Orwell missed it; 1984 has come and gone. Americans are not controlled by a Big Brother regime; our living rooms aren't bugged by an ominous electronic eye monitoring our every move; and most Americans are better off financially in the 1990s than any other people in the history of the world.

Since bad news sells, however, the would-be prophets give us what we want and capitalize on our fears all the way to the bank.

WHATEVER HAPPENED TO THE GREAT DEPRESSION?

Tom McGill from Louisville, Kentucky, who was my boss when I worked in the marketing division of International Milling (now International Multifoods), told me his perspective of the Great Depression of 1929.

"I didn't even know one was going on," he told me. "I was a young man starting out and had just bought a new Buick convertible."

"But what about all those stories people tell?" I asked him. "I thought everybody went broke during the Depression."

"Certainly the Great Depression was bad, and I'm not downplaying the pain it caused," he answered. "But the real truth is—not everyone suffered like we've been led to believe."

It's true that about 25 percent of Americans were out of work during the Great Depression, but that certainly wasn't everyone.

Doomsayers today predict that an economic collapse—worse than the Great Depression—is inevitable. But, even in the 1930s, the country did not sink into Third World status as some had predicted. In fact, the United States bounced back as new creative ideas were formulated to get the nation on its feet.

On Black Monday in 1987, however, the shock of the crash overshadowed the fact that America had survived and prospered since the Great Depression of the 1920s. The day after the market crash in 1987, investors hurriedly sold millions of shares of stocks and bonds in an effort to salvage as much of their investment portfolios as possible. Most people reacted out of fear.

That was a big mistake. Why? Because those who held on to their stocks or bought stocks at rock-bottom prices have profited greatly in the last few years. No wonder Ravi Batra's theory about "the great depression of 1990" never caught on.

It's true, however, that since 1990 the United States has been experiencing an economic "correction." Unlike other recent recessions, this one has been particularly long and brutal—but it's not even close to being a depression.

During the 1992 presidential election, the current recession became the main issue. As a result, the campaign rhetoric centered around jobs and the economy, playing on the fears of American voters. Months before the election, the doomsayers were at it again; this time showcasing Larry Burkett's book *The Coming Economic Earthquake*, with its gloom-and-doom predictions about America's future.

What is the theme of that Christian best-seller? William C. Melton, an economist at IDS Financial Services, calls Burkett's theories "repackaged Ravi Batra." Does that mean that all doomsayers and their messages are largely alike?

Perhaps. The writings of most doom-and-gloom authors— whether secular or Christian—have several characteristics in common.

1. They say they aren't predicting anything.
2. They make predictions in spite of what they say.
3. They set dates.
4. They theorize using a sequence of possible events leading to the prediction.
5. They present themselves as experts in the field in question.
6. They tend to distort facts and confuse numbers to support their case.

7. They make attempts to analyze the economy.
8. They create a reactionary environment, often to their followers' detriment.

When it comes to doomsday predictions, unfortunately, religious writers top them all.

DATE SETTING

Some Christians rush to buy any book predicting the fall of our government, the moral decay of our society, or the imminent "economic earthquake disaster of unparalleled magnitude."[1] Yet, these same readers know—from the books they bought several years previously—that predictions about the future seldom come to pass. Remember Edgar Whisenant's book, *88 Reasons Why the Second Advent Could Be in 1988?* That is a classic example of recent date setting.

Whisenant's sixty-seventh reason suggested that the Soviet Union would achieve world domination between 1987 and 1993. As a result, an attack on the capitalistic world was predicted to occur precisely on October 4, 1988, at 5:00 P.M.[2] At that moment, he figured the Soviet military would be at its maximum potential, America would be embroiled in a difficult election, and the United States would be suffering from a deep depression reminiscent of the 1930s.

On the morning before the expected return in 1988, I found several hundred doomsday books on my church doorstep. After reading two paragraphs of Whisenant's theology, I trashed the entire box. That evening, a local church bought thousands of dollars of television time so Whisenant could go on the air and warn the Bay Area about the impending doom.

Today most Christians don't even remember Edgar Whisenant and his predictions. That's why I am convinced that this latest round of doom-and-gloom speculation will soon be only a faint memory in the minds of most Christians. That is, except for those who follow the doomsayers' advice and find themselves in a financial fix with no way out.

In *The Coming Economic Earthquake*, Larry Burkett writes that Ravi Batra used the date prediction in *The Great Depression of 1990* as a gimmick to sell books.[3] But Burkett himself says he is going "to step out on that proverbial limb"[4] with his prediction that the "earthquake" will probably happen somewhere between the years 1994 and 2006.[5] With all due respect, there seems to be a similarity here; if not monetary, then at least the attention-getting aspects of date-setting are in full play.

As a seminary-trained pastor, I have studied eschatology—the biblical theology of the last days. I understand that numerologists place great emphasis on the year 2000, or thereabouts, as the time when all things, as we know them now, will come to an end.

As we move closer to that year, the prophetic preachers will spout their beliefs about the coming Antichrist, and paranoia among Christians will reach extreme bounds. I believe that entire churches will dive into disillusion as numerologists focus on the idea that the Bible teaches that the number six—which represents the Antichrist—is complete in the year 2000. They will proclaim that the number seven, which represents the millennial reign of Christ, starts with the first year of the twenty-first century. Using questionable mathematical calculations concerning the Second Coming, doomsday prophets will present their predictions as unquestionably accurate.

As this decade grinds to a halt, it is possible that one or two religious cults will arise and deceive many Christians. Because their teaching will be more biblical than other false religions—such as the New Age movement—these new cults will attract a large following. They will convince many that the Second Coming of Christ has already occurred but that we did not physically see Him when He came. The same lie deceived many in the 1800s, when several well-known cults got started. Unfortunately, such false teachings about Christ's return are still hanging around today.

That's why I'm so cautious about accepting any theories based on date setting and mathematical arm twisting. Surely Christians have better things to do with their time than trying to figure out the day and the hour—which Jesus said no one knows except the Father.

THEOLOGY, NOT ECONOMICS

Do we really need Christian economics? If so, then why stop there? Why not Christian chemistry, Christian medicine, or Christian political science? The Bible does provide principles that apply to every realm of life, and those are certainly not irrelevant to economics, science, or any other academic study. Christianity, however, is not mainly concerned with any particular field of discipline or learning. Instead, it is concerned with the eternal and everlasting—God's relationship with humans and His redemption of humankind.

What people believe about the last days or the end times usually determines how they approach life in the here and now. Some look at the future with fear, while others view the future with hope.

• *I can only advise one course of action: Plan for a future you can't predict.* • • • • • • •

The study of eschatology centers around four predominant teachings. Permit me to review these in an effort to clarify my point. The different views focus on the Millennium, or the thousand years when Christ will reign on earth, and the Great Tribulation, or the seven-year period when the Antichrist will rule the world.

- Premillennialists believe that Jesus Christ will return and rapture the Church before the period of the Great Tribulation and the subsequent Millennium.
- Postmillennialists set Christ's return and the rapture of the Church as occurring after the Great Tribulation and the millennial reign. They believe Christians will go through the tribulation period.
- Amillennialists do not believe there will be a literal thousand-year reign of Christ on the earth.
- Post-tribulationists believe that all Christians will go through the Tribulation and Christ will return after the Great Tribulation.

In addition, there are the mid-trib-ers who predict that Christ will return in the middle of the Tribulation period—after three and half years—and before the Millennium.

It seems to me that the economic chaos mentioned in Christian doomsayers' books would probably occur at the ushering in of the Antichrist. So, if you are of the opinion that you will go through the Great Tribulation, you might give credence to such claims. If you don't, I can only advise one course of action: Plan for a future you can't predict.

Although I certainly believe we are living in the last days, I don't know that for sure. The only thing I can do is prepare myself spiritually for Christ's return. However, I know of no way to properly prepare myself economically except to follow the basic principles taught in the Bible—principles that, I believe, work in any economic, social, or political climate. I certainly would not sell my house, cash in my retirement, and wait for the Antichrist to appear.

One morning not long ago, a phone call from Austin, Texas, came into my office. The gentleman on the other end of the line was insistent. "Sherm, listen to me and don't argue. Sell all my assets."

"What for?" I asked.

"There's going to be an economic crash, and I don't want to be caught."

"When?"

"In about seven years," he answered.

"Do you realize you will take an enormous penalty plus have to pay a lot of taxes?"

"I realize that, but I want to sell anyway."

"I'd rather not do that, Fred," I answered in disbelief.

"Sherm, sell me out, and send me the money so I can spend it while I still have it."

"Okay, Fred, it's your money, but listen to me first."

I knew he believed the doomsday theory that all money would eventually become worthless and that we'd soon be living in a cashless society.

"I'm writing a new book so people like you can see the other side of the picture. Please listen for a few minutes."

I then explained several reasons why he should not make a rash decision that would ruin him financially. After I finished, he calmly summarized my points. "Then your opinion is to hold the assets, keep putting money away and—since most of it is liquid money anyway— wait until things get a lot worse and then sell."

"That's right, Fred. If there is no economic crash, you will still have all your money."

"Okay," he agreed. "Thanks for the advice. That's what I'm paying you for."

After I hung up the phone, I sat back in my chair and thought, *Now Fred isn't in debt and has plenty of money for retirement, but he believes—because of what he has read—that all of his money is going to be sucked up in an economic disaster. In fact, he is so convinced that he's stressed out, ready to sell everything he owns and spend all his money before it's too late.* Almost every day I encounter people who, like Fred, are reacting to the economic doomsday message with fear and confusion.

Unfortunately, the authors of such books have become economic alarmists and have gone beyond stimulating justifiable concern to creating paranoia and panic. If they truly want to help people, they should not make inflammatory statements nor use their financial adviser status to scare their followers into making foolish mistakes. I'm sure that is not the intent of most authors who write on economic issues.

IF, WHEN, MAYBE . . .

If people like Fred are going to base their financial futures on someone's predictions, they will certainly want to know that the author's facts and figures are correct. With an inexpensive calculator, a little knowledge from *The Wall Street Journal*, and the economic figures published by the U.S. government, we can deduct that some of the discussion in *The Coming Economic Earthquake* is erroneous.

For instance, Burkett claims that cutting defense spending by 25 percent would save the government $10 billion annually. How can that be when, in 1991, the defense budget was $326 billion and a 25 percent savings would equate to $81 billion, not $10 billion?[6]

In another book titled *Investing for the Future*, Burkett suggests that the current, posted on-budget debt of $4 trillion is a farce and that the real debt of the federal government is closer to $8.5 trillion. Using that figure as his basis, he predicts that "by 1996, at the current rate of deficit, it will take all of the taxes paid by all taxpayers to pay the interest on the national debt. The federal government will be spending money at the rate of approximately $7 billion per minute!"[7] It is that kind of statement—made without presenting evidence to back it up—that sends the average person into a financial frenzy.

After predicting America's economic downfall, Burkett claims there will be another depression; when, we don't know precisely, but he writes: A "logical projection is the last half of this decade when government debt reaches the $10 trillion mark and the annual deficit reaches $1 trillion a year!" That hair-raising prediction is followed by the morbid pronouncement, "Depression in a debt-run economy is as certain as death. The question is not IF, but WHEN."[8]

Paradoxically, Burkett claims that, in spite of all that, the economy will recover. Circumstances may then be quite different, he proposes, in that we would no longer use currency as our medium of exchange.[9]

The "key to surviving," however, is to be debt-free and to "have enough cash on hand to buy good assets when the prices are down."[10]

But if we will be living in a cashless economic order, how can we buy *anything?* Won't cash be worthless? In fact, isn't that why Burkett encourages his readers to become debt-free, self-reliant, and to take austerity measures? Because legal tender and paper will be obsolete. Apparently, the situation will be quite serious because Burkett accents his theory with language such as, "earthquake," "bankrupt," and "the greatest economic calamity of the millennium."[11]

To avoid poverty in this new economic order, Burkett counsels his readers to pay off their houses by cashing out their retirement and ignoring the penalty and the taxes incurred as a result. He writes:

> Currently, if you take an early withdrawal on a retirement account, you will have to pay additional taxes and a penalty. . . . Even so, it still makes economic sense to take the penalty and pay the taxes just to know your home is debt-free.[12]

It's my opinion that this kind of specific advice—given without exceptions and failing to take the person's individual circumstances into account—leads to trouble. It's the perfect example of why I feel compelled to write this book.

Burkett's final warning in *The Coming Economic Earthquake,* however, includes this disclaimer:

> I believe I have done what the Lord asked of me: I have warned you. If I am wrong and you do all the things I have suggested, the worst that can happen is that you will end up out of debt and be more involved with our political system.
> If I am right and you do nothing, you'll end up losing everything you own and be totally dependent on the very system that created the mess we are facing. Keep in mind that God has everything under control. You can do your part by giving sacrificially to the Lord's work; if you do, you cannot lose.[13]

I'm afraid that I must respectfully disagree. I believe you have a lot to lose. In fact, if you follow through with some of Burkett's suggestions, you may have nothing left to give to the Lord's work, let alone support your family.

WHAT WILL CRASH?

In *Investing for the Future*, Burkett advises his readers to invest their cashed-out retirement money in mutual funds—the same securities in which their retirement fund had been invested before they removed their money.[14]

If an economic crash is coming, what will crash? The government? Companies? Industry?

What makes all those "no load" mutual funds earn interest? Every financial adviser knows that some mutual funds—no load or those with sales loads—invest in government agency securities such as FHMLC (Federal Home Loan Corp.), Sallie Mae (Student Loan Corp.), Ginnie Mae (Government National Mortgage Association), and so on. Mutual funds also heavily invest in corporations by buying their stocks and bonds.

It seems to me that Burkett's investment advice in *Investing for the Future* contradicts his premise in *The Coming Economic Earthquake*. If I believed this country were going down the tubes, I wouldn't write a book on how to invest money in the very places that would collapse. That would certainly wipe out the retirement money I had invested and was trying to protect in the first place.

Investment counseling is a complex, ever-changing occupation that requires daily monitoring needed to keep up with current trends. That's why the government requires certain licenses and registrations for qualified investment and financial advisers. The same is true for doctors, lawyers, and CPAs (Certified Public Accountants)—all of whom must pass certain tests and meet required standards before they are allowed to practice in their areas of expertise.

DOOMSDAY ENVIRONMENTALISTS

Economic doomsayers remind me of the environmental prognosticators who base their opinions on emotion rather than fact. Their "Save the Planet" slogans activate our fears, forcing us to accept their conceptions about what the future holds. Although the rhetoric may sound fresh and catchy, their ideas are as old as the hills. The radical environmentalists are another example of how the purveyors of para-noia create unwise decision-making climates.

For instance, two hundred years ago predictions of mass starvation created great concern throughout the U.S., Canada, and England. Apparently, several philosophers had conjured up the idea that people all over the planet would starve to death. But they were wrong. Today hunger is still a concern, but starvation exists only in isolated areas of the world where ignorance, war, or religious deception prevail.

For decades, environmentalists have claimed that we're killing the planet and destroying our natural resources with pollution. By our very nature, however, we create pollution. Back in the early years of our nation's history, raw sewage caused disease and plagues that killed thousands. As a result, it didn't take long for thinking people to solve the problem by devising indoor plumbing, underground sewers, and waste treatment plants.

I can remember, in the mid-century, when homes and buildings in America were heated with coal and factories polluted the air with smoke. Today, because of higher standards and more efficient equip-ment, air pollution has been drastically reduced. Except for some isolated cases, it is my opinion that pollution is by and large under control in this country.

What about the animals? If we don't do something, won't they all become extinct? Many of the species God created were extinct long before industrialized America started doing business. Yet, if we listen to the environmentalist doomsayers, we would believe that dinosaurs died from eating Styrofoam cups or choked to death on plastic soft drink containers.

No one wants to preserve our natural resources and the beauty of this great nation more than I do. That's why I'm pleased to see mea-sures being taken to correct some of our pollution problems. The fact that we are confronting environmental issues and things are getting better gives me hope for the future of our nation and the earth.

Let's imagine a worst case scenario. Take an area that is the most densely populated on earth, has no natural resources, and must import every drop of its water. What do you think would happen? The envi-ronmentalists would say, "It is doomed!" Yet, Hong Kong is just such a place and has become the most thriving free-market economy in the world today.

The environmentalists are always overpredicting. I do not believe that the oil spill from the Valdez accident in Alaska or the oil flow resulting from the Persian Gulf War ever reached the epidemic proportions environmentalists claimed would happen. In fact, I think these areas of the world will eventually purify themselves naturally and be pronounced environmentally clean.

> • *The electronic economy has changed the way the markets operate, but I don't believe it has . . . created financial chaos.* • • •

In spite of all the diseases, plagues, and natural disasters humankind has experienced in the last six thousand years, people are living longer today than at any time since Noah's Flood. Still, the environmentalists cry, "Our planet is doomed!" and the public jumps to meet their demands. Like the environmentalists, economic doomsayers get excited about the state of things at the moment and overpredict the outcome.

Like our environment, America has experienced some turbulent times—with recessions and depressions—but, like nature, our nation has always recovered and, in fact, has become stronger after each economic downturn.

NO MORE MONEY?

Joel Kurtzman, a secular doomsday writer, sounds another alarm in *The Death of Money: How the Electronic Economy Has Destabilized the World's Markets and Created Financial Chaos.* His fears center around the economic life and soul of our nation—money.

According to Kurtzman, money no longer exists because of the trillions of signals between interlinked computer terminals in search of choice trades in hot markets. He believes that swift capital flows can derail markets when they reverse course.

To prove his theory, he cites how that happened in 1987 with the U.S. stock market crash and again with the plunge of Japanese markets in 1990. He also assumes that the European markets almost collapsed in September and October 1992 because of lightning-speed electronic trading.[15]

Kurtzman asks, "How can there be equilibrium if money becomes transformed from something solid and substantial, with demonstrable equity value such as silver or gold, into something new, strange, and ethereal?"[16] It is true that the electronic economy has changed the way the markets operate, but I don't believe it has destabilized the world's markets and created financial chaos as Kurtzman suggests. Like most doomsday writers, he tries to present an emerging global economic system beyond the control of regulators.

To build his case, Kurtzman makes the claim that the volatility in the "electronic economy" adds a couple of percentage points to the cost of doing business each year. He also believes that fickle portfolio managers who demand high returns have forced General Motors, Ford, and IBM "to buy billions of dollars" worth of their own stock to keep the price high rather than investing that money in new research and development.[17]

Where did he get those rather obscure and ambiguous numbers? As Glasgall points out, "There are no footnotes in *The Death of Money* and a serious lack of bibliography."[18]

The Death of Money has many factual errors. Kurtzman claims that banks get overnight loans to shore up their reserves from the Federal Reserve. That isn't true because the banks lend between themselves when the need arises.

When I read that Kurtzman believes that the people who spawned automatic teller machines have created a "speculative explosion" that threatens to destabilize the world economies, I couldn't help smiling. Religious doomsayers have been preaching for years that the electronic age will usher in the Antichrist. As a result, they see the Social Security numbering system, electronic banking machines, and bar code scanners as part of a worldwide scheme centering around the number 666 and the mark of the Beast.

Let's face it, the era of the Antichrist will be ushered in whether the proper electronic equipment is in place or not. The end times are God's timing, and we must be careful about tying in technological progress with doomsday myths.

If transmitting capital via computers can make money easier to manage and companies more profitable by lowering their costs, then shouldn't we exploit the technology rather than try to stall it because we are afraid it will usher in doomsday? Besides, electronic money can't bring about doomsday any faster than advancing the technology of the automobile, train, plane, food processing, or medicine has hastened our demise. (Well, the food processing might be in question!)

In fact, the way the world exchanges goods has changed many times since the dawn of creation. Electronic transfers are just another step in the evolutionary process of how trading is accomplished. Those of us who have nothing to fear call this phenomenon progress.

I'll never forget the day I took my grandfather to the bank to show him how to use the ATM machine. "Look, Grandpa," I said as I inserted my card. "See how simple this is."

As Grandpa stared at the screen and tried to decipher the instructions, a voice from the automatic teller suddenly spoke.

"Good morning, Sherman," it said in robotic fashion.

Grandpa jumped back, and shouted, "I'm not touching that thing! It's too spooky for me!" Shaking his head, he walked away and waited in the car while I finished my transaction.

I can understand why older people often fear change, but who wants to return to the days when there were no electronic calculators, computers, or the convenience of ATM machines? I don't. Advancing technology has enhanced our living standard, allowed us to communicate more easily, improved medical treatment, and in many ways has helped to spread the gospel.

BANKRUPTCY 1995?

Not long ago, while waiting for my flight, I picked up the last copy of the best-selling book *Bankruptcy 1995* at an airport bookstore. At that point it was number five on the best-seller list and rising. It is the doomsday book of books.

No heavyweight boxer ever delivered a blow like Harry Figgie does in *Bankruptcy 1995: The Coming Collapse of America and How to Stop It*. Reading it is akin to watching *Nightmare on Elm Street*.

Who is Harry Figgie? He is the chief executive officer and founder of Figgie International, a diversified Fortune 500 corporation, which includes Rawlings Sporting Goods as one of its twenty-eight companies and takes in $1.3 billion in annual sales. With an MBA from Harvard University and a law degree, Harry Figgie was President Reagan's co-chairman of Private Sector Survey on Cost Control.

The book opens with a mind-boggling statement in the introduction:

> In 1995, the United States of America, as we know it today, will cease to exist. That year, the country will have spent itself into a bankruptcy from which there will be no return. What we once

called the American Century will end, literally, with the end of the American way of life—unless you and I act now to pull ourselves and the country back from near-certain oblivion.[19]

Among the doomsayers, I tend to side most with Figgie's analysis, though my enthusiasm is limited, of course. What I appreciate about his opening statement, above, is that although he paints a rather dire scenario for the near future, at least he emphasizes that there is the possibility of our doing something to avert it. He speaks of "oblivion" to be sure, but at least he says "near-certain oblivion."

Figgie is certainly qualified to write on the subject matter proposed in his book. His presentation of facts makes his opinions difficult to dispute. To prove his point, Figgie plots what the national debt and the federal deficit had been in the past and what it was projected to be in the year 2000. Beginning from the founding of our republic, he charts the rate of change from year to year. He then makes this statement:

> In the year 1995, the American national debt would have grown beyond our ability to control it through taxation. Even if the government that year dedicated every penny it collected in personal income taxes to paying just interest on the debt, it wouldn't be enough. The deficit in the year 2000 would be 33 times what it had been in 1980.[20]

Wow! That statement would be enough to scare even a guy like me—that is, if I thought those figures were accurate. Unfortunately, most people will not question how and where Figgie got his statistics. As a result, they will overreact to his book the way Christians have to Burkett's *Coming Economic Earthquake*. In fact, Pat Robertson introduced *Bankruptcy 1995* to his viewers on "The 700 Club" and set off a new frenzy of panic among the religious crowd.

Just because a credible billionaire writes a book predicting America's financial demise doesn't mean everything in it is going to happen. Plenty of economists disagree with Figgie's "in-your-face, we're dead" philosophy.

I am sure that *Bankruptcy 1995* will make an impact on politicians, and it should because they are the ones who ultimately must get the message and get us out of the mess. But I do not believe our nation will be anywhere close to oblivion by 1995, or by the year 2000, for that matter. I believe we will take the steps to get our nation's economy under control.

I also want to point out that *Bankruptcy 1995* was written sometime in 1992, before the presidential election. Some of the predictions Figgie made have already been proven to be false since the economy is actually recovering.

For instance, he predicts that hyperinflation will kill us. Hyperinflation occurs when the public loses faith in the nation's currency. He says that by 1994, the annual inflation rate will climb to 22 percent and rise more than a point a month. Interest rates will be running at 30 percent or more. Overseas, the dollar will be worthless, and foreign corporations will buy American companies for the technology and then shut the companies down.[21]

Here are the facts. There is not a shred of evidence that interest rates are going to rise beyond what they are right now (i.e., the end of 1993, when this book went to press). In fact, most economic experts agreed, as far back as 1990, that by the end of the century, America would be in stagflation—with a stagnant economy—or experience possible deflation, which means inflation would be at or below the zero mark. Inflation at press time was 2 percent; that's a far cry from rising toward 30 percent, as *Bankruptcy 1995* predicts.

WRONG AGAIN

As soon as the recession of 1990–93 began, doomsday advisers were sure it would spell the end of the American economy—and the rest of the free world. Listeners and readers were told, "Look what's taking place in Germany. That's what's going to happen to us!" Talk about gloom.

It's true that Germany holds the key to important economic policy not only in Europe but for the rest of the world. But are things really as bad as the doomsayers predict?

I recently returned from Germany where I conducted seminars and gave financial advice to Christian U.S. military personnel living there. From all indications, the German economy appears especially strong and seems to be weathering the worldwide recession very well.

A few weeks before my trip, however, investment advisers were following the lead of certain economists who were predicting the fall of the German economy. As a result, investors were encouraged to dump their German securities and the deutsche mark. As usual, however, the doomsayers were wrong, and a huge correction began to take place in the falling markets.

Within a short time, the deutsche mark began rising against the other European currencies, and the German stock market closed at a three-year high in the fall of 1993. That fact thwarted predictions made three years previously that the German economy would be in shambles by then.

It has turned out very differently; in fact, *The Economist* magazine reported that by that period, "Industrial orders are reviving after a long slump and helped by recovering exports and an easing of the Bundesbank's monetary policy."[22]

Although the unification of East Germany with West Germany underlies their current economic problems, the Germans will survive. In fact, the recession could have a positive impact because it is forcing the government to relax its regulatory grip on the German work force.

In addition, the German people know how to attack their deficit problems. In fact, the United States would do well to adopt the German strategy. What is their plan? To take their deficit down by cutting budget spending by the government rather than raising taxes.

In *The Coming Economic Earthquake*, the author states that the post World War II economies of Germany and Argentina are "examples to avoid."[23] He fails to mention, however, the steps Germany

• *If the doomsayers were wrong concerning Germany, why should we believe their predictions about the American economy?* • • •

took after its inflationary beating from the war to become one of the strongest economies on earth. In fact, no other nation today maintains inflation discipline like Germany.

Recently, Frankfurt's role in international finance was strengthened by the Bundesbank's decision to deregulate the market for the deutsche mark. That serves to increase competition and strengthens Germany's position in international finances.

As a result, the German bond market is Europe's strongest, largest, and most important. In addition, German unification has ensured this market will continue to grow, and they are now tackling their other big problem—a central supervisory authority for securities. Germany's know-how in global finance has helped it become one of the world's most stable economies.

If the doomsayers were wrong concerning Germany, why should we believe their predictions about the American economy?

REACH OUT AND TOUCH— LATIN AMERICA

In *Bankruptcy 1995*, Harry Figgie makes a mistake similar to other doomsday analysts' when he tries to compare America to the economies of Argentina, Brazil, and Italy. I'm sorry, but I must disagree—that is like trying to compare the progress of the jet airplane with the bicycle.

The economic difficulties in those countries were caused by a completely different set of circumstances and culture than we have in America. Most of their problems resulted from the domination of the state religion that siphoned off money from the people. As a result, the church became rich while the people remained poor.

In the past few years, Argentina, however, has made changes that have stabilized the currency and shored up the economy. The turning point came with the election of the new and innovative president, who lifted government restrictions and allowed the nation to function as a free-market economy.

Many of America's foremost mutual funds are now carrying Argentine securities. That is a clear indication that Argentine bonds are a good investment. Other Latin American countries, such as Mexico, have also stabilized. A few years ago, who would have thought we would be buying Mexican stocks in record numbers?

Why is that happening? Because American corporations such as AT&T and Wal-Mart have entered into joint ventures with Mexican companies like Teléphonos (the national telephone system) and Cifra (the largest retailer in Mexico). As a result, stock in these companies has become very popular and prices have risen dramatically. In addition, Mexico's currency has been stable for three years now.

With the possibility of the passage of the North American Free Trade Agreement, Latin American economies—as well as our own— have the potential for greater growth. As a result, I believe Harry Figgie's *Bankruptcy 1995* will go the way of George Orwell's *1984*.

SIX REASONS FOR OPTIMISM

To support his theories, Figgie takes on the economists and attempts to argue his point. Readers of his book must bear in mind—as they should when reading any prophetic book—that there are two sides to every coin. The opinions of economists are evenly divided. Some agree with Figgie's analysis, and others have a more optimistic view of the economy.

Although, like Harry Figgie, I am not an economist, I like to take the more cheerful approach. Here are six reasons why I'm bullish on America:

1. *The national debt is growing from year to year, but the economy is growing as well.* Our country needs to do what any business or household should do in a crisis: Hold our debt in a sensible ratio to our income. If we do that, our economy will survive.

2. *We owe the debt to ourselves.* Who owns America? Americans do.

Americans are still far and away the biggest buyers of Treasury bills, notes, and bonds. Although it is true that many foreign investors purchase U.S. Treasury bills, they own only about 15 percent of the total amount. The remaining 85 percent are held by U.S. citizens.

On the other hand, Americans turn around and invest in foreign currencies by purchasing the British pound or the German deutsche mark.

Many people mistakenly consider America to be the biggest debtor nation in the world. Actually, America's foreign debt ratio is far lower than most people think.

The answer to keeping the economy stable is to induce more Americans to invest in America and not to borrow from foreigners. The less interest we have to pay foreigners, the less vulnerable we will be if they cash out their investments.

3. *The national debt will benefit future generations if we invest in our infrastructure.* We need to spend tax dollars on things that benefit the population. We must stop borrowing money to pay current bills such as the Savings and Loan bailout, delinquent student loans, and so on. We have to stop spending money that doesn't invest in our nation's future. If we do that, the debt we owe will be used as debt was intended to be used—to further our capacity to expand economically.

4. Interest rates are not rising in spite of the doomsayers' predictions over the past two to three years. Anyone who reads the financial pages in the newspaper or the business magazines knows that interest rates are the lowest they have been in the past fifteen years. In fact, people are refinancing their homes in record numbers.

Interest rates range from 2 percent passbook savings to 7.25 percent for some home mortgages. That is low compared to the standards set during the Carter administration. If interest rates are going to rise, there are no indications of that happening any time soon.

In fact, in some parts of the country, adjustable rate mortgages (ARM) are as low as 4.5 percent. What a bargain! Those who subscribe to the debt-free living philosophy, however, are prevented from taking advantage of this economic opportunity.

5. The country can spend itself out of the deficit if the money is going for roads and other necessary projects. That kind of spending will boost the nation out of recession by creating a demand for goods and services and jobs. The government can create money by spending more than it takes by taxes. As more people are hired by the increased demand, more cash flows to businesses, and the economy glides out of recession.

The government can leave taxes alone while it increases spending, or it can cut taxes and leave spending alone. Either scenario would increase the money supply. When this recession ends, the government must be careful to stop spending money it doesn't have.

6. Consumer confidence is increasing. Although Americans may not be on a spending spree, they are starting to buy new cars and other big-ticket items again.

During the Gulf War, people developed a wait-and-see attitude that caused them to put off new purchases. Then, in 1992, the national media, in an effort to oust President Bush, dwelled on the fact that America was in a recession. And sure enough, we got one—and the media got their man in the White House.

When consumer confidence becomes anemic, it can have an adverse effect on the economy. Like a run on the bank, consumers can hurt the nation's economy by refusing to spend during times that are actually quite normal.

Although I am alarmed at some of our government's policies, I still believe we should calm down and let the system work things out. America is far from bankrupt no matter what Batra, Figgie, or other doomsayers think. America is the strongest nation on earth, and I believe—if God doesn't bring judgment down on us—we will prevail.

HEAD FOR THE HILLS!

Imagine yourself in 1979. The economy is in deep recession. Because of the Carter administration, interest rates are at an all-time high. Home financing is next to impossible. In fact, borrowing money for any purpose has ground to a halt. Businesses are going bankrupt by the tens of thousands. American hostages are stuck in Iran, and we can't get them out. The world looks like it is about to end.

What would you have done with your bank accounts and investments if you knew the following things were going to happen in the 1980s?

1. Interest rates as measured by prime rate would reach as high as 21.5 percent.
2. Mortgage rates would hit 13.25 percent, making home buying almost impossible.
3. Unemployment would soar to 10.6 percent.
4. American businesses and banks would default in record numbers.
5. International terrorism would run rampant.
6. We would experience the worst stock market crash in history— worse than in 1929.
7. The president of the United States would be shot and wounded by a would-be assassin.

Do you sell everything you own and go to a hillside to wait for the Rapture? You could, but you'd look pretty foolish when, a few years later, the economy corrected itself. Where would you be today, in the 1990s, if you had believed that conditions in our nation in the eighties were going to persist?

Imagine if investors had refused to invest in the stock market because of all the doomsday prognostication and the negative events occurring during 1979 and the early 1980s. They would have missed out on the greatest stock market boom in history. During the 1980s, the market climbed from 838.7 to 2753.2, in spite of the crash of 1987. And at press time (late 1993), the market was setting new records around 3600 to 3700.

Many mutual funds rose in value by almost 15 percent per year throughout the decade. In a time of such volatility, the economy still thrived. So why do people begin to panic with every downturn in the economy and consider "this one" to be different? The truth is: The economy always bounces back.

DON'T PANIC!

One day, not long ago, my father phoned me at my brokerage office, obviously distraught.

"Sherman, I'm scared to death!" he said breathlessly.

"Why, Dad? What's wrong?" I asked, imagining the worst.

"I'm afraid I'm going to lose all my retirement money!"

"Why are you worried about that?" I asked, somewhat relieved.

"Last night on 'The John Ankerberg Show' (a Christian television show), I heard that Clinton's new health-care plan will bankrupt the country for sure."

"Now settle down," I said calmly. "You're not going to lose your retirement or anything else."

"But this really sounds serious," my dad replied anxiously. "His guest said that America is coming apart financially, and there is nothing we can do about it!"

"There's no need to panic," I said. "Let me tell you why."

First of all, before Clinton's health-care package ever gets off the ground, it will be radically revised by Congress. It may still have a negative impact on the economy, but it won't devastate America.

As with any new legislation that affects the public in general, people overreact at the outset. When Franklin Roosevelt first instituted Social Security, a lot of Americans were very upset. Businessmen were especially worried because they would be required to pay for half of every employee's Social Security benefits. In fact, the same kind of paranoia that exists today was rampant back then. People predicted that companies would go out of business, the economy would fall apart, and we would become a socialized nation.

Now, don't get me wrong. I am not for socialized medicine or for government interference in the lives of Americans for any reason. I do know from what I see on a day-to-day basis in my brokerage office that Social Security has benefited many older people who would otherwise have had nothing to live on during retirement. In addition, employers have adjusted their prices and procedures to make the required payments, and today it's no longer considered a big deal.

From that illustration, let me make two points. First of all, things are never as bad as they seem at first. Second, people and the economy are able to adjust to new government programs—no matter how they are designed or executed.

Isn't there a familiar verse in the Bible that we all like to quote when circumstances are beyond our control? "And we *• So, before you jump off the economic bridge, read the rest of this book. • •* know that all things work together for good to them that love God, to them who are the called according to his purpose" (Rom. 8:28).

If we really believe that, then certainly those of us who are Christians can trust the Lord to provide for us in spite of economic conditions. In fact, who's to say there won't be new economic opportunities on the horizon that we can't even foresee? Remember, it's up to each one of us to use change to our advantage.

A GENERAL PARANOIA?

As part of the dissertation for my doctoral degree in business management, my friend Dr. Demas Brubacher, who has a Ph.D. in history, helped me develop a questionnaire and conduct a survey. Our premise was that economic doomsayer books and teaching—both religious and secular—cause a paranoia in the general population that leads to irrational behavior and devastating results.

To prove this point, we polled one hundred people by telephone in various parts of the country. We selected professionals—mostly doctors, lawyers, ministers, and so on—who deal with the public on a regular basis.

We chose people who were in some way involved or at least interested in economic affairs. Some had taken part in my financial seminars, and several of those surveyed had attended seminars led by various Christian financial teachers. Many were investors in stocks, bonds, or mutual funds. Most followed some tradition of religion.

During our phone survey, no attempt was made to coerce or in-form them of the existence of economic fears. Our goal was only to determine if they were aware of doomsayers and to discover to what extent they were currently being affected by their ideas.

This is a sampling of the educational accomplishments of those who participated in the survey:

Ph.D. in Education/Minor in Business
B.S. in Business
Real Estate Broker
Degree in Marketing
Attorney in Business Management
Degree in Accounting
Mechanical Science
M.S. in Systems Management
Doctorate of Ministry

These are the questions we asked this well-informed group of people:

1. Have you read an economic doomsday book?
2. Have you been personally affected in any way by economic doomsayer theories?
3. Do you know of someone who has been affected?
4. Are doomsayer theories something you are concerned about?
5. Do you believe doomsday books cause paranoia among people?
6. Do you believe America is in financial trouble?
7. If so, do you believe America will survive her economic troubles?
8. Are your opinions based predominantly on what you have read for yourself or what you have heard publicly?
9. How much formal economic or business education do you have?
10. In your expectation, what is the time frame for a coming economic crisis?

The results of this survey are included in the graph provided.
The participants in this survey made some interesting comments

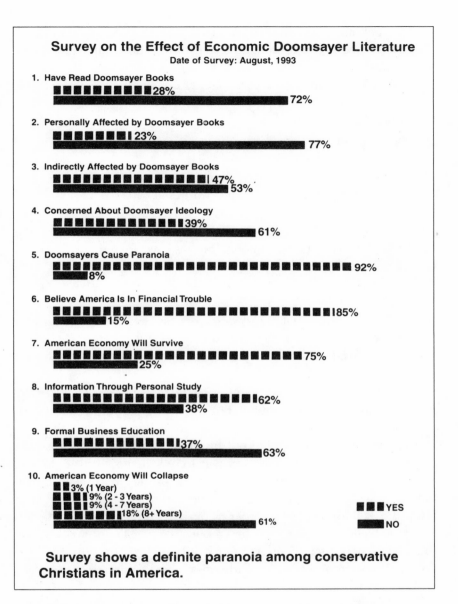

Survey on the Effect of Economic Doomsayer Literature
Date of Survey: August, 1993

1. **Have Read Doomsayer Books**
   28%
   72%

2. **Personally Affected by Doomsayer Books**
   23%
   77%

3. **Indirectly Affected by Doomsayer Books**
   47%
   53%

4. **Concerned About Doomsayer Ideology**
   39%
   61%

5. **Doomsayers Cause Paranoia**
   92%
   8%

6. **Believe America Is In Financial Trouble**
   85%
   15%

7. **American Economy Will Survive**
   75%
   25%

8. **Information Through Personal Study**
   62%
   38%

9. **Formal Business Education**
   37%
   63%

10. **American Economy Will Collapse**
    3% (1 Year)
    9% (2 - 3 Years)
    9% (4 - 7 Years)
    18% (8+ Years)
    61%

    YES
    NO

Survey shows a definite paranoia among conservative Christians in America.

about how they have responded to the economic doomsday message. Some had made drastic changes in their finances:

- "We sold all our investments and bought gold bullion."
- "We have cashed out our IRAs to pay off our debts."

- "We got out of real estate and rearranged our finances to all cash."
- "We cashed in our retirement to pay off our house mortgage; now we are heartsick and broke."
- "We quit paying our tithes to pay off our debts."

Others were making plans to help them make it through the coming economic earthquake:

- "We are going to relocate in a remote area for survival."
- "We are storing food for the hard times ahead."

One man who had followed the advice of doomsayers said, "We bought expensive solar equipment because we feared astronomical electric prices. But it never happened."

Others told us they were ignoring the doomsayers' advice:

- "We don't care what the doomsayers say; we are investing and will continue to do so because in the end if it all goes, it goes."
- "We survived the Great Depression, and we will survive this one."

One person in our survey told us how he foolishly responded to the doomsday paranoia. Believing that the price of gold would continue to rise, he cashed in everything he owned and bought gold. To make matters worse, he then maxed out his credit cards by purchasing all kinds of expensive items. His plan was to sell the goods for cash and convert his money to gold, thus making a profit. At the end of the month, however, gold prices had dropped, and his scheme fell apart. He had to sell all his gold in order to make the credit card payments.

Paranoia reaches every sector of our society. Many have reached the point where there is no sense of reality or logic in what they are doing. People from all walks of life are making unnecessary mistakes with their money.

In discussing the doomsday paranoia sweeping across our nation, one man noted this fact: "The sixteenth-century Scandinavians almost starved to death because they didn't plant crops due to end-of-the-world prophecies." Unfortunately, that is exactly what is happening today. For most Americans, our investments come from savings, stocks, and bonds instead of farm crops. Many, however, are digging up their seed and throwing away their futures because of fear. I can't believe God is pleased by such foolish and irresponsible actions.

CANCER-CAUSING CRANBERRIES

In 1957, when I was eleven years old, medical experts reported that cranberries may cause cancer. That startling information scared me beyond reason. I had already witnessed the death of one relative from cancer, and I didn't want to meet the same awful fate—especially by eating cranberries.

That year our family traveled to my grandmother's house in Abilene, Kansas, for Christmas. As usual, my grandmother had a beautifully decorated table with food fit for a king. At dinnertime, the bowls and platters were passed among the twenty or so relatives, and I waited with anticipation as the turkey and gravy and mashed potatoes came my way.

Then I watched in horror as person after person spooned out my grandmother's famous cranberry salad. In the past, I had looked forward to tasting

• *Are the doomsayers right or wrong? I honestly don't know, but neither do they.* • • • • • • •

those cranberries myself, but not that Christmas. I took one look at the salad and without even being tempted, let it pass. I wasn't even going to touch a cranberry!

That was 1957, and I haven't had a cranberry in my mouth since. But what about the millions who have continued to eat cranberries in the past thirty-six years? I haven't read or heard about any cancer deaths related to those little red berries.

Still, the experts continue to condemn food after food and find cancer-causing agents in almost every natural and man-made product. Someone has said, "You can't save yourself by not eating and drinking, 'cause if the food don't kill you, something else will."

A few years ago, the "experts" told us to throw out the wooden cutting boards we used in our kitchens because bacteria from decaying food could grow in the porous material. So, upon their advice, we all bought plastic cutting boards. Recent studies reveal, however, that bacteria actually live much longer on the plastic cutting boards than they do on the wooden ones. Now they're telling us to toss the plastic and retrieve our old-fashioned chop blocks from the garage.

I'm not saying the experts are always wrong. But let's face it, we can go to extremes in any area of our lives, whether it's eating and drinking or buying and selling. With godly wisdom, the right information, and common sense, we can make intelligent and responsible decisions about our lives and our money.

I'M NOT WORRIED!

When men of influence set dates and predict the future, people read their messages and react accordingly. That's what concerns me. No wonder Jesus warned us:

> But of that day and that hour knoweth no man, no, not the angels which are in heaven, neither the Son, but the Father. Take ye heed, watch and pray: for ye know not when the time is. For the Son of man is as a man taking a far journey, who left his house, and gave authority to his servants, and to every man his work, and commanded the porter to watch. Watch ye therefore: for ye know not when the master of the house cometh, at even, or at midnight, or at the cockcrowing, or in the morning: Lest coming suddenly he find you sleeping. And what I say unto you I say unto all, Watch. (Mark 13:32–37)

We should always live cautiously with an eye toward the sky and a heart tuned to the voice of God. He is the source of truth—not the latest book on the best-seller list.

Are the doomsayers right or wrong? I honestly don't know, but neither do they.

There are reasons to believe the economy could collapse, but there are many more indications that it is a long way from being "over." It is certainly not time to panic because there are many ways this economy can be strengthened. Let's not be swayed by every wind of prediction but, instead, consider the facts before we make adjustments in our current financial status.

My prayer is that Christians will not base their financial decisions on someone else's negative opinion about what the future holds. Overreacting or making serious changes in your financial situation without considering proper, professional advice could prove to be disastrous.

So, before you jump off the economic bridge, read the rest of this book. Like many other Christians, I am optimistic about the future and believe God is ultimately in control. If God wants to shake up America and use our economy to judge us for our sins—and nobody knows whether He is going to or not—then we cannot stop Him. If judgment is inevitable upon this nation in the near future, then there is nothing we can do to protect ourselves or relieve the situation.

If America is going to experience the economic chaos described in doomsayers' books, I'm not worried. Why? Because I believe I won't be around to witness it anyway. If the catastrophic events described by the doomsdayers occur, I believe it will be after the Rapture of the Church. Then it won't matter whether you are out of debt, have your house paid off, or anything else for that matter. Even if you have money in the bank, it won't be worth anything.

Larry Burkett says that if you follow his advice and he ends up being wrong about the future, at least you'll be out of debt. Maybe so, but with all due respect to brother Burkett, you may also be broke.

If your retirement money has gone to pay off your house and America doesn't go down the tubes around the turn of the century, what will you have? No mortgage interest deduction; more income tax to pay; a house in need of repair; no money to fix it up; and no income for the years to come.

Don't base your financial decisions on fear. If you do, all your maneuvering will ultimately backfire.

IS THE END NEAR?

In *Investing for the Future*, the author writes that "we will see a severe decline of the U.S. economy because God's Word promises it."[24] He then quotes Deuteronomy 28:43–45 as evidence that America's decline will be the result of God's judgment on us as a nation:

> The stranger that is within thee shall get up above thee very high; and thou shalt come down very low. He shall lend to thee, and thou shalt not lend to him: he shall be the head, and thou shalt be the tail. Moreover all these curses shall come upon thee, and shall pursue thee, and overtake thee, till thou be destroyed; because thou hearkenedst not unto the voice of the LORD thy God, to keep his commandments and his statutes which he commanded thee.

I believe those verses predict God's judgment upon Israel if she turned away from Him and followed other gods and did not keep His commandments. Does that mean the economic conditions in America reflect God's impending judgment on our nation too?

The author of that book thinks so, but his interpretation of those verses differs with many well-known Bible commentators—Matthew Henry, Strong, Barnes, Young, Adam Clarke—who agree that it is a warning to Israel alone. The proposal that this verse is talking about America is, in my opinion, based on supposition and, therefore, is doubtful, at best, in terms of America's future.

Doomsayers and their negative talk about the economy merely set up a smoke screen for the real problems facing our nation. I'm much more worried about the moral decline this country is facing than I am about any economic collapse. If American Christians wake up, realize what is happening, and restore decency to this country, the economy will take care of itself.

God has blessed America because it is—no matter what many say—still a Christian nation. For more than two hundred years, America has continued to evangelize the world and take the gospel to the four corners of the globe. But there are still millions who have not heard about Jesus Christ, and thousands of people do not have the Bible in their own language. I believe God intends to keep America strong until He has accomplished His purposes.

If, however, God is finished with America, then the government is powerless to avert impending disaster. Life as we know it will be over, and there is nothing we can do about it.

Is the end near? It could be and, taken at face value, many of the signs of the times seem to signal Christ's soon return. Keep in mind, however, that Christians as early as A.D. 100 were predicting the future by the events they saw happening in their time.

What if you had lived in the Dark Ages or during the Spanish Inquisition? What would have been your response if you had seen Christian believers dragged from their homes, burned at the stake, and tortured beyond belief? You would probably have thought, *It's all over!* But that was more than five hundred years ago, and we are still here today.

During World War II, Christians thought Hitler had all the characteristics of the Man of Sin. More recently, some preachers actually named Henry Kissinger as the Antichrist, and others considered Gorbachev to be the new ruler of the coming one-world government.

Remember the bomb shelters and air raid drills of the 1950s? Today, they are only a faint memory for most baby boomers, especially since the recent fall of Soviet communism has lessened the threat of nuclear annihilation and changed the way we view our world.

I agree that the amazing historical events of the past few years may be pointing toward a grand climax, but will it happen in our generation? That is the million-dollar question. No one knows except God—and believe me, He's not leaking information to only a privileged few.

MYTH TWO:

America Is Going Down the Tubes!

. . . .

On October 5, 1989, as I sat in my study at home, waiting for the opening game of the Bay Area World Series between the Oakland Athletics and the San Francisco Giants, my expectation of a great evening of baseball suddenly ended. The TV went blank, and the world around me fell to pieces.

Books tumbled off shelves, the chandelier swayed, water in the hot tub sloshed over the sides. The house pitched and rolled as I held tightly to the sides of my easy chair, hoping the ceiling would not come crashing down on me. Although I had experienced tornadoes in Kansas and hurricanes in Florida, never in my life had I gone through anything as frightening as that earthquake.

Immediately, I thought about my two sons, who at that moment would be on their way home crossing the Martinez Bridge over the Sacramento River at Benicia. Frightful predictions about bridges buckling and tossing hundreds of cars into the water came to mind.

The dark, dank Nimitz Freeway in Oakland, where I had sat gridlocked in traffic many times, also flashed before me. For years, scientists had talked about what might happen to the supports of the two-tier highway if an earthquake as large as this one ever hit us. Thankfully, within hours, all of our family members had been accounted for, and everyone was safe.

. . . .

When the dust settled and the smoke cleared, the facts indicated that the earthquake had done little damage compared with what *could* have happened. No one could deny that God had been in control. Because many businesses had closed early for the World Series, the thousands who would have been crushed on the Nimitz Freeway during rush hour were safely at home in front of their television sets. As a result, few lives were lost.

Destruction was also relatively minimal. The houses that did collapse were located in the rich Marina area and had been built on sand. The hillside homes, however, had stood firm. In downtown San Francisco, hardly a window had broken in the huge skyscrapers, and buildings were mostly untouched. No one was killed by falling debris as had been ominously predicted would happen if an earthquake of that size ever hit the city.

Although eighty-six people died, that was a small number compared to what the death toll could have been. In fact, more people are killed by tornadoes every year than died in the earthquake of 1989, and more damage was done by Atlantic hurricanes in 1992 than occurred in San Francisco.

DAMAGE CONTROL

God spared the Bay Area and the beautiful Napa Valley where I live. Although I respect earthquakes, I no longer worry about surviving one. In fact, I have learned that if God wants to destroy a city by an earthquake, He can do it.

Maybe that's part of the reason why I'm not worried about an economic earthquake either. If God wants to devastate the U.S. economy, He can do it. If He wants to spare this nation, He can spare it. But, all things considered, I have reason to hope that our economy will turn around. Let me tell you why.

• *The only thing new in this world is the history we don't know.* • • • • • • •

A short time after the San Francisco quake, it was discovered that the buckling of the Bay Bridge—which was captured on videotape and shown repeatedly on the news—was caused not by the earthquake but by human error. Previous inspectors, it was learned, had failed to notice that several dowel pins were too short. As a result, one section of the bridge expanded and buckled, tossing one car into the bay and killing one person. Within a month, however, the bridge was repaired and back in operation.

That thought gives me hope for our economy. Human mistakes have been made by our government, but that does not mean the "economic earthquake" will be as devastating as some predict. In fact, we may not even feel the ground shake. As the decade wears on, the economy could even grow stronger if we repair our bridges and get our house in order.

I find reassurance in another factor. The damage from the 1989 San Francisco earthquake was minor because the city had learned from the 1906 quake and prepared in advance.

Our government learned some valuable lessons from the stock market crash of 1929 and the Great Depression that followed. As a result, we have economic safeguards in place that did not exist sixty years ago. In addition, our government still has time to prepare before any kind of economic devastation occurs.

I believe the economic engineering available to this country will help us solve our problems before it's too late. Except for anything God may have in His plan, I am confident that by the end of the decade, our economy will still be standing firm.

NOTHING NEW

People often ask me, "Have recessions happened before?"

"Of course," I answer. "History repeats itself all the time. The only thing new in this world is the history we don't know."

Robert Conquest, delivering a 1993 Jefferson Lecture titled "History, Humanity, and Truth," said, "Only if one is without historical feeling at all can one think of the intellectual fads and fashions of one's own time as a habitation everlasting."[1]

That's what's wrong with doomsayers; they view everything in the light of what they see happening at the moment. To make matters worse, they ignore history, distort history, or are dishonest about history in proving their points.

History is important in every phase of our lives. The more we know about it, the more well-rounded we are. For instance, I teach my church religious history. Why? Because it helps people determine whether their church or denomination was founded on God and New Testament doctrines or on human tradition and false teaching.

Economics is the same as religion. We study history to find out if what is happening to us at the present mirrors anything in the past. By doing that, we can assess whether—as in the case of doomsayers—their philosophies are fact or fiction. We can also determine if the possible outcome of our current situation reflects any outcome of the past in a similar situation.

FRENCH INFLATION

One thing we know from history: Inflation often brings on recession. How do we know that? Because history has repeated itself time and time again. A look back at capitalism in its earliest stages makes the point clear. Charles Mackay, in his book *Extraordinary Popular Delusions and the Madness of Crowds,* described the inflation created in France in the early eighteenth century.

> For a time, while confidence lasted, an impetus was given to trade which could not fail to be beneficial. In Paris especially the good results were felt. . . . Bread, meat, and vegetables were sold at prices greater than had ever before been known; while the wages of labor rose in exactly the same proportion. The artisan who formerly gained fifteen sous per diem now gained sixty. New houses were built in every direction: an illusory prosperity shone over the land, and so dazzled the eyes of the whole nation, that none could see the dark cloud on the horizon announcing the storm that was too rapidly approaching.[2]

What caused this devastating inflation that became the worst experienced by any country in the world up to that time?

The blame can be traced to John Law's plan, which included developing territory owned in Mississippi by France. Law, a gambler, exploited the French government with the idea that the country could achieve prosperity by increasing the supply of money. As a result, a bank was started under Law's control, and he issued bank notes at a premium, promising to redeem them with precious coins.

Law issued small numbers of notes at first. When it became evident that his company would prosper through the Mississippi development scheme, however, he issued stocks and promised fabulous dividends.

According to economist and historian Clarence B. Carson, "The whole thing came to a head in 1720. The government of France made his stocks the official currency. There was an aura of prosperity in France as the country enjoyed a temporary boom."[3]

What are the results of inflation? Carson explains:

> Inflationary prosperity, even when the feeling of prosperity is dominant, resembles nothing so much as the gain a dog makes when he is chasing his tail. After all, the higher prices one receives for his goods mean nothing if he must pay equally high prices for what he buys.[4]

Paris had never seen so much elegance and luxury. In the end, however, France did not have enough gold to redeem the paper created, and the Mississippi bank stocks became worthless. The French government called in everyone's gold jewelry and ornaments to try and shore up the economy, but every effort failed.

A half century later, the French Revolution, rooted in the despair over the collapsed economy, turned the nation—and a few heads—upside down.

A WAGONLOAD OF MONEY

America experienced the effects of inflation early in our nation's history. In the 1770s, inflation ran away with the colonial economy. The Revolutionary War had created a financial crisis that the Continental Congress attempted to solve by printing paper that unfortunately won the epitaph "not worth a continental." Although the bank notes could be redeemed by the States, nothing of value backed them up.

To make matters worse, in an attempt to hasten the demise of the newly formed American economy, the British counterfeited the currency, creating financial chaos. Before long, the people refused to accept the worthless money for goods. In reacting to the problem of 1779, George Washington is known to have exclaimed, "A wagonload of money will scarcely purchase a wagonload of provisions!"

At the same time, America's debts to both England and France plagued the fledgling economy, but those were eventually absorbed and offset by the expansion that occurred in our nation after the war.

According to John Adams, however, inflation caused other problems: "Every man who had money due him at the commencement of this war, has been already taxed three-fourths part of that money. . . . And every man who owed money at the beginning of the war, has put three-fourths of it in his pockets as clear gain. The war, therefore, is immoderately gainful to some, and ruinous to others."[5]

As a result, the United States experienced its first depression. Although some individuals suffered personal loss and certain areas of the country were affected, the nation as a whole did not go under.

How did the early Congress fix the problem of rising prices, shortages, and depression caused by the depreciation of the money supply? They learned from the mistakes of past governments.

Our forefathers were so attuned to the history of the French that, as part of the Constitution of the United States, a law was enacted prohibiting the U.S. government from making any money legal tender. They did what France had done and made notes redeemable only by precious metals.

During the Civil War and shortly after, the United States departed slightly from the currency laws. In fact, the financial crisis of 1866–69 was created when the government printed unsecured paper currency to pay the debts accrued during the War Between the States. Although many businesses suffered, the nation survived. Later, Congress redeemed the notes in gold, which emerged as the dominant backing of currency until after World War I.

FIXING THE GREAT DEPRESSION

By 1929, the Federal Reserve Banking system was in place but could not prevent fears of inflation or stop depressions. When the stock market crashed in 1929, caused in part by the huge increase of credit expansion by the Federal Reserve in 1925, the whole system was crushed by the debt load.

Before the crash, credit had been readily available, and the term "Roaring Twenties" explains the good times that easy money brought. The margin accounts of brokerage firms had set new highs because stocks were loaned on credit to investors.

When the market crashed, however, demands were made for more liquid money. As a result, many people rushed to their banks and withdrew their money. Bank after bank failed until the country sank into the worst economic downturn in history.

To get a feel for the times, watch the classic movie *It's a Wonderful Life*, starring Jimmy Stewart. If you've seen it, you'll remember the scene where the fearful townspeople—reacting to false rumors—make a run on George Bailey's Building and Loan. In a desperate effort to keep the family institution from going under, George uses his honeymoon money to pay off angry depositors. Most banks, however, did not have enough cash on hand to cover the accounts of all their depositors at once. In two months—January and February 1933—more than four thousand banks failed.

How did the government fix the problems left by the Great Depression of 1929 to 1933? Several remedies were used:

1. Banks declared "banking holidays" in which virtually all banking transactions were stopped for a day. We still use this system today.
2. President Roosevelt stopped all redemption of currency in gold. Congress called in the "gold certificates" much as they did later with "silver certificates" in the 1960s.
3. No private obligations could be paid in gold because such demands became illegal.
4. The price of gold was raised from around $20 per ounce to $35 per ounce where it stood for many years. That drew a lot of the supply of gold into the United States as world markets sold their gold to this country.
5. All banks were closed, and only those declared to be operating on a sound basis could reopen.
6. Deposits in banks were guaranteed up to $5,000 by the federal government. That system eventually became the Federal Deposit Insurance Corporation, which today covers deposits up to $100,000.

Today we have a complex banking system, but our currency is no longer backed by gold or silver. The banks that make up the Federal Reserve System, however, are required to keep a percentage of their reserves against deposits in a Federal Reserve Bank. The Federal Reserve's main action is to expand the money supply, to issue controls regulating the flow of money, and to expand credit.

Can worthless paper money run a government economy with no commodity (e.g., precious metals) to back it up? The answer is, "Yes, it can."

Our Federal Reserve notes are legal tender for payment of goods and services that we receive and use to pay our public and private debts. Needs are created in this country, and they must be paid with something. In the United States today, Federal Reserve notes—dollar bills—are the only legal tender we have to pay them. Called fiat money, it is not redeemable by any commodity in any fixed amount.

As a result, our economy runs on exchanges and is actually an ingenious credit system. One of the functions of money in the first place is as exchange privilege. Our monetary system works on the principle that we are giving credit with our notes or money and then receiving something in return in the form of goods or services.

To refute the doomsayers, inflation has not been a problem between 1989 and 1993. Why? Because the government has learned how to control inflation with this kind of currency. That doesn't mean, however, that we won't continue to experience periodic economic downturns.

RECENT RECESSIONS

History has taught us that depressions occur every century. A recession, however, occurs whenever business activity declines, unemployment increases, and the money supply dwindles. In the past, recessions have occurred every seven to eight years. They happen like clockwork, and we should be ready for them.

Recent recessions since the Great Depression reflect the resiliency of the American economy. From 1966 to 1967, the economy floundered under the radical adjustments necessitated by both Johnson's Great Society and the costs of the unpopular Vietnam war.

Most of us over the age of thirty remember 1972–74 and the long gas lines at service stations. Created by a manipulation of the oil market by both OPEC and the other oil companies, higher fuel prices brought dozens of doomsayers out of the woodwork. Christians, especially, panicked, believing that the Arab nations were going to take over the world—a sure sign that the end was near. Some even accused Henry Kissinger, then Secretary of State, of being the Antichrist!

Although higher fuel prices did result in America's most severe recession to date and led to numerous bankruptcies, President Nixon kept his cool. In a rare and bold move, he implemented the seldom-used, economic survival tactic of freezing prices. As a result, life returned to normal, and the doomsayers retreated until the next financial crisis developed.

They didn't have to wait long.

The recession of 1979–82 soon developed—the result of uncontrolled inflation during the Carter administration. The Federal Reserve overreacted by allowing interest rates to rise to a record 21.5 percent. With interest higher than profits, there was a proliferation of bankruptcies and severe economic panic that almost created a depression.

Even though America experienced two exceptional recessions in a decade, the economy rebounded under Reaganomics. In fact, the longest expansion without some sort of economic correction in our nation's economic history occurred during the Reagan years.

The current recession of 1990–93, although mild in comparison to previous ones, is dragging its feet, especially in California. Part of the problem results from the low inflation rate. Investors are turning from

• *The independent spirit of capitalism provides a flexibility in the system that reverses economic downturns.* • • • • •

a seventy-year trend of buying real estate—which has plummeted as much as 30 percent in California—to investing in stocks, bonds, and mutual funds.

In 1991, $90 billion was invested in mutual funds that were tied by and large to the industrial sectors of the nation. That was more than any year since the inception of mutual funds. If investors had not done that, we would not be seeing some of the current expansion, which will eventually bring us out of the recession and the downward trend.

Mutual funds are becoming more and more popular as investors come out of the banks and look for better ways to make money. Eventually, what looked like a recession fueled by an out-of-control government will straighten itself out in part by the investment savings plan of our nation.

BOUNCING BACK

In spite of—or maybe because of—all the inflation, deflation, recessions, and depressions, this country is extremely resilient. Its tenacious attitude will catapult us into the next century as new and even more creative survival tactics result in greater prosperity for our nation.

The cycles of depression and recovery always bring new factors into the economic arena. The independent spirit of capitalism, however, provides a flexibility in the system that reverses economic downturns.

In a recent editorial titled "U.S. Thrives in Idea Marketplace," syndicated columnist Walter Williams credits our national freedom as the reason behind America's creative thinking:

> Despite widespread educational rot, Americans have managed to walk away with most of the Nobel Prizes and other awards for several decades. Does that mean Americans are inherently intellectually superior to the rest of the world? Forget it! The main reason is that we have virtually complete freedom in the idea marketplace.[6]

How does that freedom benefit us economically? Williams explains that "freedom in the marketplace forces out inefficient producers and transfers those resources into the hands of more efficient producers. Losses function to weed out failures, and profits function to encourage success."[7]

That makes sense—at least to everyone but the federal government, who, according to Williams, does things backward by "rewarding failure and punishing success." The evidence goes beyond our own nation. Around the world, it's obvious that "the larger the role played by government, the more impoverished and restricted the citizenry."[8]

As long as America has the ability to produce more than any country on earth, continues to educate the world as well as ourselves, has the unsurpassed freedom to innovate new technology, and maintains worldwide demand for our goods and services, we will survive. I'm not the only one who thinks so. Recently, the CEO of a Fortune 500 company told me, "If I believed all this doom and gloom garbage, I'd sell my business and try to survive on a secluded island somewhere in the South Seas."

I don't believe America will go the way of Third World nations. In fact, I'm convinced that, as our nation experiences the fallout of Clinton's tax-and-spend policies in the next few years, Americans in

1996 will elect a president and Congress who will encourage greater freedoms in the marketplace.

I recently saw a magazine cartoon that showed two donkeys talking in a bar.

"I'm worried about the Republicans," the first donkey said.

The second donkey replied, "Worried? Everybody knows that we control the White House and Congress. The GOP is powerless to stop us! Don't worry, we'll get full credit for everything we do."

"Exactly," the first donkey replied sadly.

How true! When one party is in control, policies are made according to the philosophies of that party. Disappointment with the Clintons and other government leaders will probably create a backlash against liberal politicians in the next election.

KEEPING TRACK OF THE TRENDS

Prior to Ronald Reagan's election as president, the American economy was a mess. During the Reagan years, however, glorious achievements were accomplished through unprecedented economic expansion. By 1990, the expansion had finally fizzled, but we still had the longest period of growth in our nation's history.

Robert L. Bartley, editor of *The Wall Street Journal,* in his book, *The Seven Fat Years: And How to Do It Again,* gives the facts about Reagan's presidency and how it has affected the economy in the decade of the nineties. He notes that, during the Reagan presidency, eighteen million jobs were created, and the country's GNP had been lifted by 31 percent. In addition, America's personal income rose 20 percent per capita.[9]

Bartley, however, doesn't face the reality that the Reagan years borrowed from the future, putting the strength—but not the possibility—of the recovery in question. One thing is certain: We will have a recovery because of the powerful new forces—such as innovative computer and robotics technology—unleashed in the 1980s. But it will take time.

Back in 1968, the same factors we see today were at work. Although the GNP (Gross National Product) reached new highs, only 84.3 percent of plant capacity was being used. At the same time, factory orders dropped 4.6 percent in January 1968, the largest drop in eleven years.

Why was that? The answer lies in the capital boom of 1963–67. During that time, the capital expenditures produced a surplus of capacity that ran ahead of current needs. In a sense, we have the same thing happening today. The boom of the 1980s produced surpluses ahead of current needs.

If we look back to the mid-1970s, it's easy to see that the problems resulting from overcapitalization during the sixties had corrected themselves. In fact, the economy was in recovery until Carter killed it—just as Bush killed the Reagan boom.

We can learn a lot by studying past trends. It helps us understand that the factors we are seeing in our economy today have happened before.

According to Michael Prowse, writer for *Harvard Business Review*, a partial decline does not mean there is a total decline of the American economy. In his article "Is America in Decline?" he notes that sales by the largest American companies in 1979 were equivalent to 58 percent of the Gross National Product. In the 1980s, expansion size was the enemy, and companies grew out of control. As a result, many collapsed under the weight of inefficiency. In 1989, sales were only 42 percent of GNP by these same companies—a drop of 16 percent.[10]

Prowse suggests that the United States has not lost its competitive edge in global economics because of the adjustments being made by big business to maintain their competitiveness. Current attempts to trim and retrain will make companies efficient and competitive both at home and abroad.

Those attempts are often thwarted, however, by the quagmire of federal bureaucracy, the weight of inefficiency, and the cumbersome size of the companies. In fact, part of the reason for the sluggishness in our economy right now is the inability of huge companies, which are mired in bureaucracy, to adapt to the economic changes taking place.

Look at what's happened to Sears. They ignored the trends in pricing and kept their stores in high-rent shopping malls. Kmart and Wal-Mart, on the other hand, discounted their products and constructed their own buildings, not only in cities but in rural areas as well.

When Sears finally decided to go the discount route, their prices were still higher than other stores and the public knew it. And, with a new discount mart in practically every American community, the need for Sears' massive catalog department diminished, making it obsolete. As a result, the Sears catalog became a collectors' item, and unprofitable Sears stores all across America were closed.

Sears' first quarterly earnings for 1993, however, showed the largest profits in the company's history. Too bad they couldn't have broken out of their bureaucratic bottleneck a few years sooner. But at least they had the courage to change.

SETTING THE STAGE FOR RECOVERY

That brings us back to our original question: Is America going down the tubes? If the big companies decline, is America's economy going to collapse as a result? The answer is no.

Why? Because while the big companies were declining, a host of smaller companies were being birthed. More new entrepreneurs entered the marketplace in the 1980s than at any time since the 1950s. The start-ups during the Reagan years unshackled stagnant, giant conglomerates and brought to the nation a host of opportunities that, beforehand, did not exist.

Innovative computer companies started up and saw sales skyrocket; steel companies began downsizing and specializing. The just-in-time delivery system of producing goods only when needed resulted in new production strategies that are now standard for industry. In fact, fresh, innovative companies are now leading the older, bigger corporations and competitors into new markets. That means more jobs will be created, and the recovery will continue.

The name of the game is "trends." Companies that misread current trends or, like Sears, take too long to catch on, may not make it.

Let's compare the strategies of two well-known fast-food chains. Taco Bell grew at 25 percent in 1991, whereas McDonald's growth was under 5 percent. What made the difference?

During the 1980s, McDonald's raised prices over inflation, making them too high for the average family. In addition, they expanded their menu, which meant it took more employees to prepare the food. Profits decreased as a result. Instead of sticking to hamburgers, they offered pizzas, barbecue, chicken, burritos, and other specialty food items.

An April 15, 1993, a *Wall Street Journal* article noted that "the

McLean Burger should be called McBomb." Why? It tasted bad and didn't meet the needs of the people who eat at McDonald's.

Taco Bell, however, stayed with their original philosophy:

1. *Aesthetics*. They look, smell, and sound like a Mexican restaurant.
2. *Menu*. They serve only Mexican style food.
3. *Price*. Every item is around a dollar or less.

As a result, Taco Bell did not have to raise prices or expand its menu. McDonald's has finally caught on. They have lowered prices to under a dollar or increased the size of existing products (like the MegaMac) and ignored pressure to expand to a dinner hour menu.

Burger King, however, is making the mistake of trying to be all things to all people. When families go out for dinner, they want to get dressed up and go to a real restaurant with waiters. A sit-down dinner at Burger King, with or without table service, will never appeal to most Americans.

On the other hand, if Burger King promoted the uniqueness of their flame broiled burgers—as opposed to those fried by McDonald's and Wendy's—they could create a new market niche in our cholesterol-conscious society.

To survive in today's competitive climate, companies have to keep abreast of current trends and make changes accordingly. Those who don't will go the way of the dinosaurs.

POSITIONED FOR CHANGE

According to Harry S. Dent, Jr., author of *The Great Boom Ahead: Your Comprehensive Guide to Personal and Business Profit in the New Era of Prosperity,* there are two economies in America. One economy centers around the old companies, like IBM, GM, Sears, and so on, which have been maturing and consolidating. New companies such as Wal-Mart and Microsoft are entering into the old economy with innovative business practices and, as a result, are reaping rewards.

Five years ago, who would ever have thought that the retail and industrial giants of America's prosperous postwar years would be facing financial difficulties, if not extinction? Change is always difficult, but it is also inevitable.

Toward the middle of the last century, new inventions, bankrolled by enterprising investors who had a vision for the future, created the Industrial Revolution—and, as a result, transformed the way Americans earned a living.

In the early 1900s, the assembly line, masterminded by Henry Ford, increased productivity, making it cheaper to manufacture tires, automobiles, oil, and food products. Harry Dent points out that within a few short years, the assembly line changed the world in the new industrial age between 1910 to 1924. By 1920, fueled by the enormous expansion in our nation, a new word had entered our vocabulary—*inflation*.[11]

During the 1920s, trains and ocean liners were in their glory years. Within a few years, however, the automobile and the airplane had transformed America's modes of transportation both locally and internationally, replacing railroads and ship lines.

Today, America and the world are positioned for another dramatic change. The next revolution will revolve around communication technology and is, in fact, already replacing the old way of doing things.

In the past few years, the Japanese and Europeans may have taken over our old industries—such as steel, clothing, and automobile manufacturing—but resilient Americans have created, are creating, and will create new economies for the future. Already in the United States, we have fifty million micro-based computers whereas Japan and Germany have only five million each. In other words, America's homes and businesses have ten to one the number of computers of any other industrialized nation.

The Japanese make computers, but they don't use them. In fact, some companies are still operating out of ledger books and using typewriters instead of word processors. Why? It is a means of employing more workers. As a result, the Japanese have far too many people processing their service-oriented industries.

Although Japanese workers produce almost as much as Americans per capita, they live at a 40 to 50 percent lower standard of living. Japan may be strong in a few industries that export to the outer world, but their own economy is weak and in serious trouble. By contrast, America's ingenuity and competitive spirit keep our economy afloat.

Walter Williams, writing in his syndicated column, supplies a case in point in an article titled "U.S. Thrives in Idea Marketplace":

> Choose areas of competition where Americans beat the rest of the world coming and going. One is computer software; we are the software champs of the world. No matter where people buy their computers, they depend on brilliant American minds to make and develop software programs. . . . Billions upon billions of dollars are being made by software companies. Most started out on a shoestring with "junk" (read "high-risk") bonds—like Bill Gates, chief executive officer of Microsoft, who has made us happier and happier at cheaper and cheaper prices.[12]

Hands down, America is the computer software capital of the world. In fact, Harry Dent in his book *The Great Boom Ahead* states that microcomputer-based technologies pioneered by entrepreneur Americans will replace all the technologies brought to the market by the Japanese in the past. That's one reason why he envisions a great boom ahead for America. So let's stop looking back and look forward.

History proves that whenever a society gets pessimistic about its future, you can be sure great things are about to happen. There is no reason to believe history will not repeat itself again.

PLAYING CATCH-UP

Two areas where we've seen extreme fluctuations in recent years are in real estate prices and in the number of exported goods.

Until the early part of this century, the U.S. government was still giving away land for folks to settle in the West. Acreage was cheap. As the country expanded, however, land became more expensive. For nearly seventy years, investors have made a bundle of money investing in real estate. In recent years, however, the market has changed once again.

With inflation slowing to a dead halt, real estate prices can no longer go up at the rate they once did. For years, California has ignored the economy in the rest of the nation and raised its prices above inflation. That's why today an enormous correction is taking place, and real estate prices have plunged as much as 40 percent in some areas of the state.

Another area where change is taking place is with exported goods. At the beginning of this century, the United States became an international hub for imports and exports. Although prosperity increased, it also left the nation subject to both internal and external recessions. The more expansive and industrialized America became, the more complex the reasons for economic fluctuation.

That's what happened during the Great Depression of the 1930s. Both an internal and external downturn occurred when European countries cut off agricultural trade in an attempt to become autonomous. That downfall in international trade greatly slowed our own economy.

While studying toward my Ph.D. in Business Management, I wrote an essay that included historical background on the depression of 1878. The • ***Don't cash out your retirement and move to the backwoods of Arkansas yet!*** • • • • • • • cause of that depression? Internal stagnation. Why? Because, at that time, there were few railroad facilities west of the Mississippi River, leaving America with no way to expand.

As a result, industries in the East lacked sufficient markets and went into overproduction to keep operating. The subsequent economic stagnation created high unemployment. Finally, with the development of five major national railroads, virtually every section of the new western frontier was connected with eastern production. As a result, America experienced a dramatic expansion on a higher economic plateau that lasted three decades.

Today, conditions are similar to those of 1878. America cannot expand until underdeveloped countries of the world, like China, catch up. With no skilled work force, inferior buildings, and a weak infrastructure, China has a long way to go. American companies, however, are determined to invest in this giant Eastern nation in hopes of tapping into the cheap labor and massive consumer base.

American industry is almost at a standstill. Because of this lack of expansion, the huge work forces of mega companies are no longer required. This, however, has created an opportunity for entrepreneurs to "mine" the lode of displaced workers from big corporations. As a result, a score of smaller companies is putting the labor force back to work. In a few years or so, the larger corporations will be less of a factor in the GNP than today, and our economy will be prospering as enterprising, new companies employ more and more workers.

I believe it is only a matter of time until all these factors—coupled with the cooperation of government—work together to put the economy back on its feet. In other words, don't cash out your retirement and move to the backwoods of Arkansas yet.

AMERICANS AREN'T STUPID

The doomsayers, using selected statistics to make their point, rant and rave about the danger of installment credit debt. That's the debt the average household owes and pays off by the month.

I agree that many households in America are having the life choked out of them because of debt. But the real truth is that installment debt is declining in America. Of the personal disposable income per household in 1989, 19 percent of the income went to pay off such things as credit cards, car loans, and so on. In 1993, that figure was down to a little less than 16 percent of disposable income. It may not seem like a lot, but, believe me, that 3 percent decrease in personal borrowing is significant!

Economist Robert Brusca of Nikko Securities, however, says not to be too optimistic about Americans running out on a buying spree. He claims current interest rates on auto loans, credit cards, and so on average about 11 percent. Someone with a median income of $30,000 and average installment debt of $4,800 is paying $528 in interest costs each year. If that person received an increase in wages this year of 3 percent, or $900, the after-tax deductions would leave him only about $675. That would barely cover the cost of the installment debt.

As a result, people are still paying down debt rather than borrowing more because consumer loan rates are so high and wage growth is so low. At this point, that's the best investment Americans can make.

Americans are not stupid. They understand when demands of recession are affecting their household economy, and they adjust. People are also saving money. Among the hundreds of clients I personally service, most are putting more money away than they used to.

There are many reasons to believe the changes coming in the next few years will be positive ones for our nation rather than changes that will bring about an economic collapse.

RECOVERY ON THE WAY!

Today certain indicators show that our economy is far from total collapse. In fact, the economy is recovering as I write this chapter. Why? One reason is lower inflation.

We have to return to the 1950s to see a mirror of what is happening today. Like the 1950s, we have come off a decade of super growth and great returns in the stock market. In the 1950s, stock dividend yields were higher than inflation, so stock prices did well.

Today, as in 1950, dividends on stocks exceed inflation. That means investors are making good returns on their investments. This is important because dividends have accounted for 40 percent of the average growth of stocks for almost seventy years. If inflation stays low, that can help stabilize the economy.

Does that scenario paint the picture of a nation on the verge of an economic earthquake? No, it indicates just the opposite.

Many economists do not believe inflation will move ahead of dividend yields on stocks for many years to come. In fact, the stock market will probably continue to perform at 10 to 12 percent levels just as it has done since 1936. Because of our current problems, we may not see the huge gains we had during the 1980s, but we will probably have the opportunity to earn good returns on our investments.

Certain factors occurring in our economy make the outlook on inflation appear positive. As you read this list, notice how certain existing conditions that we generally consider to be negative actually help correct adverse economic situations.

1. The Economy Has a Chronic Employment Problem

Although layoffs in manufacturing and service industries in the early 1990s have hurt many people, productivity is increasing. Why? Because of the increased demand to meet the needs of the nation.

Employment losses do not necessarily mean the demand for goods and services has ceased to exist. In spite of higher unemployment, manufacturers must still produce for the needs of the nation. As the demand increases, more output must come from those industries that have not been affected by high unemployment. As a result, the impact of unemployment nationwide is lessened.

2. Global Economies Are Not Synchronized

Our economy is not necessarily affected by the economies of other nations. As a result, American industry is not pressured to raise prices by higher demands around the world. That makes the United States the world's number-one exporter and lowest cost producer.

Even during economic downturns, America still produces and exports more goods than any other nation. You may find that hard to believe since that fact contradicts the negative picture of America's productivity painted by our national media.

3. Commodity Prices Are Declining

As a result, America's trade deficit with other countries continues to shrink. Whenever the prices of America's exported products are high, it makes our goods more expensive on the foreign market, and that deters foreigners from buying our goods. Declining prices, however, make it more attractive to invest in our products.

4. Real Estate Has Lost Value

The deep recession in the commercial real estate market has created a powerful deflationary influence on the economy. At the same time, housing affordability has risen approximately 20 percent since 1990, making it possible for more Americans to own homes.

5. The Dollar Is at Its Strongest

A strong dollar puts pressure on prices influenced by the dollar in foreign markets. In turn, American companies cannot raise prices, and that adds to deflation. In addition, foreign prices remain low, making it possible for Americans to spend fewer dollars to pay for foreign products.

Inflation growth will remain low for some time, which should stimulate our economy once other sectors of our GNP start to move forward near the end of the decade. Now is no time to jump off the economic bridge and commit financial suicide. The government can still lower the deficit and fix the economy. Before you accept the philosophy that America is going down the tubes, check out the other side of the world.

WHAT EVERY GOOD RECESSION NEEDS

In *America, What Went Wrong?* Donald L. Bartlett and James B. Steele raise some valid concerns about America's economy. To build their case, however, they draw several erroneous conclusions.

1. Tax Reforms Favor the Rich

I disagree. Tax reforms almost always favor middle-class Americans because it is good politics. For one thing, the largest bloc of voters are middle class, and politicians like to use the promise of tax reform, such as tax cuts, to get votes.

Conversely, tax hikes hurt the middle class the most. They often get the brunt of the increase. The rich, on the other hand, are able to discover tax loopholes.

2. Employers Are Cutting Costs

The doomsayers want us to believe that the number of Americans qualifying for pensions and health insurance is declining rapidly. That simply isn't so. Savings are beginning to grow in America, and that is largely due to the increase in money contributed to 401(k) plans, 403(b) plans, and personal qualified plans for retirement.

3. American Jobs Are Going to Be Lost to Mexico

As I predicted, the U.S. Congress voted to ratify the North American Free Trade Agreement (NAFTA) sometime in late 1993 or early 1994. Opponents of NAFTA still argue that jobs will flee America and end up in Mexico. That may not necessarily be so.

Laurence Hecht and Peter Morici, writing in *Harvard Business Review*, put a different twist on the issue of companies relocating south of the border:

> Any company considering a move to Mexico must balance the risks and rewards based on the long-term bottom line, not the latest free-trade rhetoric. With or without NAFTA, Mexico will still be plagued by potholed highways, commonplace corruption,

environmental messes, and a history of deep state involvement in the economy.[13]

In other words, the problems associated with relocating in an underprivileged country may outweigh the positive aspect of lower wages. Government regulations in Mexico make it even more difficult for factories to locate there. In the end, the cost of doing business in Mexico may deter industries from locating there.

Morici and Hecht continue:

> Companies that require a reliable, non-transient work force, for example, may find it necessary to provide their Mexican employees with improved roads, schools, health care, housing, and child care. Some U.S. commentators have called for taxing the maquiladoras to raise money for local housing and environmental cleanup. With increasing media attention paid to extreme examples like toxic wastes polluting the streets of Mexican colonias—the illegal shantytowns where many maquila workers live—the costs of doing business in Mexico won't remain hidden for long.[14]

That's why I don't think there will be a mass exodus of American based companies to Mexico.

4. The Top 4 Percent of Americans Are Earning Collectively as Much as the Bottom 51 Percent

So what? The top 4 percent earners in America are also providing jobs for the bottom 51 percent.

In the next chapter, I document the insanity of trying to deter the rich from getting richer in this country. That kind of Robin Hood government policy will only cost Americans their jobs. Why? Because the rich will not invest in the economy if all their incentives to invest are taken away.

In *America, What Went Wrong?* Bartlett and Steele conclude that what happened in the Reagan-Bush years is a repeat of what happened in 1913. At that time, widespread discontent resulted in the first progressive income tax. Then, in 1933, disillusionment led to the New Deal and a contrast between those who struggled and the few who prospered. This, they say, created the current rift between socialist and capitalist ideologies—between the working class and those on welfare—which is tearing the nation apart.

To compare Reaganomics to the New Deal, however, is to compare apples and oranges. Let's consider the differences.

In the 1930s, under the New Deal, the federal government set farm prices above current market levels. Farmers were paid to plow under their crops and to store grain in warehouses rather then sell their products on the open market.

It's true that the New Deal created jobs by funding huge projects such as the Tennessee Valley Authority (TVA), but competition was limited because the government itself competed with private industry. Does that sound like Reaganomics? Far from it.

The problem with Bartlett and Steele's claim is that they provide little, if any, explanation for the reasons behind their concerns about today's economy. Let's take a more pragmatic approach.

IS THE RECESSION OVER?

Economic changes are inevitable, and they happen for four reasons:

1. Bad decisions by policy makers
2. Inevitable economic changes
3. Pressure caused by technological changes
4. Global competition

Change always brings some negative thinking because change can be painful. Change, however, especially in the economic arena, may not mean what declinists predict. Let's look at some issues that reveal the significance of an economic downturn. These are, indeed, different from what doomsayers tell us is happening.

Downturns increase equality among industrial nations. America has been the dominant economic power in the world for many years. A change in that status was inevitable. Our nation's relatively slower growth rate signifies growing equality among all the industrialized nations rather than an internal problem with the U.S. economy.

Economic declines since 1973 are worldwide and are not confined to the U.S. economy alone. In other words, the American economy is not uniquely sick.

Americans can no longer assume that U.S. products are superior to those produced by every other nation. When other countries successfully compete, it threatens the American sense of uniqueness and destiny. The growing equality among the nations of the world forces America to focus more on its own problems and conditions. Yet that kind of introspection produces discomfort and fuels the ammunition for defeatists who write texts on decline and fall.

In the last few years, however, global competition has had a positive effect by challenging American companies to improve the quality of their products. Today U.S. made cars are rated higher for safety than Japanese automobiles, and the number of assembly defects has dropped dramatically.

Will the economy collapse? Perhaps someday, but not in the economic climate of the 1990s. In fact, I believe that whoever gets elected as president of the United States in 1996 will find a recovering economy.

Americans are confused. On one hand, doomsayers are predicting the decline and fall of the American way of life, and others, like myself, are saying, "Hold on." How can we defuse the problem of conflicting data? There are no easy answers, but if history repeats itself and economic indicators remain positive, the stagnant recession will end.

Let's look at nine reliable indicators that could signal a turnaround in the economic climate:

1. The Stock Market
2. Consumer Confidence
3. The Money Supply
4. Housing Starts
5. Business Orders
6. Durable Goods
7. Layoffs and the Statistical Work Week
8. Unemployment Claims
9. Exports

1. THE STOCK MARKET

Business Week reported in its March 3, 1991, issue, "If the Dow Jones Industrial Average passes the 3000 mark, it could spark renewed confidence. This would boost demand." If that is correct, then the economy has been on the road to recovery for some time, albeit very slowly. But that's exactly what some economists had predicted would happen because of the nature of this past recession.

The Dow Jones at the time that article was written was at a high of 2955. In 1993, new records were being set almost every day at over 3600! That's even better than the original prediction. What does all this mean?

If past trends are any indication, and I certainly believe they are, the stock market will start rising about four months before a rebound. That signals that consumers, businesses, and manufacturing are starting to have more confidence in the economy. As a result, economic conditions in the nation will revive.

Wall Street prognosticators, however, have been preaching the woes of a bear market up and down the highways. (Bear markets occur when the prices of stocks are falling or declining, and the bull market indicates that the stock market is rising.) David Shulman, chief equity strategist at Salomon Brothers, predicted, "Investors could get hit with a 10 percent correction any day now."

James B. Stack, editor at Inves Tech Research noted, "We're seeing the frothy symptoms of an over-heated market. When you look at market sentiment, the indicators are flashing red."

Money manager Charles Mintor recently told *USA Today*, "Stocks are in for a blood bath. The financial pain will be awesome."

With all that frightening rhetoric, no wonder Americans are confused. But is such talk worth our fearful attention?

I don't think so. In fact, many economists consider such concerns about technical indicators to be overblown. For every statistic that supposedly signals a bear (or declining) market, one can be found that suggests the bull market will continue. Even if there is a correction sometime soon, it is unlikely that we will enter a sustained bear market.

Doomsayers might as well accept the fact that ups and downs in the economy are a way of life. When one economic factor is going down, another is going up.

2. CONSUMER CONFIDENCE

After the Persian Gulf War, consumer confidence plummeted by 40 percent. When people have negative feelings about the economy, consumers become tighter with their money and suspend the purchase of big-ticket items in their budgets, like new cars. As a result, the reduced need for production plunges industries into recession and depletes profits. That, in turn, stops spending and increases manufacturers' inventories.

If, however, the indexes that measure consumer confidence show an increase of 5 percent for two or more months, spenders will be returning. Indicators are now showing increased demand for goods and services as the GNP begins to rise. However, we shouldn't rely on that indicator alone. The characteristics of current consumers also factor into how we spend our money.

Who are the current consumers now? The baby boomers.

Born in 1946, shortly after the Second World War, I am one of the true boomers, and I can attest to what economists are saying about my generation. As we grew older and our children's college education and our own retirement became more important, we middle-aged boomers saved more money.

Harry Dent describes the impact of the generation wave of the baby boomers. This wave, the largest generation in history, consists of those born after the Second World War in the United States, Canada, and England. According to Dent, baby boomers moved quietly into the work force in the 1970s, bringing a new wave of ideas and technologies. As a result of such innovations, they earned money and spent it. They bought houses, became successful, and then moved into the power structure.[15]

> • *If the boom happens, the credit problem among consumers will wash out, and the economy will return to normal.* • • • • • •

Dent notes that large generations eventually bring huge changes in society. Every five hundred years, huge population births occur in which new inventions and technologies are born. These major population spurts cause the world to change much more rapidly. For instance, just prior to the discovery of the New World by Christopher Columbus, the printing press was invented and gunpowder was developed.

According to Dent's research, people buy certain items at peak ages in their lives. For example, more potato chips are sold to forty-year-olds than to any other age group. Any product on the market can be analyzed in this way to show how an economy changes as large sectors of the population age.

As the current baby boomers continue to grow older, the economy will fluctuate with changes in technology, products, purchasing power, and styles of business. These economic changes in large sectors of the population, throughout the entire industrialized world, create cycles of inflation and deflation along with respective levels of interest rates.

Dent foresees an economic boom for 1993–94 since the lower interest rates were already in place a year ago. The baby boomers are at the age for serious spending, which he predicts might continue well into the next century.

At the end of the 1990–93 recession, baby boomers should have more discretionary income since their kids will be out of college and their mortgages will be paid off. As a result, we could see one of the biggest spending sprees in history. They will buy more houses, cars, and furniture, and some economists see this trend continuing until 2010–15. If the boom happens, the credit problem among consumers—caused in the 1980s by banks too eager to approve huge loans—will wash out, and the economy will return to normal.

3. THE MONEY SUPPLY

Another factor to watch is the money supply—or M-2, as economists call it—which refers to the amount of money in circulation. To keep the economy rolling, the federal government tries to increase the money in circulation. In the past couple of years, that action has helped to offset the tight credit policies adopted by the banks.

The next strategy the Federal Reserve adopts is to lower interest rates, which allows the economy to pick up steam. That is exactly what is happening today. The money supply is increasing, credit policies are being loosened, and interest rates are at the lowest in more than thirty years. That should bring the amount of money growing at a 2.5 to 6.5 percent range, which is healthy for the economy.

4. HOUSING STARTS

New home construction needs to grow for three or four straight months before an end to recession can officially be declared. This recession today, however, is strange in some ways. Certain pockets of the country, such as Atlanta, Georgia, are experiencing housing booms while others, like California, are still in deep recession.

If the Federal Reserve policies of easing money work, housing starts will increase. Right now mortgage rates are at the lowest since the 1950s. In most sections of the country this advent of lower interest rates has sparked an increase in the housing market.

We could have a boom instead of a crash because interest rates fell to the bottom in early 1993, and the impact has not yet been realized. Typically, falling interest rates do not have their bearing until a year or so later.

As a result, housing is more affordable because of lower inflation and lower interest rates. Places such as Lexington, Kentucky, for instance, rarely experience a housing decline because of the strong economy there. In fact, builders in the city tell me they are as busy and homes are selling as fast right now as during any boom in recent history.

California, on the other hand, has another set of problems. Because of the high income needed by families to survive there and the state's excessive regulations and taxes, the effect of the lower interest rates will not speed recovery as quickly as in other areas of the nation.

5. BUSINESS ORDERS

We'll know our economy is coming out of recession if capital spending on manufacturing sites and equipment by businesses grows for three to four months. That will spur employment as new jobs are created through increased orders and expansion.

By the middle of 1993, doomsayers were already being proven wrong. Business indicators showed expansion as new equipment was purchased, and the unemployment rate began to fall. Lower interest rates also make it easier for businesses to borrow money.

One of the things that plunged the country into recession and bankrupted thousands of businesses during the Carter administration was the ridiculously high interest rates—some as high as 22 percent. That venture almost bankrupted the entire nation. In fact, I can remember how relieved I was to get the bank to loan money on my new home at 14.5 percent!

6. DURABLE GOODS

When manufacturers' orders have had a chance to rise, industrial production starts to grow shortly after. That is a positive sign that the economy is coming out of recession because new jobs are created, and personal income will climb as a result. That scenario automatically creates a demand for goods by consumers and businesses, and it is already happening.

This increase in the purchasing of durable goods by consumers is one reason the stock market is rising. Large corporations like Wal-Mart, Kmart, Microsoft, Intel, McDonald's, Pepsi Cola, and others are showing huge increases in profits. Even auto manufacturers, such as depressed Chrysler, have new hope for the future.

Industrial production needs to increase 4 to 6 percent for two straight months to indicate a rebound.

7. LAYOFFS AND THE STATISTICAL WORK WEEK

During a recession, companies lay off workers and then cut the work week for the remaining hourly employees. In order for the recession to be over, the statistics reflecting the average work week must increase.

Before companies begin to hire back laid-off employees, they usually increase the hours of the employees still in the company work force. As soon as production hours at the place where consumers work are brought back to normal, confidence in the economy will improve.

As I travel and conduct seminars across America, I meet people from all walks of life, and I have come to one conclusion: The way people feel about the economy in general depends on the positive or negative financial condition of the company where they work.

For instance, I talked to a young couple who said to me, "What recession? We both just got a pay raise." That family is not worried about the economy. In fact, their main objective is to better their life-style and, taking advantage of the low interest rates, they just purchased a new home.

On the other hand, I also talk with people who have been laid off for months. In California, jobs are still scarce, making confidence in the economy shaky at best. Since 1991, California has lost almost 800,000 jobs.[16] California's experience can help us understand the rest of the nation's situation.

Where did the jobs go? To New Mexico, Nevada, and Texas. Businesses and industries are relocating because California's worker's compensation costs are 50 percent higher than in neighboring states. In Nevada, employee health insurance is half what employers are forced to pay in California.

Many companies are fleeing California for another reason. City, county, and state governments put so many regulatory restrictions on businesses that compliance has become a nightmare. Living in California is almost like living in a Third World country. A company that wants to plant a tree in Los Angeles needs permission from eight different agencies. If you want to chop the same tree down and make furniture out of it, you need forty-seven permits.

Recently, Intel, the largest U.S. manufacturer of computer chips, decided to move its production center from California to New Mexico. Why? Like other industries, Intel left because of California's huge tax on new production equipment. New Mexico offered Intel a package that included tax reduction savings of more than $100 million. Intel accepted the deal, and California lost the jobs. When one manufacturing job is lost, it often takes with it two or three more jobs in service-related business. With the loss of jobs go millions of dollars in tax revenue generated from the incomes of employees. To make matters worse, the state's unemployment compensation program must now fund workers who are left without jobs.

During good times, California's strict state regulations were asphyxiating. With this recession, rigor mortis has set in. Recently, however, the state legislature voted to remove the tax on new production equipment even though it will cost the state $600 million in lost revenue next year. That should encourage industries to think twice about leaving the state, and hopefully, will bring an end to the recession. California lawmakers need to make further changes along this line, and the rest of the nation should learn from mistakes made there.

Rising incomes and new jobs will start to come back if the work week increases for three or four months. The statistical work week is an accurate indicator of recession or boom in the economy.

. . . .

8. UNEMPLOYMENT CLAIMS

Two or more months of decline in the jobless rate will show that the economy is recovering. The current recession began in late 1990 and showed some signs of being short-lived when employment rates increased. Rates then double-dipped at the end of 1991, stagnated, and some believe that rates will triple-dip.

When the labor market deteriorates, recessions are inevitable. For most companies, the highest expense is labor. When costs need to be cut, unfortunately, workers are laid off. If too many laborers are jobless and receiving unemployment benefits, a recession can turn into depression. Fortunately, the doomsayers who are predicting a depression like the 1930s don't have a leg to stand on because unemployment figures are declining and signaling recovery.

9. EXPORTS

During a recession, export service is important for recovery. If Americans are stalled in spending, there is the possibility that other countries will buy our products, especially when the dollar is down on the foreign exchanges.

As foreign nations strengthen economically, that creates a demand for the goods manufactured in the United States. If countries like Japan and Germany get into economic trouble and can't control their economies, however, it could stall America's recovery. More and more the United States is dependent on those nations for economic growth.

Fortunately, there is a worldwide demand for American made products. Why? Because, by and large, American workers make the best products on earth. There is one exception, however. America paid a dear price for poor quality when it became obvious that the Japanese made a better car. As a result, the glut of foreign imports helped hasten the recession of 1990–93.

Our auto industry did learn an important lesson: They can no longer pander inferior automobiles on the American public. There are indications that American automobile manufactures are now doing a better job.

On the other hand, most American products know no equal. From fast food and clothing to other durable goods, America's products are coveted by the rest of the world. As the desire of foreign youth for

American material goods heats up around the globe, the demand will increase, creating more jobs and strengthening our economy well into the future.

While I was visiting in Budapest, Hungary, a new McDonald's restaurant held its grand opening, and I stood in line for two hours (and lucky then) to buy a Big Mac.

Across town at the opening of a store carrying Levi's jeans and other American clothing, only ten or so people were allowed in at a time. When I saw that the line of customers extended two or three deep for blocks, I was tempted to remove the Levi's I was wearing and auction them off to the highest bidder. Modesty, however, over-came my capitalistic spirit.

Watch the export indicator. In the future, it will have a lot to do with recession, boom, or recovery. If the export business increases for one full quarter or declines for one full quarter, that will indicate where the economy may be headed.

WHEN LITTLE IS BETTER

A few years ago, and perhaps even now, most of us were convinced that the bigger companies were the mainstay of our economy. As corporations gobbled up the smaller companies in the same way big farms wiped out the small farm, we thought it was for the best. Because of changing times, however, it is becoming apparent that big is not necessarily better.

Like the government, huge corporations grew too large and cre-ated a reverse evolutionary path. As a result, our economy has reverted back to doing business the way our forefathers did when our nation was first founded—as independent, creative entrepreneurs. Today, in the 1990s, the small business has once again become the backbone of the future U.S. economy.

Is that really true? The proof lies in the stock market. Blue chip-pers alone will not enhance the market; it is small capital business stock that mutual fund managers are buying. Why? Because small businesses are often profitable, pay good dividends, and have strong potential for growth.

According to Dunn & Bradstreet Corporation, 57 percent of job growth in 1993 will probably come from small business and the so-called micro-economy.[17] Companies grossing under $5 million annually account for 40 percent of the nation's employment.

I believe the expansion of small business, over a period of time, will keep the country from declining economically. Why? Because small businesses are not bogged down in bureaucratic red tape. As a result, they are able to grow, make a profit, and pay good dividends.

If our lawmakers are smart, they will stop focusing industrial policies on big business and, instead, provide support services to the hundreds of thousands of mid-size and small businesses keeping our economy afloat.

Why are computer software companies, like Microsoft, so innovative and prosperous, and yet able to produce high-quality products at reasonable prices? Because Congress has yet to muddy the waters with licensing laws and regulations that mandate who gets into the software industry and under what conditions. At this point, software entrepreneurs can still develop, test, and update their products without much government interference. Let's hope it stays that way so smaller, innovative companies can continue to prosper. And you and I can benefit from their creativity.

THE LAND OF OPPORTUNITY

In the Bay Area of California, where I live and work, nine military bases were scheduled to close in 1993 and 1994. As a result, thousands of civilians were to lose their jobs. Napa, home of the Mare Island Naval Base, and several surrounding cities have depended, in part, upon the resources that the base has generated for more than one hundred years. You can imagine the impact its closing would have.

Although the loss of thousands of jobs further hurt the already weakened California economy, I believe creative entrepreneurs, if allowed, will turn chaos into celebration. The West Coast will survive because of the innovative thinking of enterprising business people.

Governor Pete Wilson says that California "has the largest number of self-employed persons in the country, with small and mom-and-pop businesses representing 75 percent of the job creation in California."[18] That should tell us something about where the future of America's economic growth lies.

With a little help from the government, in the form of lower taxes and less government red tape, small businesses all over the U.S. will thrive. If that happens, ultimately the rest of the world will loosen tightened regulations and bring expansion instead of further decline.

I believe the opportunities in America are unlimited. One woman who attends our church has been working on a technical invention for more than twenty-five years. Just recently she received her patent-pending status, and it looks like within a few months her dreams will be realized. This invention, which I must refrain from disclosing, could revolutionize a certain part of the automobile industry.

Another woman in our church is also experiencing tremendous success—in spite of a tragic divorce after more than thirty years of marriage. As soon as their last child was grown and married, Carolyn's husband mercilessly left her with only thirteen dollars and nothing to live on.

Fortunately, Carolyn had a real estate license and had worked part-time on occasion with a small firm. Determined not to let her situation defeat her, she decided to get her broker's license and start her own realty company. Today she has turned her small business into a successful and thriving venture. Recently, Carolyn's real estate company was honored by Coldwell Banker as the number-one office in the United States of twenty employees or less.

The doomsayers are wrong. This is still the land of opportunity. Even in our present economic downturn, people are doing incredible things. Americans are resilient. With ingenuity and determination, many are operating businesses out of their garages, spare bedrooms, and basements.

R. Lee Sullivan, writing in *Forbes* magazine, tells the story of Timima Edmark.[19] In an effort to make her drab ponytail a little more exciting, Timima made a device out of a piece of plastic and a knitting needle. She shaped it like a loop with a handle and made financial history as a result.

After paying $5,000 to patent the invention, she then set out to sell it. Company after company, however, turned her down. Not being one to give up easily, Timima decided to manufacture and market the product herself.

She cashed in her savings, paid for a mold, and found a plastic maker who would do the tails for fifty cents each. Then she advertised the Topsytail in *Hairdo Ideas* and other such magazines and had first orders of $1,000. Her nights were spent stuffing envelopes and filling the orders. In a couple of months, she was making $2,000 a month working out of her bedroom.

Her big break came when the editor of *Glamour* magazine tried the Topsytail. As a result, the new product was featured in the February 1992 issue. Within a few days, Tamima had $100,000 worth of orders and hired her cleaning lady to stuff the envelopes.

After buying advertising time on television to market the product, she sold approximately 250,000 Topsytails at $10 a piece in just a little more than twenty months. That's $2.5 million in sales in less than two years! The cost to make this tool? About twenty-two cents each. Even Edmark says her "profit margins are obscene."

It can be done in America. Edmark's own tip is, "No matter where you work, have your own company ready to go."

As a hedge against recession and lost employment, it's smart to have options in mind. Stretch your imagination. Innovative ideas and hard work can net a standard of living you may have never dreamed possible. This is truly the land of opportunity.

One good thing about an economic downturn is that it makes us think. Today, individuals, small businesses, and even large companies are thinking and changing. That is healthy for our nation and the world.

Is America going down the tubes? Thinkers know better.

MAKING IT WITH SALSA!

Let me tell you about one such thinker who has touched my life in a special way.

I met Gil Holiday when our church was still meeting in a small concrete building. At that time, most of the folks who were looking for a new church visited our church last—largely because of the cramped and unpretentious facilities. Now that we have our new building, however, that fact has changed, and Napa Valley Baptist is first on the list for many new folks in our area.

I'll never forget the Sunday that Gil, a robust man in his sixties, and his British wife, Shirley, came to visit our little church. Something about them excited me. A couple of Sundays later, the Holidays joined our church.

Delighted to have them as new members, I greeted them after

the service. "I'd like to stop by your home someday so we can get better acquainted," I suggested.

"Great," Gil replied. "Come as soon as you can. We live in Rutherford."

I knew right away that they were located in the heart of the beautiful and wealthy Napa Valley. As I drove up a great stone driveway to a huge mansion (which I later learned had been owned by the famous trial lawyer Melvin Belli), I thought, *Man, how in the world did our simple, little church ever attract these rich people?*

After parking the car, I glanced over my shoulder at the surrounding gardens, complete with fish pools and immaculate landscaping. In the back, a magnificent yard showcased the lighted tennis courts and luxurious, heated swimming pool.

As I entered the beautiful manor, Gil and Shirley graciously greeted me and ushered me into the splendidly decorated great room.

Unable to stand the suspense any longer, I bluntly asked, "Gil, why did you and Shirley join our church?" In my mind, it seemed to me that people with such wealth would want to attend a more attractive and sophisticated church.

"I like the church, and I like your preaching," Gil answered candidly. "Besides," he continued, "you know what is going on in the world. You're informed, and it comes across in your messages."

As flattered as I was by his comments, I still could not reconcile their obvious wealth with attendance at our simple church.

Sensing my confusion, Gil explained the situation. "This estate where we live is not ours. Shirley and I are the caretakers, and I am the chef for a wealthy San Francisco family. They only come out to the vineyard on weekends, and we are responsible for preparing meals for them and their guests."

With that matter cleared up, I felt much more at ease.

Although they appeared to be ordinary folks who simply loved the Lord, I soon learned that Gil Holiday is no ordinary chef. He is a master who constantly experiments in the kitchen.

In fact, Gil's culinary genius and his frustration at being unable to find a good-tasting salsa (a Mexican style sauce) on the market led him to rectify the situation. After experimenting at length with several different combinations, Gil finally came up with a salsa recipe that was just right. When I first tasted the finished product, I knew he had a winner!

In an effort to market the recipe, Gil Holiday and his son contacted the H.J. Heinz Company. It seems that, for some time, Heinz had been trying to come up with a recipe of its own in its kitchens. Salsa outsells ketchup worldwide, and Heinz had no salsa to sell.

As a result, the chef of the Heinz Corporation flew to Napa Valley to meet with Gil. After tasting the salsa recipe, the Heinz chef decided they could not make a comparable sauce so the company struck a deal with the Holidays.

One Sunday morning, I was thrilled when Gil Holiday presented me with one of the first jars of his salsa to be produced before it hit Heinz's worldwide market. Gil, who has served God most of his life and has dedicated himself to serving others, will reap the results of his efforts and God's blessings. By the time you read this, you will probably be able to buy a jar of Gil Holiday's Napa Valley Salsa in your local grocery store. When you do, remember this story and the fact that America is still the land of opportunity.

ONLY IN AMERICA

Americans are still rising to the top. Since its founding, this nation has offered countless ordinary people the opportunity to reach the stars. In fact, the very people selling doomsday books are among those getting rich and benefiting financially from the America they say is going down the tubes.

But they aren't the only ones. One of the most dazzling examples of recent success is previously unknown Rush Limbaugh. In fact, Rush's delirious rise from the host of a local radio talk show to a nationally syndicated TV and radio celebrity has made his name a household word.

Rush is having, and will continue to have, tremendous influence on what happens in American politics. Bluntly articulate and unparalleled in his field, Rush's huge broadcasting success revolves around his strongly conservative views on politics, religion, abortion, gay rights, taxes, and foreign trade.

In spite of his radical right-wing philosophy, Rush has received various broadcasting awards, including accolades he says he never believed his liberal counterparts in the media would agree to give him. In addition, his best-selling book, *The Way Things Ought to*

Be, sold more than 2.5 million copies in 1993, and his second book may meet or exceed that number of sales. Only in America!

Volumes could be written about people who have succeeded in this great land. Failure is no barrier in America. In the land of opportunity, it is possible to fail and then try again because failure is never the last word. It is only a barrier to those who don't have the courage, energy, or faith to tap into the resources this country offers.

Is America going down the tubes? I don't think so. There is still plenty of fight left in this nation. No, I'm not naive; I simply refuse to believe the pessimistic, fatalistic sentiments of the doomsayers. And neither should you.

MYTH THREE:

The Deficit Is Killing Us!

· ·

I have done some freelance consulting work for some rather large companies. I continue to do this kind of work at times for churches and Christian-owned businesses. At times, I am called in to do an analysis of a company's business plan. In an effort to get to the root of a problem, I scrutinize the company's accounts receivables and accounts payables, its computer systems, and even look into the salaries of the top executives. I have never been accused of being timid; I want to leave no stone unturned in my analysis, in order to best help my client.

During one project, I did a two-month study of the inside workings of an electric wiring company that employed seven hundred people. On the verge of bankruptcy, management was talking about filing Chapter 11, and, in an effort to reorganize, called me in to examine the situation.

When my analysis was completed, I met in a plush upstairs office with the chief financial officer, the CEO, the chief accountant, and two secretaries.

"Mr. Smith, what's your conclusion?" the CEO asked.

For days, I had been trying to decide how to word my report to these guys. Now the moment of truth had come. I could smooth everything over, or I could give it to them straight.

· ·

Taking a deep breath, I began. "My conclusion is that your executive parking lot looks like a Mercedes Benz dealership, and you live in these multi-million dollar homes above your plant," I said boldly, pointing toward the window. "You're taking too much money out of your business to support your luxurious life-styles. If you keep up that pattern of spending, you're not only going to destroy this company, but you will put seven hundred people out of work!"

It takes a lot of guts for an outsider to speak so frankly to the top executives of a large company. As I anxiously waited for a response, however, my courage faded and the thought crossed my mind that I could be thrown through the window, land flat in the parking lot, and be hit on the head by my free-falling briefcase.

What seemed like twenty minutes was actually only a few seconds.

Abruptly, one of the secretaries slammed her hand down on the table and said, "He's exactly right! That's what I've been telling you birds for five years. You're taking too much money out of the business!"

Everything got quiet. Finally, the CEO stated, "Thank you, Mr. Smith. You may go."

Although no one other than the courageous secretary responded to my analysis, I was relieved to get out of there with my life and my briefcase in hand.

YOU KNOW WHAT'S WRONG

When it comes to the U.S. government, most Americans are like that savvy secretary. You know what's wrong: Congress spends too much money and doesn't put enough capital back into the economy. For years the deficit has been allowed to get out of hand because politicians believe that spending keeps Americans happy.

I agree that we must fight to reduce the deficit because the larger the deficit, the lower the nation's productivity. Reduced productivity eventually affects the long-term growth of the economy and, in the end, lowers our living standards. That's why most Americans want a change.

Just getting rid of the deficit, however, won't guarantee prosperity. Look at what happened to Great Britain and Japan in the 1980s. Although operating at a large surplus, the British economy didn't flourish—it shrank. Interest rates and inflation in England shot up dramatically. Japan balanced its budget in 1991, yet its economy— by Japanese standards—is in shambles.

In spite of evidence to the contrary, doomsday economists are singing the same old tune: If the United States government doesn't get spending under control and reduce the deficit, our nation will sink into economic disaster. Doomsayers love to use phrases such as, "We're stealing from our children!" and "The house of cards is falling down!"

The myths surrounding the accumulation of our national debt represent the ultimate in analytical absurdity. Experts who want to divert our attention away from economic prosperity use the term *debt* because of its emotive nature. Even Christians who preach that America needs to eliminate its deficit in order to solve our economic problems are barking up the wrong tree.

ECONOMIC THEOLOGY

Just the word *deficit* sends most Americans into a hand-wringing frenzy. They're scared to death that our nation's economy will collapse before they can collect Social Security and worried that their kids will never fulfill the American dream. But are such fears and anxieties warranted?

It is true that the last two decades have witnessed a phenomenal increase in the national deficit. Although that has created justifiable concern, it has also exacerbated the paranoia that our economy is on the brink of disaster. Some argue that George Bush lost the 1992 presidential election because he failed to sufficiently address this very concern.

If Americans truly understood the meaning of the word *deficit* in pure economic terms, however, they could relax. But that's hard to do when the media continues to pump out misinformation and a flurry of doomsday economists foster confusion. In spite of what you have read and heard, the deficit does have a functional place in our economy.

Robert Eisner, a professor of economics at Northwestern University and one of the most respected economists in the U.S., wrote this profound statement in the *Harvard Business Review:*

> Everybody wants to reduce the deficit, whether they know what it
> is or not. Almost everybody talks about federal budget deficits.
> Almost everybody is against them in principle. And almost no one
> knows what he or she is talking about.[1]

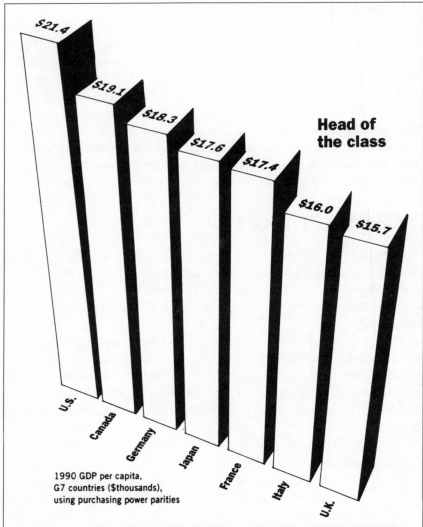

$21.4

$19.1

$18.3

$17.6

$17.4

**Head of
the class**

$16.0

$15.7

U.S.

Canada

Germany

Japan

France

Italy

U.K.

1990 GDP per capita,
G7 countries ($thousands),
using purchasing power parities

**U.S. has consistently had smallest number of shares in spending,
but as this chart points out, we have the largest output per capita
and the fastest growth rate of any country in the world.**

In many ways, the subject of the economy is like theology. As soon as you mention God, suddenly everyone is an expert on the Bible. If you bring up the deficit, anyone who reads the local paper or watches the evening news has an opinion.

To make matters worse, Christians go one step further and combine the two. As a result, we have "economic theology" fueled by the teaching that all borrowing is bad. That attitude transforms itself into a paranoia about the government as a whole, creating feelings of indifference and hopelessness.

I can understand such feelings, especially when the deficit is used as fodder to fan political ambitions and fuel hidden agendas. For decades the Republicans have blamed the Democrats for adding to the federal deficit. And who can forget the last presidential election when Reaganomics took the heat for Americans' woes, and the deficit became a campaign priority?

Politicians on both sides use statements such as, "If we don't get it under control, the deficit will kill us all." Like the legendary monster amoeba that ate New York City, the deficit lurks in the darkness waiting to swallow up our savings and digest our paltry retirements. As a result, we eagerly vote into office anyone who claims to be our savior from this supposed, horrible fate.

DEFICIT VS. DEBT

Adding fuel to the political fire is the latest burst of economic doomsayers on the best-seller lists. Doomsday authors splash the deficit horror across their pages and throw the federal "debt" around like a four-letter word without defining its meaning. I have yet to read one economic doomsday book that actually explains what the deficit is. For a moment, let's put our fears behind us and try to determine the difference between deficit and debt. Let me try to define this sometimes mystical and misunderstood term, the *federal deficit.*

The federal government creates deficits by borrowing money to expand economic growth in hard times. That results in a shortage or deficiency of money; in other words—debt.

The deficit is created when government expenditures exceed the amount taken in by tax revenues. In other words, spending exceeds the amount of money collected. When that happens, the amount spent over and above must be borrowed, and that adds to the deficit.

Debt, on the other hand, is the amount owed and not paid back at any given time. At least that's the way our government handles debt.

The government looks at debt much differently than does the

household or business that borrows money. What's the difference? The government goes into debt to itself. It borrows from itself and doesn't necessarily have a timetable to pay it back. That's why the federal debt can struggle on for years and years and seemingly never be paid back.

- *Let's put our fears behind us and examine the difference between deficit and debt.* • • • • • • • • Some doomsayers try to compare the national deficit to household debt. "People who do this don't know anything about the government," Rush Limbaugh recently said on his radio talk show. And he's right. Government and households do not operate in the same way.

It is not analogous to compare complicated government and business accounting procedures to the management of a simple household budget. That's like comparing the way you manage your children to the task of administrating the thousands of federal workers employed by the U.S. government.

A household cannot spend more money than it takes in, but the government can create funds through unlimited borrowing. Although a household budget is limited by its actual cash income and available credit, the government can raise its budget to fit the amount of money it *intends* to spend.

In households, a deficit occurs when expenses to be paid are greater than the family income. The result is a shortage that must be made up before it depletes the household finances.

The problems in our economy are not the result of the government's going into debt; it is because the government—like people who go bankrupt in their businesses or default on their mortgages—spends out of control. The problem is spending, not borrowing. Fortunately, many families run their households much better than the federal government manages the nation.

Businesses and corporations, on the other hand, use a method of accounting for deficits that is different from that of households or the government. Every company in the United States would operate on a deficit if it showed its accounting the way you and I run our household finances.

For instance, private businesses exclude capital outlays and charge only depreciation when accounting for their profits and losses. If the company is growing, the current investment is almost always greater than depreciation. When past investments are averaged, the company can keep its balance sheet in the black. Otherwise, it would almost always have a deficit, and in theory it does. Because of separate capital accounts, however, companies do not report such losses.

This explanation may be confusing to those who are not familiar with business practices, but the point is: Companies and businesses can write off their debt.

The United States government, however, does not distinguish between current expenses and capital outlays. If the federal government used private sector accounting methods, then the deficit would immediately decline. Why? Because such accounting procedures ease the figures normally programmed into the deficit definition.

> • *Some doomsayers compare the national deficit to household debt. That's an inaccurate comparison: governments and households operate differently.* • • • • • •

Don't get me wrong. I am not advocating that we spend more than we take in. But I do know that, over the long haul, the government needs to be managed like a business and not let the debt become greater than the revenue collected. I also know that we have to create deficits because, in times of recession or base economic slowdowns, we must borrow—and that creates deficit.

Well-known economist Robert Eisner considers deficits germane to American economic life and states: "Much of what is written and said about the damage done by federal budget deficits is sheer nonsense, no matter how often repeated."[2]

DEFICIT MYTHS

Let's look at some of the myths about the federal deficit that need to be dispelled.

Myth #1: The Federal Government Will Go Broke Unless It Gets out of Debt

Unless a government designs itself to commit economic suicide—which has happened in countries often used as examples in doomsayer books—we won't go broke. Why not?

First of all, the government is sovereign. It can do as it pleases. When governments are faced with insurmountable deficit problems, they raise taxes. That is the position of nearly every government on earth. In the case of the United States, we also sometimes print more money. The Federal Reserve buys Treasury securities, and the country stays itself against any bankruptcy problems.

Robert Eisner wonders why Ross Perot claims that we are spending our children's money. "Our children's money has not yet been printed," Eisner says, "and will, of course, be printed or supplied when our children need it, in whatever quantities the interaction of the monetary authorities and our banking and financial system then determine."[3]

Myth #2: The Debt Being Passed On to Our Children Will Be Too Much for Them to Bear

The perpetrators of this philosophy do not comprehend that most of the debt we owe, we owe to ourselves. Even though that is a true statement, it is also true that our children will be owners of all the Treasury bills, notes, and bonds that make up most of our debt. In fact, the debt accumulated in this manner will actually be for their benefit because of the great cushion of savings. Why? Because the Treasury bills will mature, leaving our children with the cash.

That is why the interest we have to pay on the federal debt will not exceed the government's revenue and income. I don't believe the doomsday rhetoric that the economy will not be able to expand because of the interest payments. To whom are the interest payments from all this debt being paid? To ourselves.

Myth #3: Large Deficits Will Lead to Inflation

In the past two decades, our government has run up some very large deficits. Today, inflation is down—and down sharply, at only around 3 percent. Some economists think inflation could run lower and may even hit deflation by the end of the decade. I will leave predicting the inflation rate to others, but I will reiterate the facts.

In the United States, big deficits have brought lower inflation, and lower deficits have brought higher inflation. Recessions bring on lower inflation, and booms trigger higher inflation because of the increase in revenues through expanding business.

To make a blanket statement that deficits lead to inflation is a myth.

Myth #4: Deficits Hurt Everyone and the Economy in General

That is not true. Deficits are not bad if they generate purchasing power for American business.

People with more wealth will spend more; that is a fact, not a myth. Part of the wealth in this country rests in qualified plans full of retirement securities financed largely by the federal government.

If a person owns hundreds of thousands of dollars in government securities, he or she will eventually spend some of it—or a lot of it— on goods and services that benefit the nation. If the public holds the government debt, the public is provoked to consume. As the nation retires on debt that the government owes itself, goods and services increase through productive spending on the part of the consumer.

GENERATIONAL ACCOUNTING

Laurence J. Kotlikoff, professor of economics at Boston University and author of *Generational Accounting: Knowing Who Pays, and When, for What We Spend,* makes the point that we cannot measure the deficit in any one fashion. He says that we should quit focusing on the deficit. Instead, we should figure out how to measure the debt, its effect on our current generation, and what effect that will have on future generations.[4]

He makes the case for generational accounting, which calculates how much the generations now alive will pay in net taxes over the rest of their lives. His method determines the present values of the government's bills plus the sum of its current and future spending on goods and services.

What does this method of accounting indicate? There must be a change in net taxes, or future generations will be taxed to the hilt. On that, the doomsayers and I agree.

What percentage of income will our grandchildren pay in taxes? By his accounting method, Kotlikoff estimates 71 percent! That's a

38 percent increase from the 33 percent rate currently faced by the generation born in 1960. The longtime game of "passing the generational buck" needs to be halted by the government.

How do we control taxes for future generations? We stop spending on welfare reform and other non-beneficial programs that take from the income of the government but do nothing to benefit the consumer who pays those taxes in the first place. And who are the taxpayers? The middle class—you and me—that's who the Clinton administration has pinpointed to pay for expensive welfare reforms.

Although most people are obsessed with the federal deficit, our real focus should be on the budget. We need to ask, Does the budget add to the deficit without benefiting or stimulating the economy? Unfortunately, in most cases, the answer is yes.

Certainly, we do not want to pass on to our children a fiscal burden so great that they cannot bear it. To prevent that from happening we need to elect lawmakers who will exercise restraint and be held accountable for their actions. Congress will only get its house in order if it is forced to do so by American voters.

• *There must be a change in net taxes, or future generations will suffer; on this, the doomsayers and I agree.* • • • • • • • When did the deficit nightmare actually begin? For the answer we have to go back more than twenty years. In the 1972 Watergate scandal, the Republicans under Nixon were accused of stealing campaign information from the Democratic headquarters located in the Watergate Hotel in Washington, D.C. As a result, President Nixon (whom I consider one of our great presidents, and history will bear me out) resigned from office in disgrace.

The Democrats, sensing the mood of discontent in the nation, pounced upon the opportunities afforded them at the time. As a result, Congress passed legislative acts limiting the president's power to impound funds. Those budget reforms took effect in 1974.

That means taxes went up, but taxpayers got very little back in return. That scenario escalates whenever we have a Democrat-controlled Congress and a Democrat president.

What is the answer? As part of our deficit reduction policy, the federal government must renew the discipline of spending control.

TWO STEPS BACK?

One of the first principles of public finance states: Efficiency in government spending is furthered when the costs of government programs are borne by the beneficiaries. In other words, current taxation ought to be used for government spending that yields benefits for the current taxpayers. Right government spending can, in itself, bring expansion if the budget provides for things of a productive nature.

How can a deficit coexist with an expanding economy? The answer lies in a cooperation of reduced budget spending.

Everybody knows that many public programs do not benefit society. The right side of economics would be to cut wasted spending, which would ultimately contribute to a deficit reduction. For instance, between 1985 and 1989, during the Reagan years, the federal budget declined from 6 percent to 3 percent of GNP. Why? Because Reagan cut many of the abuses out of the welfare programs.

Politicians like to blame the ills of America's economy on the American public's penchant for overconsumption. Yet, it is the government that spends America's tax dollars and calls it "good investment." That's like the pot calling the kettle black.

The advent of Johnson's "Great Society" in the mid-sixties and its adverse effect on the economy has never been reversed or repaired. During that time, the government unleashed its enthusiasm for welfare programs through public spending and has never let up. We need to stop taking one step forward and two steps back.

THE RAT IN THE WOODPILE

If deficit growth is ultimately destructive, then the federal budget—not the deficit—is the rat in the woodpile. Why? Because the resources used to pay for the benefits of government are worthwhile, no matter how they are financed—whether the money is borrowed or collected through taxation.

Debt incurred by the government should be used to finance spending benefits that accrue in the future—such as new highways and better education. From 1982 to 1989, when Reaganomics was in effect, federal capital investment outlays correlated with the federal budget deficit and mirrored one another. That's the way it should be.

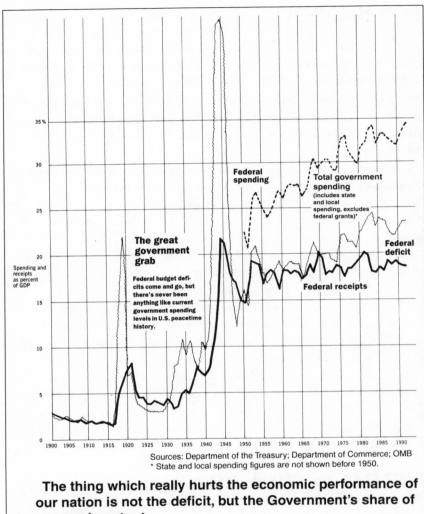

35 %

30

25

20

Spending and
receipts
as percent
of GDP

15

10

5

0

1900 1905 1910 1915 1920 1925 1930 1935 1940 1945 1950 1955 1960 1965 1970 1975 1980 1985 1990

Federal spending

Total government spending
(includes state and local spending, excludes federal grants)*

The great government grab

Federal budget deficits come and go, but there's never been anything like current government spending levels in U.S. peacetime history.

Federal deficit

Federal receipts

Sources: Department of the Treasury; Department of Commerce; OMB
* State and local spending figures are not shown before 1950.

The thing which really hurts the economic performance of our nation is not the deficit, but the Government's share of economic output.

Do you think the federal investment in social welfare programs justifies the huge sums of money the federal government spends? Of course not. Much of the capital the government uses for investment would be put to better use if returned to the private sector. The federal government is too large to operate efficiently.

Dollar for dollar, do we get our money's worth from the federal government? Jim Payne, director of Lytton Research and Analysis, has noted that the marginal cost of a dollar of federal revenue is $1.65. That means federal investment spending is only efficient if the return on that dollar of spending is at least $1.65. If the return is anything less, the government cannot be efficient.

Federal investment spending is just like any other kind of spending. You either break even, or you lose. Federal spending does not return dollar for dollar of its spending. Why? Because the government operates so inefficiently that the return on the investment is far less than the money invested.

Where does the money go? Sometimes to fund homoerotic "art" or to build a "super collider" we don't need. Only some government spending actually benefits the taxpayers— like military defense and Medicare for the elderly. If the federal government doesn't undertake its activities for the benefit of state and local governments, then it shouldn't undertake the activities at all.

> • *America's economy is sick, but that's nothing new. The illness, however, is a chronic condition, not a terminal disease.* • • •

During the 1979–82 recession, many building contractors would have gone broke if the government had not contracted out HUD projects in some of the more economically depressed areas of the country. In fact, our family construction business survived during that time because we received contracts on HUD building projects. That's an example of how the government can use tax dollars to benefit both the public and local businesses.

A TERMINAL ILLNESS?

As a child growing up in the fifties, I heard President Eisenhower warn that the national debt was $287.5 billion. Even then, I worried about the deficit. But that was before I knew what I know today.

Doomsayers have warned us about America's deficit time after time and predicted collapse after collapse. Today the deficit is infinitely larger than it was in 1956, and the doomsayers are sounding the alarm once again.

America's economy is sick, but that's nothing new. Like a complaining hypochondriac, it always has aches and pains in some form or another. The illness, however, is a chronic condition, not a terminal disease. Every now and then, our economy takes to bed and develops severe symptoms. But, even then, it is far from being on its deathbed.

Still, doomsday economists diagnose the economy's sickness as terminal and make predictions about how long it has to live. Anyone who thinks the economy will stop cold in its tracks during the next decade has ignored the economic changes that have taken place in the past. In fact, now that the Cold War is over, our national debt is no worse than it was after we won World War II.

Doomsday predictions based on the conditions we find in our economy today are unfounded. In the last ninety-two years, there have been very few times the economy has not had its problems. In 1974, our economy was in much worse shape than it is today. We had double-digit inflation, the Watergate investigation was rocking the country, and the oil embargo had raised prices at the pump to new national levels.

By contrast, as we head into the mid-1990s, the price of gasoline has come down, and even housing is more affordable. In fact, mortgage rates have dropped to levels not seen since 1950. The stock market is up 40 percent; exports have doubled in the last four years; and, including the recent downturn, unemployment claims are at a two-year low. In addition, business inventories are thin, and that will help set off a pickup in manufacturing when the recovery heats up.

The fact is that the GDP (Gross Domestic Product) is nowhere near the proportion required for an economic collapse.

WHO IS ADVISING PRESIDENT CLINTON?

The doom-and-gloom prophets—whether they be secular economists or religious financial teachers—always look for the worst. Why? They may have a personal agenda to promote—either their political ideas or their end-time eschatology, depending on the source.

Unfortunately, some of America's most negative economic prognosticators are advising President Clinton today. These are the same guys, who, during Ronald Reagan's presidency, made some rather bold and pessimistic predictions.

Let's look at a synopsis of the predictions and advice President Clinton's current team has given the nation in the past.

1. Economist Walter Heller said in 1979, when the Carter administration wanted to raise GDP to 3.5 percent, that he did not believe

the deficit was inflationary, nor that it would crowd private borrowers out of credit markets or reduce private economic activity.[5] That tactic backfired, however, and the prediction proved to be false. The Consumer Price Index rose by 13 percent, and inflation skyrocketed to 18 percent, leading a Carter administration official to say, "There's a feeling that events are beyond our control."[6]

2. When there was talk of a tax cut in 1980, John Kenneth Galbraith joined a group of advisers who predicted that the tax cut would be inflationary. In effect, he said that a tax cut would show a lack of wisdom and would put pressure on prices.

Ronald Reagan ignored the advice and signed into law, in 1981, the supply-side tax cuts. The consumer price index plummeted to 4.5 percent and even further to 1.9 percent in 1986. As a result, the economy boomed.

Later, in 1987, Galbraith said of the Black Monday crash, "This debacle marks the last chapter of Reaganomics. It is a product of supply-side economics—the irresponsible tax cut, the high interest rates that bid up the dollar, and subsidized imports."[7]

History has proved that Galbraith was not only unfair but also off base. Reagan got the blame in 1987, but did he get the credit when the stock market rose to new heights in 1992? No, but he certainly deserved it.

3. In 1982, David Stockman, then director of OMB (Office of Management and Budget), forecast "deficits as far as the eye can see" during Reagan's presidency.[8]

Yet in spite of his critics, Ronald Reagan took the nation out of recession in 1982, created eighteen million jobs, and produced $2.5 trillion dollars in GNP growth—the greatest expansion in American history.

The deficit obviously did not stop the nation from experiencing expansion as Stockman, and the other Keynesian economists, had said it would. In spite of the Keynesians' predictions in the early eighties, interest rates went in the opposite direction. Instead of going up with lower taxes, they went down with the tax cuts. In fact, by 1987, interest rates had fallen to 8 percent and now (at press time, late 1993) are around 4 percent.

After they were proven wrong, the Keynesians suddenly were on the side of cutting taxes. That was a strange move since they normally like to raise taxes to decrease the budget.

Who are the Keynesians? Economists who adhere to the 1930s writings of British economist John Maynard Keynes. They believe, as he did, that governments should engage in deficit spending in hard times in order to spur a lagging economy. On the other hand, Keynes proposed that governments should balance budgets in good times and pay off their debts with surplus money.

It's that kind of thinking that has added to the monetary inflation of the twentieth century. Why? Because if deficits crowd out private investment, then they cannot be expansionary.

Writing in *The National Review*, Stephen Moore said that Keynesians' cautioning about the evil of deficits is the equivalent of Madonna preaching against smut.

4. In 1984, Robert Reich (who, by the way, is now Clinton's secretary of labor) wrote that having a chronic budget deficit "is an overconsuming evil with insidious long-run consequences for American might and influence."[9]

5. Paul Krugman and Larry Summers, both Clinton economic supporters, predicted an "Inflationary Time Bomb" during the Reagan years. Yet, every year until 1988, the liberal economists were disappointed that the inevitable tax hike never happened and the economy continued to expand.

Reagan was coerced into a modest tax increase, far short of what the liberal economists wanted, and within two months after the 1987 crash, there was no evidence of permanent damage on the economy.

Those economists who predicted—and hoped for—a Reagan disaster are today advising President Clinton. In addition to their political agenda, they have only one other matter on their minds. Guess what it is.

RAISING TAXES

Yep. Raising taxes. Like most Democrats, President Clinton and his party think raising taxes will fix the deficit.

But as we have seen, the deficit isn't the entire dilemma. How we get rid of the deficit—that's the problem. There is a right way and a wrong way to fix it.

Congress knows we need to get the deficit under control, and I believe we will. However, it will take longer and make matters worse if our elected repairmen use the wrong tools. One of their favorite ways of greasing up the economy is to pour on more taxes. However, tax increases only gum up the works. We have only to look at recent history for evidence of that fact.

In the early sixties, President John Kennedy proposed incentives somewhat like Ronald Reagan's, and the economy expanded. When Jimmy Carter

• *"If 10 percent is good enough for God, it should be good enough for the IRS."* • • • • • • •

came into office, his fiscal policies caused America to eventually end up in a deep recession with interest rates that choked the life out of business growth.

The longest economic boom in American history came during the Reagan years. Why? Because Ronald Reagan cut taxes. Most Americans fared better in the 1980s than at any other time in their working lives.

Although there is room for debate on this issue, I believe the problem with the economy in the 1990s is not the result of Reaganomics but because President Bush abandoned Reaganomics. Bush went back on his famous "read my lips, no new taxes" campaign promise. As a result, the economy faltered, and voters punished him in the 1992 presidential election.

Instead of raising taxes, there are other ways to reduce the deficit and stimulate the economy at the same time. Here's what I would like to see our government do.

Institute a Flat Tax

The tax laws are so complicated that CPAs can no longer keep track of them all—and even they are calling for simplification. Almost half of taxpaying Americans have to pay someone to help them complete tax forms. Why? Because between 1981 and 1989, more than eight thousand subsections were added or amended to the Internal Revenue Service Code. Eight thousand!

A flat tax would cut loopholes for major corporations, making the tax basis more fair for the rest of us taxpayers. Simplifying tax laws and overhauling the system would help lower the deficit by putting more cash in the system.

My favorite bumper sticker reads, "If 10 percent is good enough for God, it should be good enough for the IRS."

Cut Government Spending

As discussed earlier, the key to economic success—whether it be in the family, business, church, or nation—is not to spend out of control.

Cut Taxes on the Middle Class

Someone has said, "Thieves rob banks because that is where the money is." The same philosophy applies to our government. The middle class is taxed to death because that is where the money is.

If the average taxpayer had more money in his pocket, he could spend more and, thus, help stimulate the economy.

Increase the Job Market

Government needs to work hard to increase the job market by spending tax dollars to make improvements to the infrastructure instead of doling out money for social programs. If the government insists on spending, then let the money be put to good use. For example, America's interstate highway system is in desperate need of repair. Money spent on new roads would create millions of new jobs and benefit the transportation of products at the same time.

Don't Overtax the Rich

Overtaxing the rich will not ensure our survival. We need to encourage entrepreneurs and those with large amounts of capital to invest in America and not take their money overseas. I will elaborate more fully on this point in the next section.

THE ROBIN HOOD EFFECT

In America, we have a preconceived notion that the rich make life miserable for the rest of us. Actually, the opposite is true. Some people blame their poverty on the rich. They think, *If the rich weren't so greedy, I could have a bigger piece of the pie.* That's why a lot of people—and politicians—like the idea of robbing from the rich to give to the poor.

Being greedy, however, has little to do with being rich. Greed is an attitude of the heart. Some of the richest people I know are the most humble, dedicated Christians you will ever meet. On the other hand, some of the poorest people are the most proud and selfish. You can be homeless or living on welfare and still be just as greedy as the rich and famous.

Our nation thrives today because rich entrepreneurs invested in our country when it was only a fledgling group of colonies. Sure, they made money in return, but they risked their own capital in uncertain ventures. The same is true of businesspeople today.

On the other hand, we have created a subculture of welfare dependents who want to live like the rich but have no desire to offer anything back to society. Instead of working, some people expect the government to support them for the rest of their lives. That philosophy has stripped away incentives and created generations of families who are unproductive and uneducated.

It's not just the uneducated, however, whose incentives are misplaced. Some Harvard graduates are just as guilty. They despise the rich, yet, at the same time, expect exorbitant salaries and perks from high-paying government jobs. They want the best of both worlds by hoping to sap the wealth out of those who have earned it.

Politicians may win elections by spouting the Robin Hood theory of robbing from the rich to give to the poor, but in the end who really suffers? Taking money from the rich only keeps the wealthy from expanding their horizons. When the rich retreat to their villas in France, it's the working man who loses out.

In an *Inc.* magazine article titled "The Enigma of Entrepreneurial Wealth," George Gilder emphasizes that point:

> If we smear, harass, overtax, and overregulate them [the rich], our politicians will be shocked and horrified to discover how swiftly the physical tokens of the means of production collapse into so much corroded wire, eroding concrete, scrap metal, and jungle rot. They will be amazed by how quickly the wealth of America flees to other countries.[10]

We have only to look at Hong Kong to see how that can happen. Today, entrepreneurs are fleeing this thriving British colony and setting up business elsewhere. Why? Because in 1997, Hong Kong will revert back to the control of mainland China. Everyone knows that capitalism cannot coexist with a communist-style government.

Some politicians, however, want us to believe that the socialization of America will benefit everybody. How? By creating a nation where the distribution of wealth is equal. We have only to look at the fat cats of communism to see how that idea worked in reverse. The bureaucrats robbed from the private sector—not to give to the poor, but to provide for their own exorbitant life-styles.

If the rich suffer, so will the rest of the people in this nation. High taxes will not keep the rich from being rich, and more regulations won't keep them from making money. The old adage "You have to spend money to make money" applies. The rich make more money because they have more money to invest in businesses. And businesses employ people. And people pay taxes.

The rich must be allowed to take financial risks in order for our free-market economy to move forward and provide jobs for Americans.

IS AMERICA GOING BROKE?

Allowing businesses to compete freely is healthy for the economy. When companies are investing, they create jobs, which in turn creates an increase in tax revenue. The more people who are working and earning money, the more income they have on which to pay taxes.

Raising taxes deters economic growth. In fact, past tax increases levied on American citizens have netted the government no increase in revenue. Why? Because businesses stopped investing. As a result, jobs were lost, and so were the taxes those workers would have paid to the government.

Price controls and rationing will only increase the deficit. Hopefully, President Clinton won't abandon the free market principles that have made this economy stable. If he can maintain stable inflation and low interest rates, our economy will recover—albeit very slowly.

Even though Clinton's economic plan has its flaws, they are not enough to kill us. Higher taxes, however, are on the way, and that will stunt economic growth in spite of stable inflation.

None of this means America will be broke by the year 2000. The reader should not believe that a total economic collapse is imminent any more than Christian America should have panicked back in the 1950s. That's when the unbelievable statistics on the national debt were first released, putting the price tag at $287.5 billion.

The economy is strengthening. That's the most important factor. Employment statistics, retail sales, and productivity show improvement. So don't throw in the towel; there is still money for the government to tax.

FIVE LIBERAL MYTHS

When *The National Review* held a 1993 conference in Washington, D.C., seventy-eight experts were invited to give their opinions on how our nation can be revitalized. One of the most profound speeches was given by Republican Senator Jack Kemp.

Kemp's purpose was to discuss how to depose the Democrats and renew the nation in 1996. To that end, he mentioned five myths that must be dispelled. I will focus on the first four because they deal directly with the economy.

1. The American people need to sacrifice.
2. The deficit is due to the fact that Americans are undertaxed.
3. Government can create jobs.
4. Children are a drain on the resources of America and the world.
5. There is no intrinsic problem in the values of the poor.

Remember, these are myths—not truths.

Myth #1: The American People Need to Sacrifice

Like Senator Kemp, I disagree with this myth. We should not have to sacrifice in the way of paying higher taxes because we have not created the deficit. It's the spending habits of the government that have gotten us into the mess the country is in right now. That's why the solution has to come from the top down and not the bottom up.

The U.S. government must reconcile its out-of-control spending and put a system of control in place. If the government cuts back spending sufficiently, the deficit will be reduced, and the national debt will be brought under control. The solution is *not* to simply burden the taxpayers with higher taxes.

Americans have to stop letting the news media, political action groups, and lobbyists dictate our policies. As more Americans become alarmed and educated about the way things are going, the more pressure they will put on politicians to begin working out the solution to the problems.

Myth #2: The Deficit Is Due to the Fact That Americans Are Undertaxed

You and I both know that Americans are not undertaxed. What causes the deficit, then? Government waste of the tax money it already collects.

Part of the deficit problem has resulted from government's spending for the benefit of lobbyists, philanthropists, and affirmative action groups—and not for the benefit of the general population. The government asks for more taxes to make life better, and then spends the tax money on obscure studies.

The Clinton administration's decision to increase taxes won't reduce the deficit. You can bet there are plenty of lobbyists and bureaucrats waiting in the Capitol wings ready to gobble up any extra revenue. That has happened time and time again.

I live in California. The state has so many regulations and taxes that it is almost impossible to function. California, like the U.S. government, has not yet figured out if you tax and tax and tax, you destroy the base that makes taxes work. Raising taxes retards economic growth.

Corporations that have tightened their belts over the last few years now have cash. American investors also have cash. A record number of investors are putting money into mutual funds, and, because of this, more mutual funds are being established. There are literally thousands of mutual fund investments now.

Homeowners are refinancing their homes, and that has given them increased cash flow. Companies are paying down bond debt, causing the supply of long-term, non-government bonds to shrink. Credit is now freer and interest rates are lower, making it possible for companies to expand and create more jobs.

All of those positive indicators can be killed, however, by new higher taxes.

Myth #3: Government Can Create Jobs

The government doesn't create jobs; it builds bureaucracy. That's why the U.S. government is the largest employer in the world.

Anytime the government decides to create jobs in the private sector, it only adds more people to the federal payroll to oversee new projects. In the end, the "new jobs" require higher taxes and stifle economic growth.

Why? Because entrepreneurs create jobs—not government. If the government wants to help instead of hinder job creation, it should lessen the burden of regulations that impede technological advances. The government actually prevents new business start-ups that create jobs for Americans by taking away the very incentives that entrepreneurs need to survive.

Myth #4: Children Are a Drain on the Resources of America and the World

America's children are not a drain; they are our greatest resource. In order to successfully tap that resource, America needs to overhaul our entire educational system.

Thomas Sowell, a writer for *Forbes* and a Hoover Fellow, outlines how the problems of the future stem from the problems of the past in *Inside American Education.*

The problem with America's educational system, according to Sowell, is not its children; it's the educational bureaucrats. The National Education Association—the nation's largest trade union—sucks up our tax dollars by the billions and gives us illiterates in return. Yet NEA's president had the nerve to say that the problems of education were caused by the failure of policy makers to give education the money it deserves.

If we want to put America back on its feet, there is plenty we can do. Committing tax money in the right places—such as implementing good educational policy—that directly benefits the taxpayers would answer the problem.

STEPS TO ECONOMIC GROWTH

If the government creates innovative ways to finance programs, the deficit won't grow any larger. That will keep the deficit under control until other methods the government uses, including the dreaded tax hikes, start to work. Why? Because economic growth will offset the negatives of new taxes, if they are not too high.

What can be done to reduce the deficit in the meantime? President

Clinton can do nothing until the economy is stronger, but here are some steps he could take that would encourage economic growth:

1. Hold up the $150 billion appropriated by Congress for infrastructure improvements.
2. Cutting the Social Security tax by as much as $100 a month would not hurt the system.
3. Repeal the luxury tax, which penalizes industries that produce big-ticket items.
4. Repeal the Tax Reform Act of 1986, which took away the investment incentives and raised taxes on capital gains.
5. Let the banks make more loans by easing regulations.
6. Encourage state and local pension funds to lend money for public works, and possibly put a government guarantee on them.

Where does that leave us?

In 1992, the economy grew by only 3.7 percent, but with a good jolt, GDP could easily grow by 3 percent. Interest rates will stay low for some time, and that enhances the stock market. Economic growth is certainly possible in the near future, and in some places of the world it's happening now.

At a time when other major economies are in slowdown, four small economies have set records in expansion: Hong Kong, Singapore, South Korea, and Taiwan. Some religious doom and gloomers may jump on the fact that those are all Asian economies and try to tie them into biblical prophecy.

> • *I am optimistic about the future because I still have faith that the system can be made to work.* • • • •

Statistics indicate that those economies are thriving because they have lower tax rates on capital and lower tax rates on earnings than any of the other industrialized nations. These four prospering Asian countries are less than half the size of the G7— which represents the U.S., Japan, Germany, France, Italy, the U.K., and Canada. Yet, according to Peter Brimelow, a writer economist for *Forbes*, this is the only time in history "where countries have gone from rags to riches in one generation."[11]

In his article "Why the Deficit Is the Wrong Number," Brimelow suggests that the United States institute the same economic growth stimulants used by those four Asian economies: lower tax rates on capital and lower tax rates on earnings.

If that happened in our country, recovery would be enhanced. Economic performance is penalized, however, not by the deficit, but by the government's exorbitant output of money to create jobs and provide services that have little cash return and actually stunt economic growth.

Again, it is not the federal deficit that penalizes economic performance. In fact, government spending often ends up draining the economy.

For instance, a few years ago, the government allowed environmentalists to hold up the construction of a dam in the TVA in Tennessee. This important and much needed dam would have benefited the economy in that state by increasing jobs and revenue.

What was the problem? The snail darter. The project was put on hold while environmentalists completed a study—using federal funding—to determine how to preserve the snail darter. Why? Because they said it was an endangered species.

Later, however, it was discovered that, not only were snail darters not on the verge of extinction, but that millions of them existed in the Mississippi River. Such irresponsible decisions increase the federal debt by forcing the government to borrow from reserves to finance unnecessary projects.

Government spending always comes at the expense of economic growth. That's why the government needs to lower its portion of the Gross Domestic Product, which is the value of all the goods and services the country produces each year.

If the country's GDP is expanding, then the government can increase its debt. In other words, the more productive we are, the safer it is to borrow. Conversely, the less productive we are, the more we should pay down our debt.

Even with our huge deficit, however, the government is only extracting from the American economy what amounts to 9 percent of GDP. Western Europe, on the other hand, extracts significantly more—18 to 21 percent—from their economy.

Japan and the United States have the smallest government shares of any world economies. These two countries also have the largest output per capita and the fastest growth rate of any nation. That fact should send a message to President Clinton.

IT'S NOT OVER YET!

Someone asked me, "If you could give one quick solution to fix America's problems, what would it be?"

My answer required very little thought. "Clean out Congress by voting in a law that limits the number of terms they can serve. In fact, limits should be set in every facet of government—from the feds all the way down to local officials," I replied.

That would give us fewer lawyers and professional bureaucrats on Capitol Hill who serve their own interests and not their constituents'. We need more businesspeople running the government. That could happen soon since some states have already voted for term limitations of elected officials.

Another way to fix our nation's economic and social problems is to overhaul the judicial system and limit the terms on federal judges. The court system has had a lot to do with the mounting federal deficit. If violent and repeat criminals were given the death sentence, the prison population would be reduced. That would save taxpayers millions of dollars and allow government to spend money in a way which would benefit all Americans.

I am not naive. I know that the government must attack America's economic problems. I have never believed the country can live forever with the so-called "sins" of deficit spending and an out-of-control budget. But I am optimistic about the future because I still have faith that the system can be made to work.

If the tax policies of the Clinton administration fail as the same policies did for Jimmy Carter and George Bush, the Republicans must seize the moment. It will be their opportunity to recapture the credibility they gained under Ronald Reagan by becoming the antitax party.

I must also point out that both Republicans and Democrats are seemingly committed to reducing the deficit. But can they raise taxes *and* get their budgets under control? That depends on whom President Clinton listens to. The doomsayers who ranted about the dangers of the deficit were wrong during the Reagan years, and they are wrong now.

If any president—whether Clinton or a new one in 1996—can cut the deficit, balance the budget, and use legislative maneuvering to accomplish such a formidable task, there will be no economic earthquake. The end will be averted, and our country can comfortably move into the next century.

MYTH FOUR:

All Debt Is Unbiblical!

. . . .

I need to see you right away," a pastor from New Jersey told me one evening at the end of my seminar.

Sensing his desperation, I drove more than four hours from Washington, D.C., to his church on the outskirts of New York City. It was not unusual for me to do that since part of my ministry involves counseling pastors whose churches are experiencing financial difficulties.

As I pulled into the exclusive subdivision and saw the beautiful brick church situated on several acres of wooded property, I wondered, *What kind of problem could this guy have?*

As soon as I walked in and sat down, the pastor stated, "I'm in trouble."

"Are you in debt?"

"No," he answered. "The church doesn't owe a dime."

"Then how can you be in trouble?" I asked, puzzled by his answer and noting the obvious prosperity all around me.

"The church building is too small. There's no more room, few parking spaces, and the members are discouraged because people tell them the cramped situation makes them uncomfortable."

"Why don't you build?" I asked.

"Can't," was his candid reply.

. . . .

"Why not?"

"Because I've been teaching our people for seven years that we cannot ever go into debt as a church."

"Oh," I said, noting several books on debt-free living lining the library shelf behind him. I immediately knew what he was going to say next.

"Don't tell me. In fact, let me tell you," I proposed, having counseled other pastors facing the same dilemma. "After you started preaching against debt, all your businesspeople left the church."

He glumly stared at the floor. Then he said, "That's exactly right. I told them it is a sin to go into debt, not realizing that business owners often have to borrow money if they want to expand or take advantage of business opportunities. So they left."

"You know," I explained, "depending upon the type of business, most companies cannot survive without lines of credit. Those costs are built into their normal overhead. Ministers who push the no-debt philosophy drive the businessmen and women out of the church. In fact, most churches frustrate the sophisticated public with this impractical—and I might add—unbiblical doctrine."

"Unbiblical!" he exclaimed, obviously shocked by my comment. "I assumed the Bible clearly taught against any and all debt."

"No, it doesn't," I replied and went on to show him from Scripture the fallacies of the debt-free philosophy.

"What should I do now?" he asked, realizing he had been misled. "Let's go outside," I suggested.

As we walked out onto the beautiful hillside, I looked around and said, "You've got some property down there over the hill that you don't need. Sell it, and use the money to pay for the expansion on your building."

"I couldn't do that either," he replied sheepishly.

Right away, I knew the reason. "You taught the people that the property was given to you by God, and it can't be touched for any monetary purpose. Correct?"

The pastor nodded.

"I'm sorry, but I don't know what else to tell you," I replied, wishing I were able to help.

As I drove away that day, I was convinced more than ever that the debt-free trap will never work—not today, not tomorrow, not in the church, not in business, not in the family, and not in any economy.

. . . .

WHAT IS DEBT?

Nowhere does the Bible teach against debt. Instead, I believe the Bible teaches principles concerning how to handle debt.

But some Christian financial writers say otherwise. If they kept their philosophies to themselves, it wouldn't be so bad. But they enslave tens of thousands of other people with their debt-free rhetoric, putting them into financial and religious bondage. Like the Pharisees of Jesus' day, "they bind heavy burdens . . . and lay them on men's shoulders" (Matt. 23:4). Although I'm sure that is not the intention of those in the debt-free living camp, it is, unfortunately, often the result of their teaching. Whether unintentional or not, however, people still wind up feeling hog-tied as to their financial options. As a result of buying into this philosophy, they unfortunately equate going into debt with being unfaithful to God—truly putting them between a rock and a hard place. And needlessly so.

The debt-free proponents are likely to quote Romans 13:8. In fact, this verse forms the basis for their philosophy. "Owe no man any thing, but to love one another: for he that loveth another hath fulfilled the law."

To understand that verse, we must read it in context. The previous verse reads, "Render therefore to all their dues: tribute to whom tribute is due; custom to whom custom; fear to whom fear; honor to whom honor." In that verse, we are taught a valuable lesson: to render to others what is due. If things are due, then we must owe. In fact, it is impossible not to owe somebody something, sometime.

Is Paul, through the inspiration of the Holy Spirit, talking about money? First, he is writing about the debt we owe others spiritually. In Romans 13, Paul is talking about the debt of love we owe one another. He's saying, "Don't stay in that debt, but show your love." He goes on to say that we are to "love thy neighbour as thyself" (v. 9), thus teaching us how to love without falling into the sins of the world. Nowhere in the chapter does the apostle mention money.

Second, we are to pay our taxes—"tribute to whom tribute is due." How many of us pay taxes in advance? I don't, and I don't know anyone who does (unless you are self-employed and pay estimated taxes every quarter). That means there are times when we "owe" taxes, right?

Third, we are to pay our customary debts—"custom to whom

custom." Every month we run up telephone, electric, gas, water, and sewerage bills. When do you pay them? After the companies bill you. So, you actually owe money for a whole month. In addition, most mortgages are paid a month in arrears.

What about our debt to God? Do we pay our tithes as soon as our paycheck is deposited in the bank? No, we wait until we take our tithe to church and put it in the offering plate. So, for a short time before we go to church, we owe our tithes.

Living debt-free, then—for all practical purposes—is impossible. If you feel guilty because you have debt and someone has told you it is sin, don't!

In these verses from Romans, I do not believe God is talking about being in debt financially. He is admonishing us not to stay in a state of "borrowing" with our neighbor, God, or the government. I believe He is talking about not *continuing* to be in anyone's debt.

If you have borrowed a lawn mower from your neighbor, take it back when you said you would. If you have been withholding your tithes, start tithing immediately. If you've been fudging on your tax returns, adjust your statement as soon as possible. If your car payment is overdue, get it in the mail. That's rendering what is due.

Those who insist that debt-free living is the only truly Christian way to live saddle believers with an unbearable and impractical burden.

THE DEBT-FREE TRAP

As I drove toward the 100,000-watt radio station that booms out over the four states of Colorado, New Mexico, Arizona, and Utah, I wondered how the listening audience would respond to my approach to economics.

After my brief interview with the talk show host, listeners were invited to call in. The most popular question that day was, "Is debt-free living commanded in the Bible?"

As always, when my answer was no, the phone lines lit up. Although the show was scheduled to air for an hour, the station pre-empted James Dobson, Chuck Swindoll, and several other syndicated programs to accommodate the numbers of calls received from listeners.

Some callers—and the talk show host himself—were relieved to hear an opposing opinion to the debt-free living philosophy. Others, however, found my ideas offensive, and a few brothers even became hostile, calling me every name but "Christian."

Most American Christians, however, are confused about the pros and cons of borrowing money and going into debt. I meet thousands of people throughout the year, and

> • *I do not believe all debt is wrong; I do not believe that the Bible teaches it is wrong.* • • • • • •

most—when they hear a reasonable, scriptural explanation—are extremely relieved to know the truth. Why? Because debt-free living is bondage.

What are the results of such bondage?

- A businessman trying to keep up with competition may eventually go under if he refuses to get a loan to expand when market conditions warrant it.
- A family hoping to better their life-style will become frustrated and overworked if they try to live debt free.
- A church looking to increase the size of their facilities will stagnate and die if they believe going into debt is unbiblical.

That's why I reject the idea of getting out of debt at any cost.

One financial writer says in his doomsday book, "I believe I have done what the Lord asked of me: I have warned you. If I am wrong and you do all the things I have suggested, the worst that can happen is that you will end up out of debt and be more involved with our political system."[1] What is the worst that can happen if he is wrong and you follow his advice and cash in your retirement fund to pay off your mortgage? Let me tell you the facts:

- Your retirement account will be gone.
- You will take a 10 to 20 percent penalty plus all the taxes taken directly from your pension money.
- You will lose the only significant tax credit most Americans have, which is the interest on their homes.
- You will be facing the future wondering how you are going to pay the taxes, insurance, and upkeep on your debt-free home with no retirement money left.

You wouldn't bet your retirement at the roulette tables in Las Vegas, would you? Why, then, would you gamble your future on predictions about the American economy that may or may not be true?

Let me state emphatically: I do not believe all debt is wrong; I do not believe that the Bible teaches it is wrong; I do not believe everyone should pay off his or her mortgage; I do not believe everyone should be 100 percent out of debt. Now let me tell you why.

USING DEBT AS LEVERAGE

In 1990, our church—which started very humbly with a small cinder block building in 1987—had grown to the point where we could grow no further. The church owned no property and had very little money.

In the city of Napa, California, property for building in acceptable locations costs $500,000 per acre. To purchase the four acres required by the city ordinances and to build a good-sized church that could continue to grow, we needed $2 million just for starters. The building itself would cost an additional $2 million.

Hundreds of thousands of dollars more would go for our part of the street-widening project and the enormous fees our city charges churches for building permits. We soon discovered that every building law in Napa legislates against churches.

What were we to do? Miraculously, the property next door to our cinder block building went up for sale. I walked over to the owner's place and asked, "How much do you want for the house and the back acreage?"

The price he quoted left me speechless, and I walked away heavy-hearted. We needed that property, and I knew only one way to get it. I asked our church to pray.

In the meantime, we trusted God and rented a modular building, but it was overcrowded within a few months, and again we had nowhere to go.

One Sunday morning after church, the man who owned the property next to our little building walked into the office.

"I want to see the pastor," he told the secretary, and she led him to me.

"What can I do for you?" I asked, surprised by the unexpected visitor, especially since he was wearing a swimsuit.

"I want the church to have my property. I've reduced the price."

"Great!" I said, excited by the answer to prayer. "I'll get back to you."

I knew our church still did not have enough money to buy the property, even at the lower price, but time was of the essence.

What did we do? We went to the bank and borrowed the money—interest and all—and bought the property.

Later, when four acres opened up two miles from our church, we sold the original property at a great profit, bought the new acreage, and moved into a slightly larger building with plans to build a new church. Today, we have a beautiful new facility with more than $4 million in property and more expansion on the way.

That's how to use debt as leverage to accomplish a worthwhile goal. Throughout the entire process, we maintained control of the situation and used the bank and the initial loan to our advantage.

A BETTER WAY

Some Christian financial experts say that paying interest makes no sense in any economy. Let's test that idea, using the story I just told you.

Suppose I go to our congregation and say, "We would need four million dollars to buy property and build a new facility."

"Okay, let's borrow the money and do it!" they agree.

"Can't."

"Why not?" they ask.

"I learned that the Bible teaches all debt is wrong. We can't expect the government to reduce the deficit if we go into debt ourselves. Therefore, we will just have to wait on God and save the money."

"How long will it take us to save the money?" the committee chairman asks.

"At the rate we're going now, probably twenty years," I respond factually.

"But that means we'll never be able to reach out to more of the people of Napa Valley," he answers.

Suppose we decide to go that route and put money aside for the next twenty years. At status quo and given normal inflation, which is

4 to 5 percent, how much would we have saved by not borrowing the money and paying the interest? None. In fact, we would have gone further in the hole.

Why? Because construction inflation runs ahead of other industries. That means the cost of building a similar facility twenty years later would probably have doubled. Because of inflation, we would need to save for another twenty years to catch up with the increase in construction costs. Talk about chasing your tail!

"There must be a better way," you say. Fortunately, there is.

Our church took special offerings, saved money, and used debt as leverage. Since 1992, when we finished the new facility, our attendance and our offerings have increased substantially. Our short-term plans are to pay off the debt as quickly as possible so our debt-to-interest cost ratio will be nominal. As a result, we have a beautiful new building and plan to be debt-free within seven years. That's a lot better than twenty—or forty.

Now what if we had not borrowed money from the bank? Our small church would either be bursting at the seams and forced to turn newcomers away, or people would have left because of the overcrowded facilities. Either way our church would still be small and inefficient, and neither scenario furthers the kingdom of God.

Suppose we do have an economic earthquake? Our church may or may not be in debt at that time, but we still would be better off if we lost the building than if we had not built it at all because we would have reached people who might not have come to Christ otherwise. That is worth far more than any interest we would have paid.

THE COST OF DOING BUSINESS

What is interest? Interest is simply the cost of doing business.

A dentist from Tennessee called me recently and said, "I've read all the books on debt-free living, and I'm convinced the economy is headed for collapse and no one can stop it."

"Well," I said, trying to find out why he had called, "how's your practice doing?"

"To tell the truth, I'm losing patients and don't know what to do," he stated in a worried tone.

"Would you mind if I asked you some questions?"

"Shoot," he replied.

"Do you tithe?"

"Well, when I get completely out of debt, then I'm going to start tithing."

His answer didn't surprise me. A lot of debt-free-living people think that way. Because they believe debt is sin, they figure it's better to stop sinning before they start tithing.

"Do you need new equipment in order to upgrade your practice?"

"Yes," he answered, sighing heavily.

"Do the dentists you compete with have this equipment?"

"Yes." I could sense the discouragement in his voice.

"Have you lost customers because your equipment is outdated?"

"Yes, they're all going to the new guy across town."

"Do you want my advice?" I asked.

"Of course. That's why I called you."

"First of all, start tithing and quit worrying about getting out of debt," I told him bluntly.

"Second, borrow more money and buy the equipment you need, advertise that you have it, and get your customers back."

"Third, make your borrowing short term only. As your cash flow increases, paying back the loan should be no problem. That's the proper use of debt."

"What about the interest I'll have to pay?" he quizzed.

"If inflation is 6 to 7 percent, then the cost of making those same purchases ten years from now is going to be the same, or more than the interest you would save by not financing the project now and doing it later. So you will lose what you would have gained by not paying interest on the money during that time."

Those principles apply to any business. In fact, you wouldn't have a job to go to tomorrow if your corporation or place of business didn't use debt as leverage. Your company leverages through the sales of stocks, bonds, debentures, and creative bank financing. That's how they finance their business so they can employ people like you to work for them. Leverage is essential in a free-market economy.

Walt Disney knew how to use debt to his advantage. One afternoon Roy Disney—Walt's brother—was very discouraged after poring over the financial records of the Disney Companies.

Walt walked in and noticed the rather depressed look on Roy's face. "What's wrong?" Walt asked.

"We are four and a half million dollars in debt with absolutely no way to pay it off at this time," Roy replied. "We have fifteen hundred people on the payroll, which is getting harder to make each payday. It looks like we've had it."

Walt started laughing.

"What's so funny?" Roy asked.

"I can remember when we couldn't borrow a thousand dollars," Walt replied.

What's the difference between leverage and financing with debt? Leverage is debt used only for a short amount of time and only for the reason of the cost of doing business. Leverage is right, but financing with debt is wrong.

WHEN DEBT *IS* WRONG

If you cannot control debt, then you should stay out of debt. If you borrow money, and the debt becomes a millstone around your neck, you need to get out of debt as soon as possible. If you're drowning in interest charges or you're struggling to pay off your debts, you need to take radical measures.

We'll talk more specifically about how to know if you're overextended and what to do about it in part two of this book. For now, suffice it to say, there are times when going into debt is wrong.

After one of my seminars, a well-dressed gentleman came up to me and said, "I have listened to your philosophy about debt, and I agree with it. In fact, I wouldn't be worth three million dollars if I didn't borrow money."

He was obviously a rich man, but he was also a borrower. How can that be, you ask, when Proverbs 22:7 says, "The rich ruleth over the poor, and the borrower is servant to the lender"?

For one thing, the word *servant* would be better translated "obligated" in the sense he owes the lender. The borrower is "obligated" to the person who lends him money. This verse, however, says nothing about debt to the lender being wrong. Debt is only wrong when you borrow, knowing that you can't pay the money back.

We live in a credit-driven economy. God, however, has never legislated against any kind of economy, whether it be a feudal fiefdom, a communist dictatorship, or a monarchy. God has given us practical ways to prosper in any government. We have only to study the lives of Joseph, Solomon, and Daniel in the Old Testament to see that success and prosperity don't depend upon the economic system of the country where you live.

In capitalistic America in the late twentieth century, we finance our free-market economy with debt. If the Bible teaches debt-free living, then God must be discriminating against capitalism.

How many economies have there been on the earth since God created man? Thousands. Every nation develops a different set of rules. That's why it is incorrect to imply that the Bible

> • **If the Bible teaches debt-free living, then God must be discriminating against capitalism.** • • • •

is written for only one kind of economic structure. In fact, biblical financial principles—when properly followed or applied—will work in any economy, whether it be the home, church, business, or nation.

If every Christian in America stopped lending and borrowing, we wouldn't have to wait for an economic earthquake. Why? Because America's economic system would collapse for sure.

We live in a free-market economy. Our standard of living is the highest in the world because there is plenty of money available to be loaned and borrowed. Believe me, the wages of sin is not debt.

INTEREST VS. USURY

"But I'd have to pay all that interest!" a client responded one day, as if I had suggested he rob the bank instead of borrow from it.

Let's be practical. First of all, the Bible does not teach that interest is wrong; it teaches that usury is wrong. "If thou lend money to any of my people that is poor by thee, thou shalt not be to him as an usurer, neither shall thou lay upon him usury" (Ex. 22:25).

The dictionary definition of *usury* states, "Unconscionable or exorbitant rate or amount of interest charged; interest charged in excess of the legal rate charged to a borrower for the use of money."

When exorbitant and unfair interest is charged on borrowed money, that is considered usury. Loan sharks are guilty of usury, and states have laws protecting the consumer against usurious interest.

In most of the United States, it is illegal to charge more than 4 percent over the legal rate of interest set by a state unless there is a legal contract between the borrower and the lender. That's why banks can legally extract usury from the consumer for credit card debt.

When you sign a contract on your Visa or Mastercard letting them charge you 18 to 22 percent, in my opinion, you are agreeing to usurious interest.

The Bible condemns usury in no uncertain terms. Let me give you an example. Nehemiah 5:1–13 describes the hard times experienced by the captive Israelites. A drought in the land had depleted the grain stores, and famine threatened the people. Taxes were high, and the Israelites were behind on their payments to the king. In order to purchase grain and pay their taxes, they had to mortgage their homes and farms. Because money was scarce, it had to be borrowed. The nobles and officials were more than happy to lend the poor folks money, but they:

1. Charged 12 percent interest.
2. Forced them to secure the loans with their lands.
3. Took children for bond servants to be sold as collateral.

The people complained bitterly to Nehemiah, and he angrily denounced the loan sharks, saying in effect, "How could you exact usury from your own countrymen and sell them as slaves?" (vv. 6–8).

Although Nehemiah had his hands full building the temple wall, he persuaded the evil men to stop the usury, give up the mortgages, put the people back in possession of their estates, remit the interest, and give them time to pay the principal. Ashamed of themselves, the noblemen promised to do as Nehemiah commanded and agreed not to demand anything more from the people.

This passage teaches two things:

1. *It's okay to lend money to people who need it.* Nehemiah and his men were also lending money and grain to the people (v. 10).
2. *Usurious interest is wrong.* Those who continued to treat the people unjustly would reap God's judgment on themselves and their families (v. 13).

To extract high interest from a person who has little ability to repay his loan because he has fallen on hard times is against the Word of God.

What is a reasonable interest rate? Around 10 percent. In fact, that has been the accepted, universal standard by which people have loaned other people money for centuries. Even today, most people expect a return of at least 8 to 10 percent on their savings account and set up their retirement accounts based on 8 to 10 percent.

LENDING WITHOUT BORROWING?

If it is unbiblical to pay interest, as some suggest, then it must be wrong to borrow. If it is wrong to borrow, then the lender is just as guilty as the debtor, right?

You may say, but I'm not lending anyone money. Let me ask this question: Where do you put your money? In the bank? What do banks do with the money you deposit? Lend it to other people. That makes you a lender.

If it's wrong to pay interest, then it must also be wrong to collect interest. Do you put your money in the bank and let it gather interest? If interest is unbiblical, why are you collecting it?

If interest and borrowing are wrong, then you should keep your money out of the banks because they pay interest to you while charging other people interest to borrow your money.

The Bible, however, does not teach that interest is wrong. If large sums of money are borrowed to start a business or purchase goods for trading, it's only fair that the lender share in the profits made by the borrower. After all, the lender provided the means for the borrower to increase his wealth.

So is collecting interest unbiblical? Absolutely not. In Jesus' parable of the talents, the master told the "wicked and slothful" servant who buried his money that he should at least have put it in the bank where it could have collected interest. Jesus must have thought this was the wise thing to do since the parable condemns those who are afraid to invest (Matt. 25:26).

So what are you going to do with all that money you save once you get out of debt? Put it in coffee cans and bury it in the backyard? When a lady from New Mexico called and asked me to advise her about making some investments, I asked, "Where is your money now?"

"My money is in the freezer," she replied.

"Well," I said, trying not to sound too surprised, "how much do you have?"

"Forty thousand dollars."

"Why do you keep your money in the freezer?" I questioned.

"I'm afraid of a fire, and in the freezer it won't burn up."

"What if the electricity goes off during the fire?" I asked. "Everything in the freezer would thaw out and burn up anyway."

"I never thought about that," she replied.

I was eventually able to convince this woman to put her money in several safe investments where she could collect interest.

WHEN BORROWING MAKES SENSE

Most people don't borrow money for two valid reasons.

1. They don't want to pay interest. This can be a personal or practical issue, but it is certainly not a biblical mandate.
2. They have no means to pay back the loan. You need to pay back what you borrow; otherwise you are borrowing under false pretenses.

I cannot find one verse in the Bible to indicate that borrowing or lending is wrong or that charging reasonable interest is against God's law. Scripture does teach, however, that we are to be careful how we borrow or lend money.

Exodus 22:14–15 teaches one of the principles of borrowing:

And if a man borrow aught of his neighbour, and it be hurt, or die, the owner thereof being not with it, he shall surely make it good. But if the owner thereof be with it, he shall not make it good: if it be an hired thing, it came for his hire.

Simply put, we should not abuse anything loaned to us. If a man loans a horse to a neighbor and the neighbor receives a profit from the loaned horse, he has a right to payment for the use of the horse. If anything had harmed the horse and the owner had received profit, he must stand good for the horse. If the owner loans the horse free to the neighbor and the horse gets hurt and dies, the borrower must make it good. Nothing in those verses says it is wrong to borrow— whether it's a horse or money.

One of my favorite scriptures in the Bible concerning borrowing is found in Matthew 5:42. Jesus said, "Give to him that asketh thee, and from him that would borrow of thee turn not thou away."

Two principles are taught in that verse: (1) We should always be ready to give if we have the ability to give; (2) if we do not have the ability to give, we possibly have the ability to lend.

I believe that in some cases lending money is as great an act of charity as giving it. The borrower, of course, is then responsible to repay the debt, according to Scripture. In that way, lending can help the borrower develop a greater sense of responsibility. A person who gets everything free or as a handout, without being expected to repay, becomes dependent—either on the giver or, as in the case of welfare, on the government.

If the Bible condemns borrowing and "to owe no man anything," as some people suggest, why did Jesus recommend that we lend to those in need?

Debt-free promoters, in an effort to discredit borrowing, are likely to quote Psalm 37:21: "The wicked borroweth, and payeth not again: but the righteous sheweth mercy, and giveth." This verse does not say it is wicked to borrow. But it is wicked not to repay what you have borrowed.

An old adage passed down from generation to generation says: "Pay your just debts." Throughout history people have borrowed and were honorable when they paid back what they "justly owed." Paying our debts is definitely a scriptural principle.

I conduct several seminars a year in the beautiful mountain area of central Pennsylvania. After one of the sessions, a man came to me and said, "All my life I have believed debt is wrong. I thought no one could change my mind, but you have done it in twenty minutes."

"Now don't get me wrong," I replied, in case he had misunderstood. "I do believe it is better to be out of debt if you can live that way."

"To stay debt-free, I have to work two jobs," he said with a sigh. "I'm out of debt, but my house needs repair, my car is worn out, my son needs braces, and I can't make any headway because I refuse to borrow money."

Then he began to smile, as if a huge weight had been lifted off his shoulders. "During your seminar," he continued, "I figured that if I go to the bank and refinance my mortgage, I can quit my second job and still be able to make the mortgage payment and a car payment every month. With the money I borrow, I can then remodel my house, put on a new roof, and have more time to spend with my family."

Although his was an extreme case, I couldn't help admiring that man's wisdom. With a home equity loan, he would be able to leverage his mortgage over twenty years, instead of trying to pay for an $8,000 roof on a $400-a-week salary.

Debt-free living is not good for every American, and the Bible does not teach against debt. To take on debt as a means of refinancing or reducing debt (consolidations, and so on) makes sense. But no one should take on debt just because it is available.

MAKING DEBT WORK FOR YOU

In *The Coming Economic Earthquake*, the author says, "To take a stand against [government] waste means that God's people must also refuse to take FHA or VA loans. Christian farmers need to say, 'Thanks but no thanks, Uncle [Sam].'"[2]

In other words, you should help reduce the government debt by refusing government money. I must disagree. If the government is going to spend money, then, I believe, it should be for the benefit of those who finance the bureaucracy by paying their taxes.

Millions of Christian Americans have benefited—as they should—from VA (Veterans Administration) and FHA (Federal Housing Authority) loans. Those loans have allowed families to buy homes when they could not qualify for a conventional loan. Radical debt-free teachers likewise advise that churches should take care of these people. That's a nice thought, but is it scriptural?

- *Debt is only wrong when you borrow, knowing you can't pay the money back.* • • • • • •

In Acts 4, the people brought their goods—which included lands, houses, and other possessions—to the apostles. Did the first church at Jerusalem use this money to finance new homes for their members? This passage only mentions that "neither was there any among them that lacked" (v. 34). Although Christians are required to help the poor, nowhere in the New Testament did Christ leave instructions for the church to become a bureaucracy or a social welfare agency.

Suppose you do take a government loan to build or buy a new

house. Did you know that you would actually be stimulating the economy instead of being a drag on it, as some say? It's a fact that whenever Americans build new homes and move up financially, that in turn helps the economy expand.

You have to live somewhere, and you'll either pay rent or pay a mortgage. In most parts of the country, it is cheaper to buy a house and get the tax break than to rent and make the landlord rich. In fact, interest rates on home mortgages have dropped to the lowest levels since the 1950s. As a result, reasonable mortgage payments should be considered a necessary part of monthly household expenses.

CAN YOU HANDLE IT?

No American should be in debt unless the debt is advantageous to better living and doesn't threaten the long-term economic condition of his or her home or business.

When I counsel people about their finances, I know when someone is falling through the cracks. If I see that happening, I always advise, "Get out of debt. And, if you can't handle credit, don't use it." But I never advise people to get out of all debt at all cost.

Most folks don't need to be taught debt is wrong; they need to be taught how to handle credit. And if they can't handle it, they have no business getting credit.

In part two of this book, I include a section called "28 Ways to Know You're Overextended." That will help you determine where you are financially and whether or not you can handle debt. If several of those symptoms are chronic in your life, you need to take immediate steps toward getting out of debt.

Before going into debt, ask yourself, *If I did go broke, would the people to whom I owe money be adversely affected by my failure to pay?* To risk someone else's money when you're not sure you can repay it would be totally irresponsible and unfair to your creditors.

Delaying paying your debts when you have the money to pay is also unjust. Proverbs 3:27–28 states: "Withhold not good from them to whom it is due, when it is in the power of thine hand to do it. Say not unto thy neighbour, Go, and come again, and tomorrow I will give; when thou hast it by thee." Those verses are not teaching that it is wrong to owe your neighbor; they are saying it is wrong to delay paying your debts simply for the sake of holding on to the money.

In America, credit turnover is important to our economic well-being. If people hold on to their payments too long, it forces the creditor to borrow and pay more interest. That eventually hurts the lender's financial status in the long run.

WHEN ALL ELSE FAILS

In 2 Kings 4:1–7, we read about the widow of a prophet (today we would consider her a preacher's widow) whose husband had died, leaving her poor and in debt. Although he had revered the Lord and had not lived riotously and luxuriously, he died owing more money than he was worth. Now his creditors were harassing his wife.

Many people today, who live under the constant pressure of collection agencies, can identify with this woman's distress. Her situation was much worse, however, because the man to whom she owed money was coming to take her sons as bondsmen for seven years to work off the debt. In desperation, she went to Elisha for help.

He asked, "Do you have anything in your house you could sell to make money?"

"Just a little oil," she replied.

"Okay," he said, "go to your neighbors and ask for as many jars as they will loan you. Then fill each of the jars with oil."

Although the widow had nothing of value to sell, Elisha reasoned that she had credit with her neighbors. Apparently she had somehow managed to keep her credibility by paying her own debts in the past.

Elisha asked the widow to borrow pots from her neighbors and shut the door behind her so her creditors would not interrupt. Then the miracle began.

As soon as all the jars were full, the oil stopped flowing.

When she told Elisha, he said, "Sell the oil and pay your debts. Then you and your children can live on the profit that is left over."

There are five lessons I have learned from this passage over the years:

1. Sometimes we get into trouble and can't help it. Circumstances prevail beyond our control. (And we certainly don't need to go on a guilt trip over circumstances!)
2. It is wrong to go into debt just to support our life-style.
3. Borrowing is not wrong if it serves a godly purpose.

4. If our neighbor wants to borrow something from us in time of need, we should be more than willing to let him or her use it for a time.
5. Sometimes, we need a financial miracle.

If debt is destroying your marriage, your family, your peace of mind, or your health, get help as soon as possible.

IT'S ONLY MONEY

Many Americans have their values all messed up. Perhaps a little bullet biting or belt tightening would be good for us. After all, it's only money. Right? At least, that's the conclusion I came to after a long and stressful financial struggle.

The late 1970s were very difficult for those of us in the construction business in Kentucky. Like many others, I got caught overextended and was having a hard time surviving financially. A young man at the time, I wasn't used to the brutality of business pressures—at least to the degree I was being hit at that point.

For several months, I had known I would have a hard time meeting my obligations at the bank. Finally, the day came when I had to face the music. Paying my bills every Friday had been a longtime habit with me, and I hated to admit that I couldn't continue to come up with the money I needed.

"I won't be able to make my payment next month," I announced to the bank financial manager sitting across the desk from me.

"No problem," my banker said. "How much do you need to get you by until spring?"

When I told him the amount, he replied, "I can raise your escrow account by that much. Then you can just go to the window and draw the money when you need it."

"I don't think you understand, Jimmy," I explained. "If you loan me more money, I will just owe that much more come spring because this economy isn't turning around. I am going to have to sell out to pay my debts."

Later that day, feeling heavy-hearted, I walked into the office of a retired army colonel who was also a building contractor. "Sherm, you don't look so hot," he said. "Those blue eyes aren't sparkling, what's wrong with you?"

I was surprised at his perception. "Colonel, I don't think I'm going to make it. I just told the bank I can't make my interest payments in another month. I think my life is over."

"Your life is not over. Let me ask you some questions. Are you having marriage problems?"

"No, sir. Everything is fine at home."

"Are Shawn and Scott doing okay in school?"

"Straight A students."

"How is your health?"

"Great. No problems."

"Let me tell you a story. I was in Vietnam trudging through a rice paddy. It was pitch dark. I had been shot down. I had a dead navigator on one shoulder and a wounded gunner on the other. The Viet Cong were behind me with dogs, and I was wading in water up to my nose. I told God if He kicked me out of a helicopter stark naked over the Atlantic Ocean without a parachute, I would have a better chance of survival than I have now."

He paused and closed his eyes, as if trying to blot out the horrible scene. Then, throwing his shoulders back in military fashion, he continued.

"You know how I got through the next three and a half years in a prison camp? I wasn't thinking about my Cadillac. I wasn't thinking about my houses or my farm. I said, 'God, if you will let me kiss the ground in Miami and see my wife and kids again, there is nothing that will ever make me feel this bad ever again in my life.' By that time, my head was almost on the floor.

"You see, your problems are no problems at all," the colonel continued. "It's only money that you're worried about. Everything in life that amounts to anything you already have, but you aren't focusing on what really counts. You're focusing on the things that don't count. Besides, aren't you a Christian?"

"Yes, sir."

"Where's your faith? Practice what you preach."

I left the office that day with a new lease on life. There was no reason to give up hope because God had preserved everything in my life that had any value. For the first time, I got my eyes off myself and onto the Lord.

I arrived at home and walked into my den. My wife was standing in the kitchen.

.   .   .   .

"Can you give all this up?" I asked.

"What for?" she responded, bewildered by the question.

"For the Lord."

"Yes, I can give it all up for the Lord."

For months, God had been speaking to me about starting a church. I had dreams that I wanted to fulfill and ideas I needed to try. It seemed that the time had finally come for us to make a break.

When I was offered a job as a consultant in California, I knew God was leading us. I was looking forward to putting my degree in business to work, and California seemed the ideal

• *Most folks don't need to be taught debt is wrong; they need to be taught how to handle credit.* • •

place to build a new career and start a work for the Lord.

We sold what we had, paid our debts, and moved to California to begin our new life and an exciting ministry. Since then, God has replaced virtually everything we gave to Him. Isn't that what He promises to do?

GOD OWNS IT ALL

I believe God controls everything. He owns everything, and His sovereignty prevails over this world. If I believed my house was going to be destroyed by some natural disaster, I wouldn't live in an earthquake zone, a tornado zone, hurricane zone, or any other kind of zone that could ultimately obliterate everything I owned. Because I trust God to protect me, I believe He will at least warn me if something life-threatening is going to happen. That's why I live a normal life free from paralyzing fear. I drive on the highway without worrying about being killed, and I fly on airplanes knowing I could be the next statistic. I live in an earthquake zone; I take trips to tornado country; and I swim in the ocean during hurricane season.

I look at the economy the same way I look at life. Although I understand the dangerous turns the economy could take, I still trust God and all His principles. That is not to say that I skip blithely down the primrose path of life. Instead, I walk confidently, knowing we are living in the day of grace and God is not going to use cataclysmic destruction to discipline His children.

I do believe, however, that God will one day pour out His judgment on the world in the form of tribulation. On the other hand, if Jesus Christ does not return to this earth soon, I will keep attuned to the changes in the world economically and prepare the best I can.

How did Americans survive World Wars I and II? How did we survive the Great Depression and all the recessions since 1929? We survived because we adjusted to change, looked to God for His help, and trusted in His Word. What reason do we have to doubt that God won't see us through again?

MYTH FIVE:

A Secret Society Controls the World

. . . .

One day while working in my brokerage office, I received a phone call from another broker whom I had known for several years. During our conversation, I mentioned that I was writing a book on exploding the doomsday money myths.

"The chapter I'm writing now has to do with the Illuminati," I told my friend, whom I knew was not a professing Christian.

"The illumi-what-y?" he asked, obviously having never heard the word.

"Oh, it's supposedly a secret organization founded in the eighteenth century that has been plotting the takeover of the world."

"And how are they supposed to do that?" he asked with a cynical laugh.

"Well, the story goes that there is a conspiracy in the United States led by the Federal Reserve Board, the Council on Foreign Relations, and the Trilateral Commission. Their goal is supposedly to destroy America and usher in the new world order."

"You've got to be kidding!" he exclaimed. "Surely nobody really believes that kind of stuff."

I took a deep breath, wishing I had never brought up the subject. "Well, actually, this myth has been floating around in Christian circles for years and is considered by many to be the gospel truth."

. . . .

"Oh," he responded.

I knew what my friend was thinking—*Christians are so gullible; they must believe everything that comes down the pike!*

Before I could explain that many Christians, like myself, take a more reasonable and logical approach to the idea of a worldwide conspiracy theory, my broker friend quickly made a feeble excuse to hang up.

Heavy-hearted, I put down the telephone and said out loud, "No wonder the secular world considers Christians to be a bunch of flakes and nuts!"

THE BOOGEYMAN'S GONNA GET US!

When I was a little child, I believed in the boogeyman. Every night, I looked under my bed and checked the closet to make sure no one was hiding there. The boogeyman was very real to me until, one day, I grew up. The apostle Paul said, "When I was a child, I spake as a child, I understood as a child, I thought as a child: but when I became a man, I put away childish things" (1 Cor. 13:11).

Whoever made up the boogeyman myth has nothing on the folks who perpetrate the Illuminati theory. Many adults, however, believe that a secret organization founded in the 1760s controls life on this planet—especially in Europe and America. Although there is no evidence to support the idea, many folks are adamant in this belief and will argue insistently if you disagree with them. The name *Illuminati*, by the way, is just one of several interchangeable terms for such secret societies: you can plug in several alternate titles, including The Trilateral Commission, the Council on Foreign Relations, and others.

I believe this myth is a figment of someone's imagination used to create paranoia in the minds of gullible people. It is pure fiction.

Before I can refute the idea of an Illuminati, you should understand how this supposed secret organization is portrayed today. Documentation of the historical development of the Illuminati and its sinister plans to orchestrate world events, however, does not exist. All we have as "evidence" is the conclusions drawn by those who have taken world history and inserted powerful players into scenarios that may or may not have actually happened.

Accounts of this illusionary history come from various sources, such as the Christian Defense League, the John Birch Society, and certain Christian experts on prophetic events. Permit me to summarize the sequence of these episodes and the overall plot for world domination as the secret society theorists view them.

As you read the following, however, bear in mind that my purpose is to educate the reader about how the Illuminati supposedly came into being and what it does today. Do not lose your concentration and think that I actually believe any of this propaganda. I will show you scripturally that you have nothing to fear from a secret organization controlling your finances.

From this point on, I will refer to those who perpetrate the Illuminati as "secret society theorists."

WHERE DID IT ALL BEGIN?

Who are the names and faces behind the all-powerful organization that seeks world domination? Supposedly, it all began in 1776, when a Jewish man named Adam Weishaupt, who had been raised by Jesuits, broke away from the Catholic faith and founded the Order of the Illuminati in Ingolstadt, Bavaria.[1]

The word *illuminati* is derived from activities of "Lucifer" and means "holding the light." Weishaupt, who earlier had been initiated into alchemy and witchcraft, supposedly carried out his occult practices under the cover of the Freemason Lodge in Munich.

In addition to practicing occultism and Satanism, the Order of the Illuminati had political and economic ambitions. The intention of the original twelve members of the Illuminati was to establish their own world dictatorship after making the traditional institutions of the family, church, and government obsolete.

Among the early members were such rascals as Voltaire, Mirabeau, and Robespierre. "In France the most fanatical group of Freemasons, the Jacobins," also joined and later had a hand in the gruesome French Revolution.[2]

Prophetic author David Allen Lewis lists the "preliminary goals" of the Illuminati for establishing their new world order:

1. The abolition of private property.
2. The abolition of the family structure.
3. The abolition of religion.
4. The abolition of national governments.

5. The abolition of inheritance rights.
6. The abolition of capitalism.[3]

Vivian Herbert, in her 1927 book, *Secret Societies Old and New*, writes: "The Areopagites or twelve disciples of Weishaupt alone knew what the aim of the society was—to establish their own world dictatorship after clearing out established institutions."[4] One wonders how secret society theorists are able to delineate goals that the Illuminati took such great pains to hide and no one has been able to document.

In spite of all that secrecy, the plans of the Illuminati members were soon foiled when, in 1785, Bavarian officials discovered a plot to overthrow the Bavarian government. Fearful that its dissident operations would be discovered, the Illuminati went underground.

In *En Route to Global Occupation*, Gary Kah writes: "Although the Illuminati officially ceased to exist after its exposure in the 1780s, the continuation of its efforts would be ensured through the grand Orient Lodge of France. . . . Freemasonry would continue with its [the Illuminati's] plans to build a New World Order."[5]

Gary Kah builds quite a case for the Illuminati-Freemasonry connection, taking it all the way back to the ancient religion of Pantheism. From there, he traces every known pagan practice, including witchcraft, sorcery, and Hinduism, to the cults of the 1800s and today's new age thinking. Mixed in with all that, of course, is Marxism, communism, and the international banking elite!

How does that all fit together? Kah explains that the evil Weishaupt "succeeded at forging an alliance between illuminized Freemasonry and the growing Rothschilds banking network, thereby giving the order the financial means to begin to carry out its plans."[6] That idea has led to the theory that, since the 1700s, Weishaupt's philosophy "is secretly guided by a small group of powerful, wealthy men throughout the world."[7]

There is one major problem with this simplistic, two hundred-year-old approach to the satanic lust for power and control. It is not a recent historical development (as Kah proves by his own cult research); it has been going on for more than six thousand years—since the Garden of Eden.

The secret theorists, however, want us to believe that, before 1776, Satan had just been tinkering with humankind, waiting for the diabolical and ingenious Weishaupt to take his place on the world's stage.

From what I know from the Bible about Satan's character, that is definitely not the case.

THE WORLDWIDE PLAN?

The secret society theorists use more than imagination to convince us that their hypothesis is actually truth. In order to do that, they must conjure up the weapons used by this sinister organization. And what were they? Money and power.

From their secret hiding place within the Masonic organization, the group supposedly seized control of all the European monetary systems. How did they do that?

According to the Christian Defense League, it all began with the Napoleonic wars, which they say were financed by the Illuminati. However, at the time the group was financing Napoleon, it was also supporting Germany and England, who were resisting the French aggression.

Nathan Rothschild, a member of Weishaupt's Illuminati, supposedly spread a rumor that when Napoleon met his "Waterloo" at Waterloo, he didn't actually lose the war but won it. The rumor reached the shores of England, and it so devastated the British people that the British stock market fell.

To take advantage of the situation, Rothschild supposedly proceeded to England, bought all the stocks at fire sale price, and ended up controlling the European economy. As a result, he set up the Bank of England, which eventually led to

• *Could it be that Someone other than the Illuminati was controlling world events during the late 1700s—and that He is still in charge today?* • • •

his control of the banking system in the United States. This theory is not substantiated, but it doesn't stop there.

By financing certain wars, the Rothschilds and other Illuminati members seized control of European and American financial institutions and—the theory goes—still manage them today.

As a result of their lust for power, in fact, the Illuminati supposedly financed the French Revolution, which led to the American Revolution against England and France. How did they accomplish this amazing feat? Simple. These masters of control created discontent in the American colonies, which resulted in war with England—and our freedom.

If they so desperately wanted to abolish nationalism and capitalism in order to dominate the world, why would the members of the Illuminati help our fledgling nation gain independence? If the Illuminati is a satanic organization, why would it support a group of God-fearing, Bible-believing colonists? Could it be that Someone other than the Illuminati was controlling world events during the late 1700s—and that He is still in charge today?

Not according to the secret society theorists. As far as they are concerned, nearly everything that happens on this planet results from a plot conceived in the mind of Nathan Rothschild two hundred years ago and carried out by his descendants and specially chosen inductees. In fact, there seems to be no end to their meddling in the affairs of nations.

ROTHSCHILD'S REVENGE

The theory continues that during the 1700s, the House of Rothschild believed the nations were weary of war—which the Rothschilds had been financing. To initiate worldwide peace, they organized a meeting of national leaders known as the Congress of Vienna. Rothschild figured that, because the nations owed him so much money, they would capitulate and give him control of the peace congress— and the world.

The Russian czar smelled a rat, however, and foiled the plot. Nathan Rothschild apparently became so angry that he vowed to destroy the Russians, no matter how long it took. Knowing he could not live long enough to see his vow fulfilled, Nathan Rothschild pledged that his descendants would effect Russia's destruction. The Illuminati is very patient, you see.

When they weren't planning and financing wars all over the globe, the members of the Illuminati worked within the political realms of nations.

According to the Christian Defense League, the Illuminati held a secret meeting in New York in the 1850s. The purpose of this meeting? To start the Communist Party. Why? Because Rothschild wanted to foster the dissident ideas of Karl Marx.

According to secret society theorists, the Illuminati financed

Marx—the founder of the most treacherous political system the world has ever known. Rothschild supposedly gave Marx the money to publish his book *Das Kapital*, which became the forerunner of the *Communist Manifesto*.

The reason? The Illuminati believed that by establishing communism they would gain control of the entire world.

That's why the Rothschilds are given credit for the Bolsheviks' rise to power and the overthrow of the czarist government of Russia in 1917. By financing the Russian Revolution, the Illuminati fulfilled Nathan Rothschild's vow for revenge.

It is truly amazing how the Illuminati operate on such a long-range basis and are able to convince their students and descendants to carry out—in full detail—previously conceived conspiracies.

If the Illuminati bankrolled communism as a means of controlling the world, then who orchestrated the fall of communism? Today, communism doesn't exist except in Cuba, North Korea and mainland China. At one time, communism controlled the lives of more than 500 million people worldwide, who—whenever they had the opportunity—fled the tyrannical rule of that godless system. From 1989 through 1990, nation after nation overthrew the shackles of their communist governments and brought to trial the tyrants who had enslaved them.

It is impossible for any group—no matter how large and powerful—to control foreign policies or relations and their impact on world politics and economics. Anyone who reads the newspapers, watches television, or pays even the remotest attention to what is going on in the world can barely keep up with the changes.

Nations change their policies like dogs shed fleas. It is impossible for the most skilled diplomats to know how other nations are going to react to America's policies and vice versa. We have only to consider unpredictable lunatics like Saddam Hussein, the botched invasion of Kuwait, and the ensuing Gulf War to realize that most of the predictions surrounding that entire scenario never came to pass.

Think for a moment. How many economies have come and gone on the earth since its creation? How many governments have risen and fallen? Today we cannot even keep up with the new names of countries being formed and carved out of the former Soviet Union much less predict the outcome of those changes. In fact, every global map more than two years old is already out of date.

The only One who can keep tabs on the transitions taking place on this planet is the same One who has every hair on our head numbered and sees every sparrow that falls. And it's not the Illuminati.

ROTHSCHILDS' ERRAND BOY

About the same time that the Rothschilds were bankrolling Karl Marx and his atheistic theories in Russia, they were also looking for a way to control American society. According to the Christian Defense League, they first needed a co-conspirator and mastermind, whom they found in Jacob Schiff.

Born in Frankfurt, Germany, in 1847, Schiff's brilliance and abilities caught the attention of the Rothschilds, who sent the twenty-one year old to America for the express purpose of carrying out their conspiracy assignments. Because young Jacob was intelligent and extremely loyal, the Rothschilds believed that he was the one to help the House get control of America and, ultimately, the world.

How did this bright young man pull off that amazing and all-encompassing feat? With a master plan, of course. Although the Illuminati theorists don't have tangible evidence of this plan, that hasn't stopped them from devising an incredible scenario outlining Schiff's ultimate goals.

First, he was to acquire control of the American monetary system. How did he do that? Easy.

Paul Warburg, another German who was also an American representative of the Rothschild family, had become a partner in the financial institution of Kuhn, Loeb, and Company of New York. Using Warburg's influence, the Rothschilds bought their way into the businesses and families of America's wealthiest entrepreneurs.

Gary Kah explains how this happened:

> Through their U.S. and European agents, the Rothschilds would go on to finance the Rockefeller Standard Oil dynasty, the Carnegie steel empire, as well as the Harriman railroad system. The Rockefellers, who later became intermarried with the Carnegies, would go on to finance many of America's leading capitalists through Chase Manhattan and Citibank, both of which have long been Rockefeller family banks.[8]

As a result of their family ties, a bond of loyalty was cemented between these wealthy families that has never been broken. Gary Kah concludes that "much of America's corporate wealth is ultimately traceable to the old money of Europe and the one-world interests of Freemasonry."[9]

By lending and giving money to those vast entrepreneurial giants, Jacob Schiff bought their loyalties and made them cronies of the Rothschild-Illuminati conspiracy, where they have been ever since. To maintain control of these independent industrial giants, Rothschild told them that Jacob Schiff was the boss and everything was to be cleared through his office.

According to the secret society theorists, the Illuminati ended up with control of the money supply in America, and Jacob Schiff had completed the first part of his four-part assignment.

WARS AND RUMORS

During the early 1900s, it seems that the members of the Illuminati were busy on several fronts.

In spite of the temporary setback at the Congress of Vienna, the Illuminati, financed by the wealthy banking families of Europe, continued to push for world unity.

The next opportunity came after World War I, when President Woodrow Wilson, who was under the influence of Illuminati agent Colonel Edward House, tried to institute the League of Nations. This time it was Rockefeller who helped fund the venture, "which was to serve as the first political step toward the forming of a world government."[10]

Although the American people rejected the idea of this move toward globalization—much to President Wilson's embarrassment—the Illuminati did not give up. They decided to wait until the American public was ready for a world peace-keeping organization.

After World War II, the Illuminati, working through its members on the Council on Foreign Relations, founded the United Nations. In fact, the United Nations is considered to be the power behind a conspiracy whose main objective is to destroy the solvency of the United States and ultimately enslave the American people.

The Illuminati, we are told, hold to their same original goals today: Destroy all governments and religions—especially Christianity. How? Create wars in order to get control of the world.

The power of the Illuminati knows no bounds, according to those who subscribe to this myth. Secret society theorists believe the world's major wars—and many smaller ones such as the Korean and Vietnam wars—were planned, financed, and manipulated by this powerful organization.

No single organization has now or has ever had enough money to carry out such an all-encompassing project. What private person or organization has enough wealth to finance one war, much less all of them?

In fact, those who believe in the Illuminati theory say both World Wars I and II were financed and initiated by the conspiracy. According to secret society theorists, financier Paul Warburg "authored the War Finance Corporation, which allowed Kuhn, Loeb, and J. P. Morgan to finance World War I. In fact, the Federal Reserve Act and the new income tax law had been delivered 'just in time' to finance a European War. Without them, the war could not have occurred."[11]

At the same time Paul Warburg was bankrolling the Allies, his brother Max, who was head of the German S.S., was financing America's enemy—Hitler.[12]

What was the Illuminati's purpose in orchestrating and financing both sides of the world wars? To leave no nation untouched by the destruction and devastation of battle and the economic ruin that would follow. The plan was to bring the nations to their feet and then shore them up again by refinancing their infrastructure. That would take place, of course, after the nations had buckled under the control of their wealthy benefactors—the members of the Illuminati.

• **Surely there's a better and cheaper way for the Illumnati to gain control of the world than by destroying their own assets in the process.** • • • • • •

There is no historical proof, however, that any organization has ever cooperated to carry out such a preposterous plan.

Even if the members of the Illuminati were able to start a few wars, how would they control events once the battles started? And what about the aftermath of war? How could that be planned?

Surely the world wars—which were fought mostly in Europe—

would certainly have taken a toll on the very industries and institutions owned by the international bankers who were supposedly bankrolling the wars. That would cost them untold millions of their own money, not counting the billions spent to finance an expensive armed conflict like World War II.

If such a secret organization like the Illuminati does exist, surely there's a better and cheaper way to gain control of the world than by destroying their own assets in the process.

JEWS MURDERING JEWS?

In addition to starting World War II, the Illuminati supposedly had a hand in fostering the rise of Nazi Germany. According to the secret society theorists, the Illuminati was the force behind the Nazi concentration camps and the killing of six million Jews.

That seems odd. Wasn't the Illuminati mostly composed of Jewish bankers? Not to worry, the secret society theorists can explain this paradox. The fact that Jews were being killed was of no concern to these ruthless Jewish international bankers, they say, because it was worth the sacrifice to get the world to hate Hitler.

So we are supposed to believe that a group of Jewish bankers financed a horrendous war and a maniacal despot, whom they knew would murder six million of their own race, including women and children. And all for the purpose of overthrowing the very regime they had helped put into power.

As with their other bizarre explanations, the secret society theorists hope we won't ask too many questions. I, however, along with many other Christians, respect the Jewish people and believe they hold a special place in the heart of God. To portray God's chosen people as bloodthirsty, greedy, vindictive, ruthless tyrants borders on the same kind of anti-Semitism that comes straight from the pit of hell. Still, many Christians unwittingly perpetrate this kind of thinking with their Illuminati conspiracy theory.

A RHODES SCHOLAR?

Jacob Schiff, the Rothschilds' secret agent in the United States, had a second goal outlined by his benefactors. He was to find men who could be bought and promoted into high offices and positions of tremendous influence. In order to carry out this order, Schiff needed to recruit and covertly place bright young men who could be indoctrinated in the Illuminati philosophy of one-world government.

The young men were—and still are today—supposedly recruited by offering them expensive scholarships—like the Rhodes Scholarship—to universities where they are brainwashed by principles of humanism and secularism.

James Wardner, a dentist, includes this note about Cecil Rhodes in *Unholy Alliances:*

> An Englishman, Cecil Rhodes, had exploited the diamond mines and gold fields of South Africa (a British colony) and monopolized these . . . with the help of England's Lord Rothschild. . . . He spent his money to further his desire . . . "to federate English-speaking peoples and bring all the habitable portions of the world under their control." In order to accomplish this goal, Rhodes organized a secret society in 1891 which utilized the Rhodes Trust to fund the extension of the British Empire. This is the same trust from which the Rhodes Scholars are funded.[13]

Rhodes and his secret society failed miserably. During the late 1800s and early 1900s, one British colony after another rebelled against the Crown and gained independence. Today, the former British Empire is composed of only a few independent nations who enjoy certain benefits—like supporting the royal family—under the British Commonwealth of Nations; but that's about it. I don't think we have to worry about the British taking over the world.

It's true that the Rhodes scholarships were and continue to be awarded to students from the U.S. and British Commonwealth nations. Part of the plot includes planting these elitist, hand-picked scholars into high positions in government and universities in order to carry out the conspiracy and covenants made two centuries ago. In this way, the Illuminati plans to get control and keep control of the world and destroy its governments and religions.

MONEY AND MEN IN HIGH PLACES

To further their plan for world domination, the Rothschilds told Jacob Schiff to use money, sex, and bribery to get control of men in high offices and high places who could influence their respective governments. According to the Illuminati theorists, such intrigue has been going on for centuries and has enabled this all-powerful organization to manipulate the laws of nations and initiate wars all over the world.

In an effort to infiltrate the American government, Schiff first employed political stooges who had no scruples about selling out their patriotic sympathies. Using Rothschild money, he supposedly financed the campaigns of selected politicians from various states in the nation. By getting those men elected to Congress, Schiff eventually obtained the means to enact legislation that would eventually destroy the United States.

Schiff's greatest accomplishment, however, was gaining control of the Democratic party by planting politically ambitious and unscrupulous men throughout its ranks. (Republicans love this part!)

Through his influence over Congress, Schiff asked for a bill to create the Federal Reserve Board. President Howard Taft, however, would not sign the legislation into law. Not to be denied, the Illuminati waited until Woodrow Wilson was strong enough to win and backed his presidency. According to the secret society theorists, Wilson was one of Schiff's stooges and was more than willing to sell out his country for the conspiracy.

On December 23, 1913, President Wilson signed into law the Federal Reserve Board Act. Although that fact is true, it's hard to believe it was orchestrated by one man as some theorize. But it works to perpetrate the idea that formation of the Federal Reserve was Jacob Schiff's way of gaining control by appointing the members of the board—made up of selected international bankers.

In *Unholy Alliances,* Wardner writes:

> The Federal Reserve Act allowed the credit of the nation to fall into
> the hands of a few international bankers who now direct American
> policy and hold in their palms the destiny of the people. . . . There
> is a ruling elite in America and they and their imperial wealth
> know what they want and how to obtain it. They achieve their
> desires through legislation.[14]

Let me ask you: Who but bankers should be on the board of the Federal Reserve?

To answer that question, we need to understand the purpose of the Federal Reserve. This private organization is owned by banks and operates independent of government control. In fact, they answer to no one. Although those facts immediately create suspicion in the minds of most Americans, I believe the positives far outweigh the negatives surrounding the Federal Reserve Board.

Aside from supposedly lending the Illuminati members money from time to time, the major function of the Federal Reserve Board is to manipulate the flow of money in the United States. Since 1913, the Federal Reserve Board (FRB) has had the following responsibilities:

Coin money. Decide how much money was to be put into circulation. Today the Federal Reserve Board still acts in this capacity by regulating the money supply. In addition, the FRB has the power to lower or raise interest rates (prime rate), which in turn can heat up or slow down our economy.

Regulate the standards upon which our money is secured. At one time, the federal currency was backed by gold and silver but today depends on the faith and credit of the federal government. U.S. currency is better described as promissory notes based on a complicated bartering system.

The Federal Reserve wields tremendous power; there's no doubt about that. And, at times, their motives and actions must be called into question since their policies are based on economic principles that generally benefit the private owners of those banks. Often, however, what benefits them benefits the American public. In addition, their control over interest rates and the currency often forces our economy to adjust in positive ways and keeps America stable.

Which is worse? Having a group of professional financiers making the economic decisions for our country, or a bunch of Congressmen who aren't able to manage their own bank without writing rubber checks?

The conspiracy theorists, however, consider the Federal Reserve to be a sinister organization, "designed to allure, inextricably, the financial freedom and enterprise and hope of the people of America. It was designed to give ultimate power to a very small group of evil men. These are men who desire subservient behavior and ruthless power."[15]

THE ILLUMINATI AND THE IRS

Aside from the Federal Reserve Board, the only other independent government agency with that amount of power is the awesome Internal Revenue Service—the IRS. That's probably why the secret society theorists believe that the IRS and all its agencies are controlled by the Illuminati.

They also point out that all the federal regulators are international bankers and friendly to the controllers of the huge corporations, who are all supposed to be members of the Illuminati. That's why the secret society theorists blame them for the institution of federal income tax laws, which were supposedly created to enslave the common people. At the same time, the laws permit huge corporations to shelter billions in tax exempt foundations—like the Rockefeller Foundation, the Ford Foundation, and so on. Such laws are considered unconstitutional by the secret society theorists.

Who initiated this shift in American policy? Jacob Schiff, of course.

Schiff supposedly arranged for passage of the Sixteenth Amendment to the Constitution, which influenced the tax laws in such a way that the IRS could not touch the money sheltered in the tax-free accounts of the huge corporate trusts. Conspiracy theorists say that was done solely to benefit the Illuminati.

But how can one man get exactly the legislation passed that he needs and flawlessly predict how it will benefit him and his benefactors? Anyone who has studied the American economy and knows its trends realizes that no one can predict what the economy—or the American people—will do.

For a conspiracy to accomplish a work of the magnitude supposedly planned by the Illuminati, the economic legislation would not only have to be planned, but the outcome as well. Every senator, representative, and elected official, starting with local governments and emanating all the way to Washington, D.C., would have to be meticulously programmed and the outcome perfectly predicted.

THE NAACP AND THE ACLU

In addition to his political and financial maneuverings, Jacob Schiff still had time to work on the Illuminati's social policies. First on their list was to stir up racial strife in America. At least that's what members of the Christian Defense League believe.

Acting on orders from the Rothschilds, Schiff gets full credit for fostering racial tension across the United States. As part of the Illuminati's plan to destroy America, the Rothschilds conspired to create national chaos by pitting blacks against whites.

To carry out this plan, Schiff helped establish the NAACP (National Association for the Advancement of Colored People) by encouraging his rich friends to give money—from their tax-free foundations, of course—to finance the new organization. Using the NAACP as a front to carry out the Illuminati's activities, they planned to finance all subversive organizations that would incite race riots. The theorists claim that virtually every major disturbance was initiated by the great conspiracy.

In 1913, another organization, the Anti-Defamation League, was founded to oversee all Negro activist groups, including the Urban League, and any other group concerned with the interests of the black people—such as the ACLU (American Civil Liberties Union). Later, communist comrades infiltrated these black action groups and were used by the Illuminati to further their dastardly plot.

According to the secret society theorists, Martin Luther King, Jr., was an influential member of the Illuminati who carried out the orders of his co-conspirators. Many believe King's followers in the NAACP are still part of the conspiracy and blame them for every insurrection of blacks against the white race—both past and present.

TOO BIG TO BE TRUE

I could mention numerous other sinister actions attributed to the Illuminati, but let me make my point with a few examples.

According to Gary Kah, anyone who gets too close to the truth about the world conspiracy and seeks to expose it risks being murdered—like Congressman Larry P. McDonald, who, in 1993, was a passenger on Korean Airlines flight 007 when it mysteriously strayed into Soviet airspace and was shot down. Or Senators John Tower and John Heinz, who were killed in separate crashes of their small planes.[16]

I am sure there have been hundreds—perhaps thousands—of plots to create chaos in this country, overthrow the government, assassinate presidents, murder government leaders, and control our economy.

However, because of our political system, the free press, and the power of American voters, I do not believe any conspiracy could mastermind and carry out the extensive turmoil it would take to destroy this nation.

First of all, imagine the number of people such a scheme would need to enlist or buy off. To get enough people to carry on a conspiracy that affects the highest strata of society in the richest nation of the world is unrealistic. Second, it would take years to network and put into place every aspect required for a conspiracy of this magnitude.

Take the Mafia, for instance. Even in a secret organization so well-devised and connected, they seldom succeed over any length of time. During Prohibition days, the Mafia thrived for a while in racketeering, gambling, and the distribution of illegal alcohol. With government crackdowns, however, many of the Mafia kingpins were killed or put in prison where they grew old and died. And many of those who escaped the long arm of justice ended up being murdered by one of their own or by the member of a rival organization.

Time and greed are the enemies of any activity spurred by a lust for money and power over others. Eventually, the members of the rank and file of the organization rise up and topple those in control. Human nature is human nature. It didn't change simply because Nathan Rothschild and his cohorts decided to control the world.

If the Illuminati did exist at one time, it would long ago have collapsed from within. And even if those in power had been able to maintain their control, I doubt that God would allow any man-made organization to thrive for very long. Remember the Tower of Babel? God has His way of turning our best laid plans into a pile of rubble.

FUELING THE PARANOIA

Through the years, the Illuminati has been known by different names. Today, the Illuminati, we are told, reports to the Council on Foreign Relations (CFR) in America—as does every other sub-secret organization in the world.

Why? Because the board of the CFR is now and has always been composed of the descendants of the original Illuminati members. To avoid detection, however, they changed their names years ago and adopted a strategy of absolute secrecy.

If the Illuminati organization does exist today, wouldn't we find among its members those who worship the devil and practice witch-craft? After all, wasn't that the original purpose of the Illuminati—to perpetuate their evil ways? Why else would they seek to take over the world if it were not to force humankind to bow to their hellish agenda?

Instead, the conspiracy appears to be composed of bankers, politi-cians, intellectuals, military officers, businessmen, and television jour-nalists as well as Democrats, Republicans, liberals, and conservatives. You name it. Anyone who's anybody is a member of the Council on Foreign Relations or the Trilateral Commission.

According to Gary Kah, "every U.S. president since World War II, with the possible exception of John F. Kennedy and Ronald Reagan, has been either a Freemason, a member of the CFR, or a member of the Trilateral Commission. George Bush is perhaps the most prominent [conspiracy] insider ever to have attained the position of president."[17]

That premise underlies much of the paranoia surrounding the Illuminati and fuels such organizations as the John Birch Society. As a result, every branch of government is viewed as an extension of the Illuminati, and every policy or piece of legislation considered mere propaganda to further the plans of worldwide domination by those in power.

Hasn't every U.S. president since George Washington, at one time or another, had to withhold information from the general public in order to protect national security? For the Illuminati, however, govern-ment deception is a matter of course in an effort to keep Americans in the dark about issues affecting their sinister agenda. If that were true, then we'd have to also believe that our two-party political system is a huge hoax.

It is hard to accept that nearly every elected and appointed Re-publican and Democratic official from the president on down is part of a conspiracy to lie to the American people. That's not to mention the hundreds of lobbyists, special interest groups, and reporters who meticulously keep an eye on every memo, report, and piece of pro-posed legislation that crosses the desk of anyone in government. Be-cause of such scrutiny, our government is often forced to come clean and be up-front or face the consequences—which is often political suicide.

We have only to consider Nixon and Watergate, Reagan and the

Iran-Contra affair, the House of Representatives' banking scandal, and the Clinton Travel Office fiasco to realize how difficult it is for both Democrats and Republicans to hide the truth for very long.

Let's examine the two maligned American institutions—the CFR and the Trilateral Commission—and see if they truly do have a sinister agenda for world domination. Or even a suspicious one.

THE COUNCIL ON FOREIGN RELATIONS

According to the secret society theorists, the CFR is a round-table group of international leaders who have imperialistic tendencies and who continuously plan the takeover and control of countries. The plot goes back to the one devised in England by Cecil Rhodes, where it became known as the Royal Institute for International Affairs (RIIA).

Here's how one secret conspiracy believer describes the CFR:

The CFR, established in New York, July 29, 1921, was a front for J.P. Morgan and Co. (in itself a front for Rothschild banking). . . . Since 1925, substantial contributions from wealthy individuals and foundations and firms associated with the international banking fraternity have financed the activities of the Round Table Group. . . . All of these have links with the international banking family, the Rothschilds.[18]

What do the theorists think the members of the CFR hope to achieve? "By controlling government . . . the power brokers are able to control an entire country's economy, politics, law, education and day to day subsistence."[19]

The conspiracy believers consider the CFR to be the American branch of a society that wants to obliterate national boundaries and establish one-world rule. As an arm of the Illuminati, the CFR has supposedly devised ways of destroying the freedom and independence of the United States.

In *The Insiders* (published by the John Birch Society), John McManus, a proponent of the secret conspiracy theory, states:

The Council on Foreign Relations was conceived by a Marxist, Edward Mandell House, for the purpose of creating a one-world government by destroying the freedom and independence of all nations, especially including our own. Its Chairman of the Board is

David Rockefeller. And its members have immense control over our government and much of American life.[20]

The Council on Foreign Relations does exist. That's a fact. It is located in New York City on 58th Street, and you can find the phone number in the city directory. Out of curiosity, I called the offices of the CFR. They fully answered all my questions without hesitation or reservation and faxed me additional information about their organization. I must admit that their candor surprised me, and I couldn't help thinking it was not your average cover-up conspiracy.

• *The Council on Foreign Relations was founded after World War I primarily to help stop future wars—not start them.* • • • • •

So, what *is* the Council on Foreign Relations? It is a partisan group of leading men and women who study foreign relations and give their opinions on certain issues. The Council has no affiliation with the U.S. government and receives no government funding—and won't accept any. They are financed by membership dues, magazine subscriptions, and private donations.

Because their members are generally high-profile experts who have made foreign policy their business, our government officials often look to the CFR for advice. In fact, their input often helps strengthen American foreign policy decisions when a positive outcome is in America's best interests—like the fall of communism in Eastern Europe and the support of democracy in Russia.

The CFR was founded at the end of World War I primarily to help stop future wars—not start them as the conspiracy theorists would have us believe. By acting as a liaison between governments and people concerning foreign relations policies, they are able to work behind the scenes to smooth the ruffled feathers of government leaders and keep diplomats functioning within their designated guidelines.

Every discussion among CFR members—among whom are liberals and conservatives, Democrats and Republicans—is an open discussion. In fact, they publish their viewpoints in a news magazine called *Foreign Affairs*. Although they appear to take a liberal stance on most foreign policy issues, their thinking differs little from the rhetoric found in *The Washington Post* or *Time*.

Who Belongs to the CFR?

Members of the CFR are selected from specified fields and include such opposites as conservative U.N. Ambassador Jeanne Kirkpatrick, who served during the Reagan administration, and Warren Christopher, Bill Clinton's secretary of state, who was also the number two man in the Carter State Department.

During their open public discussions, members are known to have hearty disagreements among themselves over foreign policy issues. With a membership of more than three thousand that constantly changes year by year, it would be impossible not to have varied opinions. As a result, members are forbidden to speak for the council on any matter of public policy. That, however, does not prevent members from giving their own opinions on foreign policy issues.

In fact, Jeanne Kirkpatrick, one of the recent directors of the CFR, is often interviewed by news commentators on network television to provide a conservative viewpoint to foreign policy issues.

Although I am not defending the CFR, I am trying to offer a reasonable explanation for its existence. In fact, as I understand it, the CFR works like a think tank, investigating, researching, and addressing important foreign policy issues.

After all, isn't this America, where freedom of speech and a free press are heralded and coveted by its citizens—especially Christians? Why, then, do some people want to put the clamps on our more liberal citizens? Don't they have a right to their opinion too?

When you look at the names of those who are and have been listed among the members of the CFR, it's even more difficult to believe that a conspiracy is afoot. If it is, either the leaders or its members are confused about the purpose of the CFR.

Some of the reputed members of the CFR who supposedly seek to control our nation and the world include: Presidents Dwight Eisenhower, Lyndon Johnson, Richard Nixon, Jimmy Carter, George Bush, and Bill Clinton and a host of senators, representatives, governors, and other prominent political figures, including most of the government leaders before them. In addition, the cabinets of all these past and present presidents were and are composed mainly of members of the CFR.[21]

In other words, the CFR is an organization of the United States government, but the government won't admit it.

The John Birch Society makes these conclusions about the members of the Council on Foreign Relations:

> In our opinion, however, not every member of the CFR is fully committed to carrying out Edward Mandell House's conspirational plan. Many have been flattered by an invitation to join a study group, which is what the CFR calls itself. Others go along because of personal benefits such as a nice job and a new importance. But all are used to promote the destruction of U.S. sovereignty.[22]

As far as I'm concerned, those who think Ronald Reagan and Dwight D. Eisenhower were conspirators to destroy this country are on the verge of being traitors themselves. Although they may not have been perfect presidents, Reagan and Eisenhower were certainly committed patriots who proved their loyalty to America time and time again.

According to the conspiracy buffs, however, many of the trips that U.S. presidents make to foreign countries to visit with heads of state are nothing more than secret meetings to discuss the demise of America. In other words, there is no escape from the doom being planned and organized by the members of the CFR who orchestrate wars, race riots, financial scandals, and all the wickedness we have on the planet. Such a scenario borders on the ridiculous. All things considered, the CFR is like any other private organization with a membership and a cause. In fact, they have twenty-five directors who serve for a limited term staggered over five years.

With those kinds of safeguards, it would be very difficult to maintain an ongoing conspiracy. In order to secure a totally secret organization it would be better to control it by a few men exercising complete authority over a long period of time. That's what the Illuminati theorists want us to believe, but the bylaws of the CFR make that virtually impossible.

The Great Cover-Up

You may be wondering why you've never heard much about the Council on Foreign Relations.

Maybe you have. In fact, the name of this prestigious organization often surfaces in news reports whenever foreign policy is involved. So either this organization is too mundane for most Americans to be concerned about, or the media is trying to hide something from us. Which is it?

The secret society theorists would have us believe that the entire media are involved in a huge cover-up to deceive the American people and keep the facts about a worldwide conspiracy secret. Here's a sample of what they believe:

> The CFR is little known today because the media want to "control" what you know. Do not expect the media to tell you the truth since they are sworn to secrecy. The infiltration is virtually complete. We can only imagine the immensity of the cover-up when from the Council's own 1987 report we read that 262 of its members are "journalists, correspondents, and communications executives."[23]

According to the secret theorists, network personalities such as Dan Rather, Tom Brokaw, David Brinkley, and Barbara Walters are—along with other popular correspondents—members of the CFR. To make matters worse, the major television networks are "influenced by the Rockefellers' family bank."[24]

In addition, most of the major newspapers and magazines, includ-ing—among others—*The New York Times*, *The Washington Post*, *The Boston Globe*, *The Chicago Sun Times*, *The Wall Street Journal*, *Newsweek*, *Time*, and *U.S. News & World Report* are influenced by the CFR and the international bankers.[25]

If the Illuminati controls both the U.S. government and every media operation in America, then why do reporters have such a diffi-cult time ferreting out information?

Journalists tend to be highly independent and will scoop any story that promises them a Pulitzer Prize for investigative reporting. Al-though the media may be basically liberal overall, I believe they are beyond the control of any specific group—no matter how much they agree with their political agenda. Believe me, if the media had any concrete evidence linking any organization to a worldwide conspiracy, surely someone, somewhere, by now would have exposed it.

THE TRILATERAL COMMISSION

It isn't enough that the Illuminati—and the Rockefellers, in par-ticular—control the Council on Foreign Relations, the media in general, the U.S. Congress, and most publishing companies in the United States. Those are only tools to aid in achieving their main goal—the financial and political control of the world. So they have an organization designed for that specific purpose—the Trilateral Commission.

Established in 1973, its members are drawn from international business, banking, government, academia, and mass media, including David Rockefeller, chairman of the Chase Manhattan Bank, and Zbigniew Brzezinski, former national security adviser to President Jimmy Carter.

Secret society theorists believe that the Trilateral Commission was established as a vehicle for multinational consolidation of the commercial and banking interests. How did they plan to do that? By seizing control of the political government of the United States.

Barry Goldwater writes in his book, *With No Apologies*, "What the Trilaterals truly intend is the creation of a worldwide economic power superior to the political government of the nation-states involved. As manager and creators of the system they will rule the world."[26] Certainly Goldwater is entitled to his opinion, but this interpretation is puzzling to me.

The name "Trilateral" comes from a triangle of countries in North America, Japan, and Western Europe and represents the areas where most of the world trade takes place. From these geographical centers, the world is supposedly controlled through finance, commerce, and politics. The entire Trilateral organization is purportedly made up of volunteers who have sworn to bring about the demise of freedom.

How is that supposed to happen? Here is Gary Kah's explanation:

> Their strategy would involve funneling American and European
> consumer money to Japanese industrialists and Arab oil magnates
> who would promptly use it to acquire Western companies and real
> estate. This way, it would be the Japanese and the Arabs—not the
> Rockefellers and their allies, who were really the ones responsible.[27]

Weren't the conspiracy folks saying a few years ago that Japan was trying to buy America? How do they explain the fact that now Japanese investors are selling their assets in America at great discounts and taking huge losses?

MOVE OVER HONDA

Another case in point involves the oil industry, which in my opinion manipulated oil prices back in the early seventies. Now that may have been a true conspiracy orchestrated by the oil companies, but the secret society theorists like to blame the 1972 oil embargo on the Rockefellers and the Trilateral Commission.[28]

What was the outcome of that situation, however? Didn't it lead to the production of more efficient automobiles that get more miles per gallon and actually save fuel?

In 1971, the price of gasoline in our city was thirty-five cents per gallon. The car I was driving got eight miles per gallon, which was common for the big V8 engines. Today my car gets twenty-four miles per gallon, and the cost of gasoline at the pump hovers around $1.10 per gallon and less in some places. As a result, I pay no more for gasoline today than I did in 1971—all things being relative.

Secret society theorists, however, believe that was part of the conspiracy to bankrupt America. Why? Because Japanese car makers greatly profited while the U.S. auto industry "was plunged into a deep recession from which it has never fully recovered."[29]

Where would we be today if American automakers had been permitted to continue dominating prices and producing lemon after lemon? The competition from imports—which were cheaper to operate and,

• Ethical mores and scruples are a matter of the heart. No group can control the minds of men or what they might do. • • •

unfortunately, superior in quality—forced our domestic auto companies to get their acts together and produce better cars (which they have done) in order to compete in the American automobile marketplace. As a result, U.S. automakers are now enjoying increasing sales and a better reputation.

And what about Europe's recent rejection of the Maastricht Treaty that would have unified the countries of Europe? That would have brought about a breakdown in the borders between nations and instituted a European currency. Surely that's something the Illuminati would like to see happen.

If you have ever traveled in Europe, you know how annoying it is to have to exchange your money at each national border in order to pay tolls, and so on. It would certainly be much easier for tourists and Europeans to have one currency. Understandably, however, the people are afraid of losing their national identity, and they certainly don't want the Germans controlling the currency. As a result, the Maastrict Treaty is dead for the moment.

If a conspiracy exists, they apparently didn't have enough clout to get this all-important economic treaty passed. As a result, the formation of the EEC (European Economic Community) and its one European currency was set back at least ten years.

UNSURPASSED LOYALTY

In spite of their inconsistencies, the secret society theorists continue to assert that the Rothschilds and the Rockefellers control and have controlled American society for years through their many "front" organizations.

The idea of such total unity and perfect loyalty among relatives from different families and nations is unfathomable. From what we know about history and the infighting that can occur within even a single family unit, the possibility of such a large group successfully devising and implementing a planned strategy for more than two hundred years is minuscule. Not even Israel, God's covenant people, could continue to fulfill God's plan for them as a unified nation with one purpose and goal.

I don't believe anyone can control good women and men. Surely, someone, at some point, would have knuckled under to his or her conscience and cried foul. No organization is powerful enough to control idealism—not even the church and certainly not the Illuminati. Mores and scruples are a matter of the heart. No matter how many people are involved or how elite the organization, no group can control the minds of people or what they might do.

THE HOUSE OF MORGAN

When the Illuminati are not planning wars and devising America's destruction, they spend the rest of their time figuring out how to create financial chaos in the stock market and banking establishment. That's one reason why the secret theory centers around the House of Rothschild.

They are not the only wealthy family to be singled out, however.

The J. P. Morgan banking empire is also considered to be part of the worldwide conspiracy for power and control.

It is true that, during the eighteenth and nineteenth centuries, the Rothschilds were the most powerful banking house in the world. In the early twentieth century, however, the House of J. P. Morgan replaced Rothschilds in the top-ranked position and held that distinction until the 1950s. With its tremendous assets, the House of Morgan at one time was powerful enough to finance conglomerates such as U.S. Steel, General Electric, General Motors, and Du Pont and bail out New York City from bankruptcy three times.

Through the years, there has been no doubt that the Morgans and their money have been able to influence governments. According to Ron Chernow in *The House of Morgan: An American Banking Dynasty and the Rise of Modern Finance*:

> The old Morgan partners were financial ambassadors whose daily business was often closely intertwined with affairs of state. Even today, J.P. Morgan and Company is probably closer to the world's central banks than any other bank.[30]

Because of the power such a financial institution wields in and out of the banking industry on a daily basis and the influence it can have over international affairs, thousands of rumors have been engendered. The most prominent myth is that generations of Morgans are linked to the great conspiracy discussed in this chapter.

But what if the Morgans did establish their business among the bigger conglomerates? That fact by itself in no way means or implies that they were controlling those entities or powerful enough to change the course of governments—or that they even wanted to.

It's true that the House of Morgan, at one time, had a rather negative reputation among their clients and were even nicknamed "the House of Blood, Brains, and Money."[31] The Morgans apparently insisted on complete control when structuring security deals in financial syndicates that involved the cooperation of other brokerage firms. In other words, if a large company wanted to raise capital by promoting a stock sale, Morgan would insist on being the manager of the deal over and above the other firms. Such strong-arm business techniques, however, in no way prove the Morgans' involvement in a worldwide conspiracy.

Conspiracy or Bad Business?

How did the House of Morgan rise to such prominence in the banking world?

During the early part of the twentieth century, it was difficult for corporations and governments to find a financial institution to market their securities. As a result, they often turned to larger firms like the House of Morgan. Questions arise, however, when it is noted that J. P. Morgan and other bankers sat on the boards of the very corporations they were financing.

Ron Chernow details the conspiracies in which the Morgans and their banking friends were involved. Their activities mostly centered around the manipulation of the sale of bonds and government securities of large corporations and governments.

In 1913, President Wilson set up the Federal Reserve System, which created private banks in certain regions and provided the government with a bank from which to borrow money. Although the system relieved the U.S. government's dependence on the House of Morgan, the Morgans actually benefited from the arrangement by making alliances with the new banks in the Federal Reserve System. In fact, they held that powerful position for more than twenty years.

Let's face it; conspiracies do exist. But devised by wealthy and powerful people, they succeed only for a while; they do not continue on for generation after generation. Our world is too unpredictable and uncertain for such absolute control to be maintained for long periods of time. Eventually, something breaks the hold of those in positions of power.

It is obvious from historical accounts and documents that the Morgan House and other banking entities tried to wield power and monopolize the banking world. The time came, however, when circumstances beyond their control served to limit their power. In fact, no one could have predicted the events that took place in the late 1920s and early thirties—as I will show you.

PLANNING THE GREAT DEPRESSION?

For some reason, there are as many myths surrounding the Great Depression as exist about the Illuminati. Secret society theorists would want us to believe that the 1930s depression resulted from a dastardly plot devised by the international bankers who, controlled most, if not all, of the money in America at the time.

To gain a more accurate perspective, let's take a brief look at what actually brought on the Great Depression.

In the years prior to that disastrous event, America was awash with cash because people were liquidating their assets in record proportions. Hundreds of thousands of people and millions of dollars were invested in the commodity markets. Money made from the sale of oil and land was being pumped into the stock markets. As a result, the prices of stocks hit the ceiling. In fact, at one point it was thought that the stock market would even run out of stocks to sell.

Ron Chernow explains this period of overwhelming growth in the stock market: "Riding this cash boom, the American financial services industry grew explosively. Before the war, there were 250 securities dealers; by 1929, an astounding 6,500."[32] Small investors had jumped into the markets by buying on margin. That means they put money down and bought the rest of the stocks on credit.

Before the Great Depression, it was popular to buy stocks with only 10 percent down. Today regulations dictate 50 percent down to buy on margin. In addition, if the price of the stock falls, you must make up the difference immediately or your other securities will be sold to bring your account to acceptable levels.

Before the stock market crash of 1929, the markets were controlled by the banks that had gorged themselves on the very stocks they were manipulating. That left the banks in a vulnerable position, as we shall soon see.

At the same time that stock prices were rising, America—which was still largely rural—was developing a trade surplus due to the wars in Europe. The oversupply of goods eventually forced farmers to lower their prices, and many began to default on their mortgage loans. This in turn led to the failure of many small banks in rural areas.

As negative news of impending doom swept the nation, people began to sell off their stocks in a frenzy. As a result, stock prices fell dramatically. At the same time, the banks dumped their stocks, selling them at a loss in an effort to save themselves.

Frantically, people ran to the banks to draw out their money. (Remember the scene from the movie *It's a Wonderful Life*, which we discussed in Chapter 2?) The ensuing frenzy emptied the banks of cash and gave birth to the Great Depression.

To make matters worse, many families experienced severe devastation during this time because of the Dust Bowl phenomenon that had been occurring in the Midwest. As a result, that part of the country had suffered from drought for several years, which had already caused unemployment to skyrocket in industries related to agriculture. The 1929 stock market crash only added to an already weakened economy.

Although that is a simplified version of a very complicated era in our nation's history, it is clear that the Great Depression resulted— not from some far-reaching conspiracy—but from natural disaster, foreign wars, and the lack of governmental controls in the banking industry.

With that in mind, I can dismiss the doomsday rhetoric of secret society theorists who write:

> When the next great crash hits this country, as has been predicted
> by author Larry Burkett and others, remember that the "hit" was
> directed from London and through the Council on Foreign
> Relations. . . . This is the same place from which the crash of 1929
> took place and the government can do nothing about it. . . .[33]

Anyone familiar with the history of the times knows that the events leading up the 1929 stock market crash were impossible for any person or group—no matter how powerful—to plan or predict. The greatest evidence, however, lies with what happened following that terrible day.

Since 1936, the stock market has outperformed all other forms of investments, including real estate. If the Illuminati controls the money markets and wants to impoverish America, they are botching up the job. In the past sixty years, Americans have prospered more than almost any other group of people on the earth. As a result, most Americans will do anything to maintain their high standard of living and will fight to keep their share of the American dream. Perhaps that is why the United States has never lost a major war.

CHANGING TIMES

It is true that many of the banking companies, such as the House of Morgan, manipulated the markets of banking and investments (stocks and bonds) prior to the crash of 1929. There is no question they had amassed an empire and were a powerful force in the financial affairs of the world. But it didn't last.

With the passage of the Glass-Steagall Act in 1933, the ties between investment banking and commercial banking were broken, and the Morgan empire suffered a serious setback. Before the Glass-Steagall Act, a banking house could not only lend money but could also sell securities such as stocks and bonds. After 1933, it was illegal for one banking institution to hold a monopoly by controlling all the financial markets.

The Glass-Steagall Act separated the banking business from the securities business so that monopolies could no longer control the money markets and investment securities. In other words, the banking industry could not make loans and accept deposits while issuing stocks and bonds.

That law has done more than any other measure to protect our nation against the possibility of one major institution gaining control of the financial markets again. In the 1990s, however, the Glass-Steagall Act is by and large ignored as more and more banks are sliding over into the security business.

Many banks are selling mutual funds, making deals with investment houses, and, in some cases, managing their own funds. Why is that happening today? The reason lies in the changing times and in the financial struggle that many banks are facing.

The investment business produces more income than the banks can generate through the much lower certificate of deposit or passbook savings rates. Because of the lower interest rates, banks are losing millions and millions of savings dollars to the brokerage houses.

In 1992 alone, record billions were invested in mutual funds in this country. That phenomenon has forced the banks into the mutual fund business to protect themselves against losses. In my opinion, that violates some of the reasons the Glass-Steagall Act was initiated in the first place.

Because the government has not yet recovered from the Savings and Loan fiasco, it cannot afford to take on a banking crisis at the same time. If, however, the banks continue to make deals with brokerage firms and mutual fund families to sell securities, a major scandal could erupt. In fact, it's probably just a matter of time.

SETTING THE RECORD STRAIGHT

Is the House of Morgan involved in this kind of double-dealing today? No, because their financial empire was broken up in 1933. In fact, today their banking houses—J.P. Morgan and Co. and Morgan Grenfell—and their investment firm, Morgan Stanley Company, are bitter rivals.

Ron Chernow explains the mystery surrounding this prestigious institution:

> While people know the Morgan houses by name, they are often mystified by their business. They practice a brand of banking that has little resemblance to standard retail banking. These banks have no teller cages, issue no consumer loans, and grant no mortgages. Rather, they perpetuate an ancient European tradition of wholesale banking, serving governments, large corporations, and rich individuals. As practitioners of high finance, they cultivate a discreet style. They avoid branches, seldom hang out signposts, and (until recently) wouldn't advertise. Their strategy was to make clients feel accepted into a private club, as if a Morgan account were a membership card to the aristocracy.[34]

I'm familiar with this elite way of doing business because I have worked for some of the largest brokerage firms in the world. I know how they operate and how exclusive they can be, with their yachts and private clubs where they wine and dine the wealthiest of clients. I've seen their high-rise buildings (Morgan used to occupy thirteen floors of the Exxon building in New York) and luxurious office space.

The high status of these financial organizations, however, does not mean they are secretly plotting the demise of our nation. Such myths arise out of misunderstanding about the nature of business in the complex arena of investment banking.

Today, Japanese and other foreign banks are much larger than our American banks, and the banking business doesn't operate the way it used to operate. It's also important to note that the Morgan House is not the largest bank in the world. In fact, it ranks far below some of the great international banks, like Citicorp and, therefore, its influence is far less than it was in the early part of the century. Yet, there is no mention by the doomsayers of a conspiracy by these larger banks—at least, not that I know about.

The steel, automobile, oil, and all other major industries require financing today just as they always have. In the 1990s, however, the banking industry and responsibility for mortgages, investments, and so on is spread over thousands of institutions that did not exist in the past. Today, the job of financing the world is too vast and overwhelming for one banking institution to handle. In fact, that's one reason why it would be impossible for one bank to gain control and monopolize large caches of money.

The secret society theorists, however, fail to see the positive significance of this fact and, as usual, consider any kind of change to be negative. Now that the old banking institutions are being replaced by a new wave of financing criteria, they will look for ways to fit this development into their theory. They are convinced that a secret conspiracy controls the world's economic future, and no amount of reasoning or presentation of the facts will shake them out of this deception.

THE COUNTERBALANCE

No matter how vast and powerful a banking house may seem, it is not above the law. In the past decades, many financial institutions have been brought to court, tried, and convicted. In fact, in 1954, J. P. Morgan Company was involved in a huge trial relating to a financial conspiracy and was heavily fined as a result. If there is a conspiracy involving members of the U.S. Congress, the president, his cabinet, and other highly placed government officials, why would they have allowed one of their own to be tried and convicted?

Conspiracies and monopolies do exist. That's a fact. The positive side is that for every action of conspiracy there is a counterbalance. If that were not true, the entire world would be controlled by the Mafia and other such underworld organizations.

Remember the AT&T monopoly? Ma Bell got too big, so the government deregulated the telephone industry and allowed other companies to rise up and compete with Bell Telephone. Although some jobs were lost initially, in the end many new opportunities were created for the American people. That's part of the counterbalance.

The banking industry is no different. It will dominate everything it can in any way it can. Witness the junk bond market manipulation of the mid to late 1980s. Drexel-Burnham-Lambert, through the intellect of Michael Milkin, controlled and manipulated the junk bond markets and violated the law in the process. As a result, Milkin and several other conspirators went to jail, and Drexel-Burnham-Lambert was forced to file for bankruptcy.

There are swindlers and power-hungry shysters in every business, and when men and organizations get too powerful, their hold can be broken by the legal intervention of the government. There will always be crooks and charlatans. We have them in business, government, and, yes, religion. But to say that all the evils of the world are part of one huge conspiracy dating back to 1776 is false and foolish.

THE PLOT AGAINST CHRISTIANITY

In addition to their plan to control the world's financial markets, its leaders, and its institutions, the Illuminati has supposedly hatched a plot to control the world's religions. This may be their most ambitious goal of all because without supernatural intervention such a feat is impossible.

Religion—be it Christianity, Catholicism, Islam, Hinduism, Buddhism, or atheism—develops strongholds in nations and affects the role of government and its leaders. We have only to look at Poland, Iraq, Israel, and the former Soviet Union to realize that religion is the single most powerful force in the world. Religion determines the predominant culture of a nation and cannot easily be dictated or manipulated. Why? Because it is deep rooted and indoctrinated into the people, generation after generation.

Even the communist KGB couldn't completely eradicate orthodox Christianity from the hearts and minds of the Russian people. And no organization is powerful enough to manipulate the Arabs and their Moslem religion—not even the Rothschilds. That's one reason we can conclude that if there were an Illuminati, it would be a weak, pathetic organization with unattainable and futile goals.

In spite of this fact, the secret society theorists continue to spread the rumor that the most diabolical part of the Illuminati's orders to Jacob Schiff was to desecrate Christianity in the United States. Apparently every decision against religious freedom—and there are many—has been the work of the secret conspiracy. They specifically point to the Supreme Court decision that removed prayer and Bible reading from the public schools.

The theorists also consider the National Council of Churches

(NCC) to be part of the conspiracy plot and specifically blame The United Methodist Church for leading the way in violating Christian rights. Although I agree that the NCC has helped bring heresy to Christianity and undermined conservative viewpoints of Bible doctrine, that organization is certainly not the only one.

In an effort to destroy our nation's historical Christian beliefs, the Illuminati supposedly initiates all the ecumenical movements in America and around the globe in hopes of creating a one-world religion. Their goal is to force all religions to come under their authority by changing the laws regarding freedom of speech and the right to worship freely as one believes. Slowly, the conspiracy will take away our religious freedom, and Christianity will be crushed under the heel of liberalism and humanism. At least, that's what the theorists want us to believe.

But I don't believe them; I believe the Bible. Jesus said, "Upon this rock I will build my church; and the gates of hell shall not prevail against it" (Matt. 16:18). No organization or government will ever wipe out Christianity or the church. It has been tried in centuries past, but the gospel is still being preached. In spite of persecution and governmental control, people around the world are coming to know Christ in greater numbers than ever before.

• *Wise men still seek Him, and they always will—no matter what the economic or social climate.* • •

I am old-fashioned enough to believe God still is in control and Christians need to trust Him. The terrible paranoia caused by the doomsayer crowd carries little validity, and Christian America—indeed, all of America—ought to reject it for what it is: a myth.

A DIFFERENT PERSPECTIVE

During a recent trip to Europe, one thing kept jumping out at me: Europeans have a prosperous life-style. Most of them drive new or fairly new cars and live in lovely, well-kept homes on the hillsides. In fact, the villages of France, Holland, Belgium, Germany, Switzerland, Austria, and Spain are far more beautiful than our small towns and cities in the United States.

I have to remind myself that at one time those countries were ravaged by war. Throughout the countryside, the only visible signs of the terrible battles in Europe are the marks left by bombs on old buildings in the villages.

Hitler's evil empire did not succeed; Europe survived the war and even prospered as a result. The doomsayers of yesteryear who predicted that Hitler was the Antichrist who would take over the world and eradicate Judaism and Christianity were wrong.

In addition, the gospel is alive in Germany. People are getting saved and giving their lives to Jesus Christ in this seemingly secular nation. In spite of the negative effects of socialism, humanism, liberalism, and even atheism, the people of Europe are hungry for a relationship with the living God. Wise men still seek Him, and they always will—no matter what the economic or social climate. I believe that as long as America is sending missionaries, the church will prevail. Conspiracies—no matter how well thought out—will fail.

Christians need encouragement today. When trouble comes, people identify with trouble and quickly latch onto the doom-and-gloom, the-end-is-near, get-me-out-of-here type of preaching. And preachers preach it because it plays on the emotions of people who need a peg on which to hang their anxious hearts. For some reason, it provides a moment of comfort to think everyone is in the same boat. But we are not all in the same boat! Some of us have hope for the future and believe that God is still in control.

FACING REALITY

I don't doubt that many of the events the secret society theorists propose will probably happen, but their eventuality will result from the coming of the Antichrist—as predicted in Scripture—and not from some plot devised by mere man.

Even if I didn't have Scripture on my side, I couldn't accept the Illuminati conspiracy theory because of all the inconsistencies and absurd conclusions it makes. That's why I'm always surprised to meet educated, well-read, Bible-believing Christians who unquestionably subscribe to this theory. In fact, when I have questioned the reasoning and knowledge of those who disperse this kind of jargon, they adamantly defend their position as if it were gospel.

If I could get them to listen to reason for a moment, I would tell them that it is God who sets up governments and allows men to reign and rule. How do I know? Because Romans 16:26 says, "But now is made manifest, and by the scriptures of the prophets, according to the commandment of the everlasting God, made known to all nations for the obedience of faith."

God controls the nations as a means of establishing the gospel in every nation. The nations will obey God. I believe that is one reason why America exists. As long as there is one person who needs the gospel, American missionaries will probably be there to preach it.

Jesus prophesied that there would be "wars and rumours of wars" and that "nation shall rise against nation" (Matt. 24:6–7). Although some may argue as to whether Jesus is talking about our age or the age to come, one thing is clear: God makes the ultimate decision as to what happens here on earth—not the elusive Illuminati.

THE SAME OLD CONSPIRACY

The secret society theorists and I agree on one thing: There is one huge conspiracy. But we disagree on who is leading it.

I believe it originates in hell.

The Bible teaches that Satan exists and that he seeks to control people and nations and governments. I know that Satan has his secret cults and subversive organizations that go about their dastardly deeds on a daily basis. The myth that a secret conspiracy controls the affairs of the world, however, is just that—a myth.

I believe there is a conspiracy, but it is the same conspiracy that has been in the works since creation. Satan is the great conspirator, and his main plan is to derail Christians and cause as much hatred and devastation as he can.

I also know there are evil spirits in the world because Jesus said:

Beloved, believe not every spirit, but try the spirits whether they are of God: because many false prophets are gone out into the world. Hereby know ye the Spirit of God: Every spirit that confesseth that Jesus Christ is come in the flesh is of God: And every spirit that confesseth not that Jesus Christ is come in the flesh is not of God: and this is that spirit of antichrist, whereof ye have heard that it should come; and even now already is it in the world. (1 John 4:1–3)

I know the powers of Satan exist, but I don't go looking for them. As a result, they don't affect me, nor can they affect me. Anyone who goes looking for trouble with the powers of darkness will find just that—trouble. Satan has masses of people confused, and some of them are Christians.

The devil can oppress us greatly, but he will never possess us if we are Christians. He can cause only as much damage as God allows him to cause. Satan cannot take our lives by war or any other means unless God permits it.

It is Satan's job to manipulate everything, but it is God's job to keep the world under His control. No conspiracies will prevail unless He allows them to succeed in order to fulfill His purposes.

I'M NOT WORRIED

Sure, there is a dark side to everything. I believe the dark side of politics. I know there are evil men who want to rule and reign and have power. But they won't get it. They haven't had control of the world in the past, and they won't have control in the future.

There is only one time in this world when men will completely control what happens politically, socially, and economically. That is the time after Jesus Christ returns to the earth and allows the Antichrist to rule and reign for seven years. And even then, God has already arranged for that to happen because it fits into His perfect plan for humankind.

If all the events and circumstances happening in our world today are part of God's plan for the coming of the Antichrist, no one can stop them anyway. And even if the Illuminati is alive and well and meeting this very hour in a dark, smoke-filled back room somewhere to plan the downfall of the United States, I'm not worried. Why? Because I do not believe God is going to let any would-be conspirators get out of hand.

Anne Frank, the young Jewish girl who died in a German concentration camp during World War II, wrote in her now-famous diary,

> I simply can't build up my hopes on a foundation consisting of
> confusion, misery and death. I see the world gradually being
> turned into a wilderness; I hear the ever approaching thunder,
> which will destroy us too; I can feel the sufferings of millions. And
> yet, if I look up into the heavens, I think that it will all come right,

that this cruelty too will end, and that peace and tranquility will return again.[35]

In spite of the madness occurring all around her, Anne Frank held hope beyond the current paranoia of totalitarianism. Should not we, who live in the most democratic and Christian nation on the earth, have greater reason to hope?

As angry as I am about some of the unjust and detrimental things that are happening today in this nation, I still believe in the power of prayer. God still listens to His good people and will not let our nation fall into the hands of too many wicked men until He is ready.

MONEY
MANAGEMENT
TIPS

In part two, I would like to give you the benefit of the kind of financial counseling I do on a daily basis. As a financial adviser and pastor of a local church, I do much more counseling in the financial area than most ministers. Because my work and training seminars take me to the four corners of the earth, I am exposed to every kind of money problem imaginable.

I do a great deal of counseling with individual pastors, giving advice that helps them run their churches more effectively. That advice includes everything from the church's fiscal structure, financial stewardship, and budgeting to personal instruction on household money management. I also provide investment advice and execute that advice when asked.

Because of my training and experience, I believe I am relatively qualified to write on financial matters. In addition, my research capabilities allow me to make up my own mind about things without being influenced by wrong thinking. As a trained pastor with a master's degree in divinity, I am able to study the Scriptures and correlate my complicated financial education to the Bible.

Allow me, if you will, in these next few chapters to give you the advice I dispense daily to people across the country—and around the world. They are people like you, with families and mortgages and bills to pay. Most are not high-rolling investors or millionaire businessmen. All, however, face essentially the same difficulties with managing their money. Hopefully, something you will read here will keep you out of financial difficulty or help you recover if you are already in trouble.

28 Ways to Know You Are Overextended

. . . .

The American home is under attack, and many families are out of financial control. We have already learned that easy credit can be an enemy to the person who cannot control it. At the same time, when used properly, credit is a wonderful benefit of American life.

Like fire when it runs wild, however, credit can burn the flower bed of life into ashes. It's up to you to keep your spending within the boundaries of your income.

The marketing department of every American company has one purpose: Sell the product. That's why Americans are inundated with advertising and easy credit terms. Because of that, many households are in trouble financially.

Every day, and sometimes several times per day, someone calls to ask me what he should do about his credit problems. Often it is too late to help. Many Christians are losing sleep at night because of financial stress. Being in financial trouble creates a suffering like no other. I know because I've been there. In fact, my ministry evolved out of the problems I have had myself. I have experienced the sick feeling in the stomach that financial stress can cause.

About ten years ago, God began calling me into full-time ministry. In essence I believed the Lord was saying, "You've been trained

. . . .

to be a preacher, now it's time for you to pastor a church." I knew God wanted me to be more than a businessman.

I wanted to obey the Lord, but I couldn't. Why? I was in debt up to my ears. It wasn't that we didn't have money. In fact, my business was prospering, and we were living high on the hog. That was the problem. I had invested in real estate and apartment buildings and purchased cars and a big house, but none of it was paid for. Financially, we were going down the tubes, and I didn't know what to do.

I couldn't just pick up and go to California. In fact, I was probably ten years late getting there because I had to pay for all of my foolishness. That's why I want to help you avoid the trauma and stress that financial pressure brings.

Losing your car, having the bank foreclose on your home, or being kicked out of your apartment can be devastating. Collection agencies calling your house or office is embarrassing, as well as difficult to bear. The end result of financial difficulties can be bankruptcy.

You can avoid these problems by knowing where you are financially. The Bible says, "Be thou diligent to know the state of thy flocks, and look well to thy herds" (Prov. 27:23).

If you don't pay attention to anything else in this book, pay attention to the advice you find in the next few pages. One of the best ways to avoid financial problems is to never have them in the first place. Recognize when you are getting into trouble, and take the necessary steps to pull yourself out.

In part one of this book, we outlined some of the steps our government needs to take to rectify its financial problems. Our leaders need to understand what the signals are and follow up with a program to get the country out of danger. You must do the same thing.

The following twenty-eight ways will show you whether or not you are overextended financially. Here's how to rate yourself:

- If 3 or more items apply to your situation, then you are beginning to have the symptoms of financial overextension.
- 4–8 negatives means you need to take immediate steps to get your finances under control.
- 10 or more indicates that you are overextended.
- 14 or more means the red light is flashing, and you are a financial time bomb getting ready to explode.

1. YOU DON'T KNOW HOW MUCH DEBT YOU HAVE—AND ARE AFRAID TO ADD IT UP

It is the end of the month and time to pay the bills, but you barely have enough money to cover them. You have been here before—in fact, for the past several months—and the bills are getting harder and harder to pay. The problem is that you are in debt but don't know how much, and you are probably afraid to add it up. Most Americans do not know their own debt tally.

Every shepherd knows how many sheep he has. He knows when one is missing and when one is born. We are not shepherds, but we must know the state of our flocks or finances as the verse from Proverbs states.

I want to encourage everyone reading this chapter to sit down immediately and add up your debt. You may be surprised at what you find. It may not be as bad as you think, or you may owe a lot more than you ever imagined. By adding up your debt, you will get a realistic idea of where you are. It should either shock you or relieve you as the true picture of your finances comes into clear focus.

• *Like fire when it runs wild, out-of-control credit can burn the flower bed of life into ashes. It's up to you to keep your spending within the boundaries of your income.* • • •

Once you find out, you can take the necessary steps to pull yourself out of debt by devising a plan. You may need to put some controls on your credit limits or decide whether you should extend your credit at all.

2. YOU PAY MONTHLY BILLS WITH MONEY TARGETED FOR OTHER OBLIGATIONS

When you start paying your regular bills every month, you realize you are running short of money. On one side of your desk sits a list of bills you have been putting off paying because they aren't top priority—they can wait.

For instance, you have owed someone money for some time, but he really isn't pressing you to pay it back. Little by little you have been putting money aside to take care of this little deal, but now you find yourself using that money to pay the bills in your hand.

You need to get a handle on this right away. Realize that you are running short of money, and take steps to replace the money targeted to pay those bills you have not been impressed to pay.

3. YOU PAY THE MINIMUM PAYMENT ON YOUR CREDIT CARDS EACH MONTH

Most credit cards set minimum payments at only 5 percent or less of your balance. They keep the percentage low because they want your balance to keep growing. That way they earn more on the compounded interest over time.

Keep in mind: Credit card companies are not your friends—no matter how much they flatter you in their marketing letters.

One early sign of overextension is that you consistently pay only the minimum amount required. That is a an early warning that you are in the beginnings of cash flow problems.

At the least, you should be paying your monthly charges plus a little here and there on the outstanding balance of the credit card. If you don't, you'll never get ahead. This kind of credit card abuse is probably the main reason why Americans don't save money.

4. YOU INCREASE YOUR CREDIT LIMITS ON YOUR CREDIT CARDS

Credit cards are great, in certain circumstances. In fact, you can hardly rent a car without one. When traveling, credit cards can get you out of a temporary bind and are more convenient than carrying a lot of cash. Be smart and learn how and when to use credit cards for your own advantage.

Remember, credit cards are not designed for and should never be used to finance long-term debt. The cost is too high, and the compounding interest payments can get you into trouble quickly.

When you increase the limit on your credit cards, that normally means you are borrowing over your set limit and have maxed out your card. You are overextending yourself when you do this. Resist the temptation to raise the credit limits on your cards, no matter how enticing the offer from the credit card company. Remember, they want to lend you more money because, in the end, the more you charge, the more they earn on your interest payments.

5. YOU INCREASE THE NUMBER OF YOUR CREDIT CARDS

When your credit is good, it is fairly easy to get more credit cards. Sometimes when people need money and their present cards are maxed out, they apply for more cards to increase their credit limit.

Sooner or later the habit of collecting and paying for multiple credit cards will wipe you out—especially if you are financing yourself this way. If this is your problem, I encourage you to face the facts and find a way out of potential disaster.

I read about a man who had more than one hundred credit cards and a limit amounting to hundreds of thousands of dollars. That can be an expensive habit, especially if the cards carry an annual fee— which most do.

At one time, I realized I had around twenty-five different bank credit cards. When I figured the total annual fees, I cut the number of cards down to the four or five that had the lowest interest charges and no annual fee.

If you are paying an annual fee on your credit card, call the bank or institution that issues the card and ask for the fee to be waived. If they think they're going to lose your business, they will probably drop the fee. But watch your statements; it may reappear. It's a good idea to contact them every year.

Some cards promise no fee up-front, but when you read the small print, you discover that is only good for a limited time. After a while, they sneak in the annual fee, hoping you won't notice—or, at least, won't complain.

6. YOU PAY OFF CREDIT CARD PAYMENTS WITH OTHER CREDIT CARDS

No. No. No. You are overextended. Folks who do this are living on borrowed time. It will take only a few months before you will reach the credit limits on all your cards. This is financial suicide.

7. YOU WRITE POSTDATED CHECKS ON A REGULAR BASIS

Postdated checks are written for a predetermined date. In other words, you put a future date on the check and pay the bill because, at the time, you don't have the money in the bank to make it good. Or, if you want to pay a bill but do not have the money, you write the check and ask the person to hold it until a certain day when you will be able to make the check good.

Creditors hate postdated checks. In my experience with accounts receivable, I would rather the person not bother than to pay me with a check I cannot cash. Although many postdated checks I have received in the past were good on the date indicated, I had to wait a long time for my money with no interest. Sometimes, however, I was unable to cash certain postdated checks because the payee put a "stop payment" on the check. In many states that is not against the law nor considered fraud.

There is no reason to postdate checks except for the emotional relief it allows the debtor. In reality, however, you—the debtor—are actually telling your creditor you are overextended. That's not only embarrassing, it's downright irresponsible!

8. YOU SPEND MONEY IN ADVANCE OF PAYDAY AND MUST HURRY TO THE BANK ON PAYDAY TO COVER THE CHECKS YOU HAVE WRITTEN

It is Wednesday, and you have reached the deadline for making your car payment. If you wait any longer, you will have to pay a late fee—which you have done on occasion. The bank has already warned you about letting late fees mount up.

You write a check and mail it, calculating the payment will wind up in the bank's office on Thursday. The bank will ask your bank to pay the check on Friday and, since your bank takes deposits until 6:00 P.M., you have just enough time to make it from work to the bank to cover the check.

If I could ask how many of my readers have ever been guilty of this practice, I'm sure I would get a lot of positive responses, including one from me. Almost everyone finds themselves in this situation at one time or another. But, when it happens on a regular basis, it is a sure sign that financial trouble is brewing.

9. YOU OFTEN HAVE A NEGATIVE BALANCE IN YOUR CHECKBOOK

For many people, living with a negative balance in the checkbook is a way of life. What that signals, of course, is that you have no reasonable cash flow. Households are just like businesses in this respect. If there is no cash flow, there is no money to write checks.

Running a negative balance all the time in the checkbook indicates overextension because it means you are writing checks on overdraft or covering your checks in the nick of time. Some people, however, never know what their checking balance is. As a result, they write checks without a clue as to how much money they actually have in the account.

People often ask me, "How often should I update my checkbook?" I tell them, "You should balance the amount in your checkbook as soon after you write a check as possible." Every evening you should subtract the checks you wrote that day from the balance left in your checkbook. Then you will be able to determine the actual amount of money you have left in your account. Carrying forward the balance is easy and only takes a few seconds.

If you balance your checkbook every day, you can contemplate just how much money you have to work with instead of constantly worrying if you will have enough.

10. YOU RECEIVE REGULAR OVERDRAFT NOTICES FROM THE BANK

Often overdraft notices come because you don't really know how much money is in your checking account. This directly relates to the previous warning. On the other hand, some overdraft notices result because checks are written with a negative balance in the checkbook on purpose.

Overdraft notices can be costly. Some banks charge as much as twenty dollars per check. If you have several checks on overdraft, that can add up to a tidy sum, making your cash flow situation worse. How do I know? Because no one would write a bad check unless he or she was overextended. And most people who are overextended like to keep themselves in the dark about their financial situation.

To keep in touch with reality, you should reconcile the checking account statement every month. It is easy to do. On the back of your statement, the bank provides step-by-step instructions showing you how to do this. If you are still confused, make an appointment with your banker or financial adviser and learn how to reconcile your statement.

If you do that religiously every month, you will know more about your cash flow situation and avoid embarrassing and costly overdraft statements from the bank.

11. YOU PAY ONLY THE INTEREST ON BANK LOANS

You may have asked the bank to allow you to pay only the interest on a loan in order to reduce your payment that month. Paying only interest is not wrong, but it does signal that your cash is being used for something other than the loan payment. Check your finances closely if this is a problem.

You cannot renew loans forever. At some point, the bank is going to ask for the loan, especially unsecured notes.

12. YOU INCREASE YOUR BORROWING LIMITS AT THE BANK

Many people get a line of credit from their bank, and that can be good to have in case of emergencies. Credit lines are provided for short-term debt in order to leverage for a specific purpose. Some people, however, raise the credit limit to pay for problems caused by overextension.

If you find yourself having to ask your banker to raise your credit limit, you need to see what is happening to the money. Increasing borrowing limits to pay past-due bills can lead to financial chaos.

I have known people who spent out of control because it was easy for them to increase their credit limits. When the loans came due, however, they had no means to repay the bank and they lost everything.

13. YOU DON'T HAVE A SAVINGS PLAN

Some people go for years with no savings in the bank. Everyone should have a savings account, even if it means putting away only a dollar per week. Dollars mount up, and the habit brings great rewards.

Pay yourself. You pay everyone else. I recommend putting aside 10 percent of your monthly income into a savings plan. No savings means you are extended to the point where there is no cash left to save. You need to rectify such a situation immediately.

14. YOU CANNOT LIVE THREE TO SIX MONTHS WITHOUT REGULAR WEEKLY OR MONTHLY INCOME

Most people live paycheck to paycheck and could not survive very well—or at all—if the paycheck were missing on Friday or at the end of the month. Money in reserve is a great way to offset disaster. If you lose your job, it can take several months to find another suitable one.

I believe in saving money. Throughout this book, I have encouraged and exhorted the reader to save. Every responsible adult should have an emergency fund of up to six months of free money. That should come from a fund separate from or on top of your savings and long-term retirement investments.

• *Keep in mind: Credit card companies are not your friends—no matter how much they flatter you in their marketing letters.* • • • • • •

15. YOU DECREASE YOUR 401K OR PENSION CONTRIBUTIONS AT WORK

A 401K plan is a qualified investment plan that allows the employer to deduct a set amount—determined by the employee—of the employee's wages in pretax dollars. In other words, the money is deducted from the wages and contributed to the plan. The employee, however, is taxed only on the money left after the retirement deduction has taken place.

One of the beginning signs of overextension is asking your employer to suspend the contributions from your paycheck or to decrease your contribution to the 401K.

16. YOUR MORTGAGE PAYMENT OR RENT IS MORE THAN 45 PERCENT OF YOUR TAKE-HOME PAY EACH MONTH

If your monthly rent or mortgage payment has crept up this high, you have:

a. Bought a home or moved into a more expensive apartment than you can afford; or
b. Created a deficit in your household budget by extending yourself in other areas too deeply, requiring a second or third mortgage to pay the debts.

The safe figure for a mortgage payment is 35 percent or less of your monthly take-home pay.

17. YOU ARE ONE OR MORE MONTHS BEHIND IN PAYING ONE OR MORE BILLS

You do not have to be behind on all your bills to be overextended—one bill will do just fine. If you have one bill that you must put off until the next month, it could be a sign that you are on the verge of overextension.

If we incur bills, then we should have the means to pay them. Although most of us have come up short at one time or another, a continued pattern of letting the bills go indicates trouble.

18. YOU ARE BEHIND IN PAYING ALL YOUR BILLS

You are definitely overextended! People who can't pay their bills should know that they are in serious trouble. When that happens, the point of no return may be passed. Bankruptcy usually results when none of the bills can be paid.

19. YOU CASH IN SAVINGS FOR HOUSEHOLD NEEDS

Money has run out, and the only thing left to tap is the savings account. Using savings to pay for groceries, utilities, and so on is bad news.

20. YOU CANCEL AUTO INSURANCE ON ONE OR MORE CARS

I have counseled with enough people who get into financial trouble to know that automobile insurance is one of the first things they think they can live without. As a result, they first cut down the insurance to liability only. Then they cancel the policy altogether and take their chances on the highway.

When you are overextended, that seems to be a logical thing to do. It actually can be very dangerous and lead to greater problems if someone gets injured or there is a costly wreck. If you feel overextended, cut down other spending, but don't cut back or cancel the car insurance.

In many states, it is against the law to drive a car without having automobile insurance, so this is not an option for everyone.

21. YOU CANCEL YOUR HEALTH INSURANCE

Most people add to their problems by cutting out health insurance. Of course, that could lead to more turmoil if tremendous hospital bills pile up due to illness or injury.

22. YOU PAY FOR REGULAR HOUSEHOLD BILLS WITH BORROWED MONEY

Almost every person who begins to see the signs of deep financial difficulty tries to offset long-term problems with short-term fixes.

Most people who borrow money to supplement regular cash flow bills do so with the intention of being able to recover. The problem is—they have no method or means to bounce back. They just get out of the problem at hand as quickly as possible to terminate the immediate pain.

If you are paying regular monthly bills with borrowed money, you need to be jolted into reality. You should realize that this drastic action stems from financial problems that have been evident for a long time. A short-term fix is no fix at all but will only create more serious problems.

23. YOU BORROW MONEY TO PAY BILLS FROM AN UNCOMMON SOURCE

Everyone has a slush fund somewhere for emergency troubles. It can be money hidden under the mattress or reserves tucked away in the bank. Hardly anyone has not had to use this resource at one time or another.

What I am talking about here, however, occurs when all the normal sources for short-term money have run out, and the borrower is now scampering to find cash. You may even be considering borrowing money from friends or relatives. That is a definite sign of overextension.

24. YOU HAVE RECEIVED A LETTER FROM A COLLECTION AGENCY

Let your bills pile up, and sooner or later you will receive a notice from a collection agency.

There are a number of ways businesses collect debts. Banks have their own in-house collection procedures. First, you would receive a notice from your loan officer. If he cannot collect the debt, then the account would be turned over to the collection department to start dunning you for the money past due.

Sometimes businesses use outside collection sources. One of the largest is National Revenue Corporation and United Creditors. They utilize two methods. Your creditor may employ their letter-writing service first. In this non-alienating approach, a letter is sent simply reminding you of the past due account. Over time, such letters will increase in their demands. The letter-writing procedure generally does not affect your credit rating because the creditor does not report directly to the credit agencies.

If it is determined that the debt will not be brought current or paid in full, then the full service collection procedure kicks in—which could result in a judgment against you in court. Once your account has progressed to a more serious status, the bill is considered uncollectible.

At that point, the report comes from the collection agency to the credit reporting service. The largest of these are TRW, Transunion, CBI, and Dunn and Bradstreet (D&B). D&B generally provides credit rating information on companies and corporations. However, they also collect past dues.

Probably the most demanding financial agency for dunning accounts is your local credit union combined with a collection service. They know no bounds when it comes to borderline harassment.

No matter how it happens, the notice from a collection agency should be taken as a serious warning light that you are moving deeper into overextension.

25. YOU HAVE HAD SOMETHING REPOSSESSED

Watching your car being towed away down the street produces the ultimate in financial stress. Anyone who has experienced the trauma of repossession knows that he or she is over the edge. It is at this point that most people finally wake up and start looking for ways to get out of financial trouble.

26. YOU HAVE A PENDING JUDGMENT THAT CANNOT BE PAID

Some people ignore certain bills while taking care of more threatening ones. The person who isn't getting paid, however, may decide to take action by getting a judgment in court that will demand payment.

Judgments in most states give the creditor the right to back interest at the state's set law, which is usually 6 percent. The creditor then has the right to all assets that are not attached by a lien by someone else. To pay the debt, they can demand the sale of any asset.

In some states, judgments stay on the credit report for ten years and can be renewed by the creditor. Even if no action is taken by the creditor to collect the debt, the judgment will mess up your credit report for years to come.

27. YOU ARE CONSIDERING FILING FOR BANKRUPTCY

Being on a witness stand ruthlessly grilled by a lawyer concerning your debts can be traumatic. Many times creditors are there to incite the judge against you. On top of that, your credit rating can be permanently destroyed.

• *Remember, credit cards are not designed for and should never be used to finance long-term debt.* • • • • • • • •

Don't listen to advice that says when you file bankruptcy, your credit problems go away. They do not. Your bankruptcy stays on your credit file for ten years, making it almost impossible to get a credit card, new or late used automobile at good credit rates, or a new home. Banks take a dim view of people who have filed bankruptcy no matter what the reason.

28. YOU ARE PAYING YOUR BILLS WITH MONEY NORMALLY GIVEN AS TITHES AND OFFERINGS

I saved this argument until last because tithing is usually the first thing to go when finances get tight. Whenever people want to buy something or find themselves overextended, they opt out of giving to the church.

Robbing God is the greatest crime committed every Sunday morning by Christians all over America. Many folks want to give, but, because they are overextended, they must pay for their foolishness with every dime they get—including what belongs to God. When people arrive at this point, they are only digging themselves into a deeper hole. Let me explain.

You don't give your tithes; you pay your tithes. Why? Because "all the tithe . . . is the LORD's: it is holy unto the LORD" (Lev. 27:30). That's not just an Old Testament law, it is a spiritual law.

According to the tenth chapter of Hebrews, Abraham paid his tithes to Melchizedek. The tithes are what you owe; offerings are what you give to the Lord above your tithes—and with them come abundant blessings. If you withhold your tithe, however, you are robbing God, making it impossible for Him to prosper you.

> Will a man rob God? Yet ye have robbed me. But ye say, Wherein have we robbed thee? In tithes and offerings. Ye are cursed with a curse: for ye have robbed me, even this whole nation. Bring ye all the tithes into the storehouse, that there may be meat in mine house, and prove me now herewith, saith the LORD of hosts, if I will not open you the windows of heaven, and pour you out a blessing, that there shall not be room enough to receive it. (Mal. 3:8–10)

If you keep 100 percent of your money, it will not go as far as the 90 percent you would have left over after you tithe. Why? Because God has a way of exacting the tithe one way or the other. I know because God brought me to my knees on this issue.

A LOAN FROM GOD

At the beginning of this chapter, I said that as a businessman, I had overextended myself financially and was at the end of my rope. I couldn't figure out why everything was coming unraveled until one day during a time of urgent prayer I heard a voice within me say, *Sherm, you're robbing God.*

That was true. For the first time in my life, I had gotten way behind on my tithes. *No wonder God can't bless me,* I thought.

Down on my knees, I pleaded, "Lord, please have mercy on me. If You will be patient with me, I will pay my tithes and offerings. In fact, I will start tomorrow."

I owed God thousands of dollars, so I said, "God, if you will loan me the money, I will pay all my back tithes. I will catch them up and add 20 percent to that, according to Leviticus 27:13. I will pay above my tithes and offerings every week until I pay You everything that I owe."

In my mind, I worked out a payment schedule with the Lord and realized it was going to take me four years. It was a forty-eight-month loan.

As I prayed, I could see the collection angels standing on the brink of heaven getting ready to come down and zap me again. But then God said, "Hold it, boys. This man's making a deal. Let's hear what he's got to say."

The angels retreated, and the great loan committee, the Father, the Son, and the Holy Spirit, got together to consider my request.

"Well, Sherman Smith has been an honest man," the Holy Spirit said. "Although he hasn't been too honest with us in the past few months, he is an honest man overall. He's treated people right, and I think he deserves a chance. What do you think?"

When the vote was taken, they agreed to loan me the money. I got up from my knees, and a deep inner peace flooded my heart.

The next morning at church, as the offering plate was passed, I knew I had to keep my end of the bargain. Although we had no money in the bank, I quickly wrote a check for three hundred dollars. Then I bowed my head and silently prayed, "Lord, here it is. You told me You'd bless me if I trusted You."

All Sunday afternoon and night and into the next day, however, I worried that the church was going to cash that check and I wouldn't be able to make it good.

After work on Monday, I drove up the quarter-mile driveway to our house and, as usual, walked back down to the mailbox. It was a daily ritual for me to take the mail out of the box and read it going up the drive. That day I did so with a heavy heart. All I could think about was the phone call I was going to get from the church treasurer asking how I could write a bad check.

When I opened the mailbox, I noticed a handwritten envelope and opened it first. A note read, "Dear Sherman and Sharon, we know you have a problem, so we want you to accept this money as help." I held in my hand a cashier's check for ten times what I had given to the Lord the day before. I did not walk back to my house; I flew.

I rejoiced to know that I had finally come to a point in my life where I had needed to trust God, and I had done it. Even though I worried about it, He blessed me anyway because He knew my heart was right.

Now, I don't recommend writing rubber checks or even making deals with God. That is how I believed God was dealing with me personally because He wanted to prove Himself to me.

*• **If you keep 100 percent of your money, it will not go as far as the 90 percent you would have left over after you tithe.** • • • • • •*

God wants to bless you, too, but until you pay Him what you owe Him, you are robbing Him of His tithe and robbing yourself of financial and spiritual blessing.

I probably preach more sermons on tithing and giving than any other pastor I know. One Sunday morning, after I had told my congregation the story about my deal with the Lord, a man came up to me as I was shaking hands at the front door. His shirt and tie were wet, and as I looked into his eyes, I noticed they were full of tears.

"Is something the matter, brother?" I asked.

"You got to me today," he replied. "I've been robbing from the Lord."

"It's not too late to make things right," I replied.

He nodded and walked away with a determined expression on his face.

You know what he did? That man figured out the tithes and offerings he owed God for his entire life, and he gave to the church until he had paid every penny he owed.

Today whenever I talk to that dear brother, he tells me, "I'm a happy man. I'm having a wonderful life because I don't owe God any money. I owe God everything, but I don't owe Him money. I don't owe Him a tithe, and I don't owe Him an offering. They're paid."

God doesn't require all of us to pay back the tithes we have withheld during our lifetime, but let me ask you something: When the offering is taken at church, when missionaries need support, when the mortgage on the education building needs to be paid, when the church staff needs their salaries, do you respond?

If you would like to give but you can't, take this advice from someone who's been there and back. Don't hold back from God. Pay your tithes, and ask Him to help you out of your financial difficulties. He is faithful and will show you the way.

KEEPING MYSELF ON TRACK

After God showed me the way out of my financial problems, I established several financial guidelines for myself. You may want to set up your own set of rules for your personal and/or business finances. This is how I keep myself on track:

I Pay My Personal Bills Each Friday

This is a longtime, no-nonsense habit.

I Keep My Business Capital Separate from My Private Money

I almost never mingle the two. My opinion is that if my business cannot support itself, then I need to bail out. That does not mean I won't borrow money to keep the business going. I will borrow money for the business and make the business pay it back. I will not borrow from myself.

Once I have put money into personal savings, it will not come out except for the Lord's work if need be.

Leverage Is Good Business If You Know How to Leverage

Leverage is different from debt.

As I explained in an earlier chapter, our church leveraged heavily. As a result, we were able to move ahead rapidly. Although we took a "calculated risk," we thought it was better to move ahead rather than sit with no way to progress.

Forget the hype and get-rich-quick schemes. Wealth comes slowly and over a long period of time.

Entrepreneurship Belongs in Business, Not the Household

We do not spend money we cannot afford to spend. That does not mean our household is out of debt. It is not. However, our debt-to-income ratio is very low.

House Rules for Me

If I have a problem with three or more of the twenty-eight warnings on overextension, I will immediately take steps to correct the problem.

Business Rules for Me

I will allow my business capital to fall to a predetermined level and then take necessary steps to build it back up.

I am a risk taker in this case. However, if for an extended period of time I am not putting money aside in personal savings as part of my business income, I will correct the problem.

Staying in business and keeping your personal finances in order does not mean you must be rich or cannot take certain risks. Debt is not wrong if treated properly. If, however, several of the twenty-eight warnings in this chapter applied to your financial condition, then you should take immediate steps to get out of debt. That may mean changing jobs, selling assets, or strict discipline.

Seven Mistakes That Lead to Financial Chaos

N ot long after I became a pastor, a couple came to my office. From their demeanor, it was obvious that they were under tremendous stress.

As soon as the husband sat down in front of me, he said, "Pastor, I'm going to blow my head off."

Shocked, I asked, "Why in the world would you do something like that? You're a Christian. I mean, that's not a Christian attitude."

With despair in his voice, he said, "I am forty-one years old, and I do not own a foot of anything. I do not own a house, and I am mortgaged up to the hilt. Next week we are going to have to file bankruptcy because our debts are way over our heads, and we don't know how to get out of this mess."

Being a good pastor, I did what all good pastors do. I asked him, "Do you tithe?"

When the man shamefully answered no, I launched into one of my theological discourses on tithing. I stomped around my office for about an hour breathing fire and putting the fear of God into this couple.

"You are in trouble because you robbed God! How could you do that?" I reprimanded, quoting every scripture on tithing I could think of.

Finally, when I had finished, those people were on their knees. In fact, my discourse was so effective that I felt convicted myself, and the three of us were on the floor in tears, begging God to forgive us all. We prayed fervently, getting our lives and hearts right.

When we got up, the husband said, "Boy, am I glad I came to see you today. This has been worth it all." I had to admit, I felt pretty good myself.

Two days later, however, I was waiting in Bay Area traffic, looking up at the sky through my sun roof and thinking about the couple who had come to see me. What had I told them? What advice had I given them? Suddenly, like a bolt of lightning, it hit me. It was not what I told them; it was what I did not tell them that bothered me.

I had advised them to tithe and give to the church—and that was right and scriptural. But what if six months later that couple returned to my office under even more stress and said, "We tried tithing, but it didn't work. In fact, we're in worse shape now than before. So we quit tithing because we still can't pay our bills."

I had seen it happen before. As soon as Christians begin tithing, God starts blessing. They eventually work themselves out of their financial difficulties and the overwhelming stress. When they get a few extra bucks in the bank, what's the first thing they do? Run out and spend it!

God doesn't intend for us to take the increases He has blessed us with and spend it all. But that is what 90 percent of the Christians I counsel do.

TIME TO GROW UP

Imagine this scenario, which I have seen happen more than once. A guy is told by his boss that he will receive a $100 raise, beginning next month. What does the excited employee do? Starts planning how to spend that extra $100; or, what's worse, goes out and spends it before he even sees it. Then, a week later, the boss calls him back into his office and says, "I'm sorry. Not only can I not give you the raise, but you're fired!"

God's children are like most children I know. Whenever they get money, they cannot wait to spend it. That wouldn't be so bad, but kids go out and buy foolish and unnecessary things. Then when they need money for textbooks or school clothes or gas for the car, guess who gets stuck with the bill?

At some point, parents realize they must pull the plug and demand financial responsibility from their children. And that's exactly how God operates. He wants His children to grow up!

Many Christians, who have no reason to be living under any financial stress whatsoever, live under horrendous pressure. Why? Because they can't control their spending habits, or they simply don't know how to manage their money. Mistakes can lead to financial chaos. The best way to avoid financial disaster is avoid money blunders in the first place.

In my opinion, there are seven major financial mistakes that can lead to chaos. These points can be applied to every area of American life—to our government, churches, businesses, and homes. See which ones apply to you, and begin to take steps to correct them.

1. NOT LIVING WITHIN YOUR MEANS

When I was a young married man, in my early twenties, I was riding in the truck with my grandfather one day. Along the way, we passed many beautiful homes, and I commented, "Here I am struggling financially, yet all these people are living in new homes. Surely, I can't be making much less than they do. How do they do it? How did they accumulate enough money to buy a home?"

I have never forgotten my grandfather's answer. He said, "If you live within your means, you will eventually cross a line of accumulation and be able to afford many things that you now consider unaffordable." At that time, I could not imagine how such a simple philosophy could work.

In all my studies of business and the economy, I have never read about the "line of accumulation," but I certainly know from experience what he meant.

• *Most people are in trouble financially because they don't live within their means.* • • • • • •

Had I lived within my means and followed my grandfather's advice, I would have avoided many of the financial holes I later dug for myself.

In the last few years, I have discovered plenty of people who are in way over their heads. Recently in Denver, Colorado, I met with a group of Christian aviators. One pilot told me he had to get completely out of debt because he couldn't handle it. His spending had been out of control, and he was living way beyond his means. His life-style had become a bondage to him.

Although I have stated clearly in this book that I don't believe debt-free living is for everyone, some people are too undisciplined to use credit wisely. When I met with financial adviser and author Ron Blue, he said something that stuck in my mind: "One thing is for sure, if debt isn't wrong, it sure is stupid to pay credit card interest rates."

In counseling with people on a day-by-day basis, I have discovered that most people are in trouble financially because they don't live within their means. The soundest principle I can present comes from the Bible. Proverbs 21:20 says, "There is treasure to be desired and oil in the dwelling of the wise; but a foolish man spendeth it up."

There are dire consequences to not living within our means—like repossession of expensive "toys," bankruptcy, and unbearable stress. I believe not living within our means is one of the main causes of stress in America today.

2. MAKING FINANCIAL DECISIONS BASED ON EMOTIONS

I was visiting a church recently where the people were euphoric about remodeling the building. They believed that if improvements were made to the facilities, more people would attend the church, leading to financial growth. There was only one problem: These folks couldn't afford to remodel the church. Their excitement had created emotions that, if allowed to continue, could have led to costly decisions.

It is easy to get hyped up on a project, but if we can't afford it, we shouldn't do it. Jesus addressed this problem when He asked, "For which of you, intending to build a tower, sitteth not down first, and counteth the cost, whether he have sufficient to finish it?" (Luke 14:28).

More than one person has looked back, in the wake of financial disaster, and wished the consequences could have been foreseen. Emotions out of control cause us to overreact and keep us from making wise choices.

There is a thin line between faith and foolishness. We don't want to legislate faith out of the picture, but true faith comes by conviction and not by letting emotions run wild. In short, we need to separate excitement about something from the feelings we have at the moment—especially when it comes to money.

One emotion that sometimes gets out of control is "blind faith." Although God may ask us to walk this way on occasion, I do not believe it should be the way we manage our lives as a rule.

While I was a student at a Christian college in Manaus, Brazil, I met an American couple who lived by the philosophy that saving money indicated a lack of faith. They had no life insurance because they thought paying insurance premiums showed they didn't believe God would take care of their survivors when they died.

They also had the notion that segregating money for retirement in bank accounts took away from the daily, necessary needs of the family. In other words, "Don't worry about the future because God will somehow meet our needs, if we live by faith."

Now, don't get me wrong, I know what it is to live by faith. But I also know that God's Word teaches us to plan for the future.

Although those dear people in Brazil were an extreme case, I have met many others who live the same way but who have no faith in God at all. They make decisions based on emotion rather than wisdom, always hoping for a miracle, or expecting God—or a rich uncle—to bail them out. Later in life, they are disappointed to find out things didn't work as they had imagined, and they find themselves in dire straits.

3. MATERIALISM

The American way of life has always puzzled me. Americans buy things they don't need, with money they don't have, from people they don't know or care about, to impress friends who won't be their friends if they can't impress them.

Materialism is one of the scourges of the American way of life. Trying to "keep up with the Joneses" creates all kinds of unnecessary pressures and discord. Many marital problems that eventually lead to divorce can be traced directly to materialism. Pressure to maintain a certain life-style can destroy love and contentment in a home.

Although we are commanded to "be content with such things as ye have" (Heb. 13:5), God does not condemn material wealth. In fact, He says in 1 Timothy 6:17, "God . . . giveth us richly all things to enjoy." God doesn't want us to be without the daily necessities of life. In fact, He wants us to be able to afford the things we need.

The psalmist said, "I have been young, and now am old; yet have I not seen the righteous forsaken, nor his seed begging bread" (Ps. 37:25). The Christian who honors God will not go hungry.

If we put God first in our lives and desire to serve Him, He has promised to bless us with "things." "O fear the LORD, ye his saints: for there is no want to them that fear him. . . . They that seek the LORD shall not want any good thing" (Ps. 34:9–10).

The key is the motive of our hearts.

Two years ago, I counseled a couple who had inherited a large amount of money. At the time, they lived in a rundown house in a low-income neighborhood. Instead of increasing their living standard by investing in a new home, they opted to use their inheritance to buy a new Mercedes Benz and a Lincoln Town Car for themselves and a new Porsche for their teenager. That chewed up $180,000 of the inheritance right off the bat.

• *God always promises to supply our needs—but never commits to provide our every luxury.* • • •

Then they bought a boat to park at the marina at a cost of more than $150,000. Every item they purchased had tremendous depreciation and required expensive upkeep. After the husband and wife quit their jobs to live on the remainder of the inheritance, they eventually ran out of money, had to sell their house, and are now broke and in worse shape than before.

That may sound like an extreme case, but I assure you it is not unusual. People up and down the street where you and I live have new cars, boats, motorcycles, and every other item that marketing specialists have told them they need to be happy and fulfilled. The only problem is that they don't own anything outright; everything is financed.

Most Americans don't think in terms of how much interest they are going to pay before they buy something. People think in terms of monthly payments. The fact that they are going to pay two or three times the purchase price of a new car is never considered. If the monthly payment can be made out of their budget, they convince themselves it is affordable.

At the end of almost every automobile commercial on television, the final sales pitch is: "Only $199 a month!" The full price of the car is seldom mentioned because it is completely irrelevant to most Americans.

Materialism can be a dangerous trap and create ungodly longings for unnecessary things. Nice things are wonderful, but materialism will separate us from God if we're not careful. Remember, God always promises to supply our needs but never our luxuries.

4. BUYING ON IMPULSE

During my financial seminars, I often invite folks to take a walk through their garages, basements, and attics to see all the things stored away that they no longer use but that they once considered essential.

Not long ago I decided to follow my own advice. Within only a few minutes, I left my basement depressed after adding up the approximate cost of all the items we had discarded.

Whenever you are tempted to buy a new television set, VCR, furniture, or new car, stop and take a few minutes before you jump into the easy credit terms offered. I often advise people to wait twenty-four hours before buying anything and always to pray before spending money.

One day I was out with a friend when we walked by an electronics store. Before I knew it, he had bought a fifty-two-inch television set.

"Why did you do that?" I asked.

"Because the sign said, 'Easy Credit. No payment until next March!' I couldn't resist," he admitted.

Remember, retailers will do anything they can to suck you in. But you can outsmart them if you stop and ask, "Lord, do You want me to have that?" You'll be surprised how much you won't buy if you pray about it first.

Patience and practicality should always prevail. If you want something badly enough, you should have the discipline to save the money for it. We need to build our financial base before we decide to purchase any item.

In the South, which is known as the Bible Belt, everybody says, "Let me pray about it first," even if they don't mean it.

The story goes that a gentleman was having "buyer's temptation." He wanted a new car. As soon as he drove into the dealer's lot, a salesman descended upon him, showed him the kind of car he wanted, hooked him into the office, put a contract in front of him, and said persuasively, "Just sign here."

The man hesitated and replied, "I need to talk to God first."

The salesman, a quick thinker, looked at him and suggested, "Then why don't you go talk to God right now?"

So the guy answered, "Okay, I will." He walked over to a corner, put his hands behind his back, bowed his head, and prayed. After saying amen, he walked back to the salesman and said, "God says I can't do it right now."

The salesman, not one to give up easily, asked, "Do you mind if I talk to Him?"

The gentleman answered, "No, go right ahead."

So the salesman walked over to the same corner, bowed his head, and began to pray. After saying amen, he walked back to the gentleman and said, "God wants to see you again."

If you're going to pray, make sure you get the right answer the first time.

5. NOT CONSIDERING CHANGE

Someone has said, "The only thing constant is change." By paying attention to changes, we can avoid financial disaster. We need to learn from the mistakes of others so history will not repeat itself for us.

As I travel and speak to people, I meet many folks who are not saving or investing money for their future. Because they think their lives are going to remain on the same even keel, they are not preparing for economic downturns or potential personal disasters. Some are not even saving for retirement.

Many of these are pastors of churches. Because ministers and Christian workers are given the option to opt out of Social Security, many don't contribute and, instead, plan on investing for retirement on their own. Unfortunately, they seldom have the extra resources or the self-discipline to set money aside for themselves.

Again and again, pastors of churches call seeking my financial advice and asking the same question: "Should I exercise my Social Security option and get out of the system?"

In every case, I try to persuade ministers not to opt out of Social Security but to stay in the plan. Here's why:

The Social Security System Is Not Going Broke as Some Think

Most pastors who want to opt out of Social Security are convinced that the Social Security system is going to go broke and there won't be any Social Security money left by the time they retire.

That is a myth. It has been perpetrated upon our nation by the liberal media and others, and has many people worried that someone is "raiding the cookie jar" while they're not looking.

The way I see it, there are three forces that won't allow the Social Security system to run dry: old folks, young folks, and the legislative process.

First, the senior citizens: Because Social Security is so important to our society, the AARP (American Association of Retired Persons) lobby—one of the most powerful forces in Washington—will not let any politician fool with the system. Politicians need votes, and whenever one of them reaches his or her hand into the cookie jar—he gets smacked with a cane!

Second, the young people: The baby boomers, who are funding the system right now, won't stand for anyone messing with Social Security either. That's their nest egg; their future; they also stand guard.

Last, since the Social Security system is funded by a tax, Congress can always raise the contribution (tax) if conditions warrant, to keep the fund solvent. That wouldn't be a great situation from the taxpayers' viewpoint, but it would prevent the fund from going bankrupt, as some allege is possible.

Circumstances May Change

Ministers who, in the past thirty to forty years, have not contributed to Social Security are now ready to retire. While their elderly parishioners are collecting Social Security checks and enjoying their retirement, these unfortunate pastors must often get jobs just to survive.

Many ministers who took their option did not plan on being moved around from church to church. Every church—especially independent ones—operates differently. When I ask a pastor why he has no Social Security, he usually tells me that he expected his church to take care of him.

Several years ago, when I first began giving my "How to Double Your Church Financial Base" seminar, I was invited to a church in Tennessee. Just as I was about to enter the building on Sunday morning, the janitor approached me and asked if he could speak with me.

"I am seventy years old, and I used to be the pastor of this church," he said. "In fact, I founded it and preached in that pulpit for many years."

"Why are you the janitor now?" I asked, shocked but preparing myself for the answer I knew he would give.

"If I didn't sweep the floors in my own church, I couldn't survive."

"Didn't the church have a retirement fund set aside for you?" I asked.

"Nope! I never taught the church to plan for the future. What's worse, I didn't put any money aside for retirement either."

Later that morning, when it came time for me to speak to the congregation, I told them about my conversation with their former pastor. Then I said, "I want everyone here who has a retirement plan at the place where they work to stand." Most of the people stood.

"I want everyone who has some form of military pension or Social Security coming to him or her to stand." The remainder of the congregation stood to their feet.

"Now I want you to look and see who is still sitting. Your pastor and your former pastor. Shame on you," I said, rebuking that congregation of intelligent, educated people for not caring enough about those men to take care of their retirement needs.

"If a man spends his life in the ministry, he certainly should not have to get a secular or part-time job after he gives up the pulpit," I told them. That morning, the congregation came under conviction and determined to support their former pastor and begin a retirement plan for the present pastor.

Unfortunately my pastor/janitor friend died about six months after I had preached in his church. Instead of being able to enjoy his few remaining years, he had been forced to do manual labor in order to put food on the table.

Regular Social Security Payments Ensure Disciplined Savings

The money contributed to Social Security goes toward retirement, and it can't be touched. That is the number-one reason why I encourage pastors to stay in the Social Security system. Those who do not pay the Social Security tax usually intend to take the same amount that would be deducted from their paychecks by law and invest that money. Unfortunately, few pastors I have met actually set that money aside and invest it. Even those who do save for retirement are often tempted to use the money for emergencies or special needs.

If they did have the discipline to invest that money and put it away at 10 percent interest, they would have a lot more than the government would give them when it comes time to retire. That is the main complaint with the system.

• If we do what God has commanded us, He will do His part. We can never get ahead by violating one of His principles to uphold another. • • • • •

If the Social Security system were put into the hands of private management, our citizens would retire with incomes more than sufficient to meet their basic needs. Even though there is little hope of that ever happening, I advise every pastor or independent Christian worker to stay in the system.

One day I received a call from a seventy-five-year-old man who had just returned from the mission field with his wife.

"I don't have any money," he said matter-of-factly, "and I'm not calling to ask you for any. I just need some advice."

"Sure," I replied.

"I've been a missionary in Brazil for most of my life. For years, we put all our support money into the mission work and didn't set any aside for ourselves. I didn't pay into Social Security either. My wife and I kept the mission going until we no longer had the health and strength to carry on."

I listened quietly, picturing the scene I had witnessed time and time again during my student years in Brazil.

"My wife had been very ill, and I was afraid she would die in the jungle, so I gathered what money we did have and came back to the States."

"What are you living on now?" I asked, knowing that when an independent missionary retires from the field, the churches soon forget about him or her.

"We don't have any steady income," he replied. "We're pretty much on our own."

That is why most mission boards require their missionaries to have some form of retirement fund. In fact, I manage the investments of several missionary retirement accounts that require missionaries to set aside some portion of their monthly support for retirement purposes. Every pastor, missionary, or independent businessman should be part of a retirement plan.

"How are you managing?" I asked.

"We rent a little shack in the hills of northern Arkansas for $100 a month, and we usually have enough money for groceries."

I sighed heavily, wondering how to help this dear man of God. But before I could ask, he said, "Here's the reason I'm calling. Some-one gave my wife a mink coat, and I was wondering, since you know a lot of people, if you could find a buyer for it and invest the money for me so I'd have a steady income."

The sad part was that the gentlemen thought the coat would bring in thousands of dollars. After all, it was mink. I had to choke back the tears as I told him, "I'm sorry, but the coat is probably only worth $300 or even less."

"I knew it," he said in despair. "I should have put some money aside instead of plowing every cent into the projects we were doing in Brazil. I should have saved a portion. That would have been right, wouldn't it?"

"Yes, of course," I replied as gently as possible. "The Scriptures teach us to plan for the future."

If we do what God has commanded us, He will do His part. We can never get ahead by violating one of His principles to uphold another.

The Social Security system may not be the best retirement program, but at least you will be guaranteed a steady income. In addition, you should invest in a private retirement fund that will allow you to enjoy your latter years without worrying about finances.

6. GETTING INTO DEBT

This is another mistake many people make.

I have already talked about debt and the fallacies debt-free preachers are perpetrating on the Christian world. I do not believe debt is wrong, but if you cannot handle credit, you should not be in debt.

The misuse of credit cards has created financial chaos in the lives of millions of Americans—including many Christians. Paying 15 to 22 percent interest for items you probably didn't really need in the first place is irresponsible. Once the interest eats up any excess money you have coming in each month, it will start chewing into the cash you need to pay your household bills. Before you know it, you are always short on cash, and you're heading down the slippery slope to financial ruin.

Check the twenty-eight ways to know you're overextended listed in Chapter 6 to determine how far you have slid already. If several of those symptoms are chronic in your life, you need to take immediate steps to get out of debt.

If you are paying more than 18 percent of your after-tax income for consumer payments—such as your car, furniture, electronics, and so on—then you are in over your head. In addition, life-style spending—eating out, vacations, and so on—should be less than 18 percent of your take-home pay.

Overextension goes beyond the financial problems to affect both your personal and spiritual life. Do any of these situations sound familiar?

1. You and your spouse constantly argue about money.
2. The stress you are experiencing is affecting your health.
3. You can't sleep.
4. You are considering questionable ways of getting money.
5. You're always searching for an escape from the constant pressure.
6. Hopelessness and depression have overwhelmed you.
7. You've stopped praying and reading your Bible.
8. You no longer tithe.
9. You avoid going to church.
10. You're afraid to get financial counseling.

When debt is misused, financial and personal disaster always result. What can you do? Here are a few suggestions.

1. Develop a plan for paying your debts. Write a list of your creditors, the amount of payment due, and the interest you are paying.
2. Check to see if the interest you are paying exceeds the net rate of return of interest you are earning on your investments.
3. Pay off all negative interest loans from your savings accounts or liquid investments if they are not in IRAs or some sort of qualified or tax-deferred plan.
4. Keep your short-term debt (everything except your mortgage) within a thirty-six-month payback period.

If you are making car payments at a high rate of interest, get a loan at a lower rate and pay off the car. That won't get you out of debt, but it will help you reallocate your funds.

The easiest way to keep your debt safe is to control spending and use your credit lines only in emergencies. Credit is a valuable asset and should be used wisely.

7. REFUSING TO BUDGET

Every single person, business, and church should be on a budget. Households operating without a budget are like airplane pilots flying by the seat of their pants. You'll never know where you are headed, what your expenses are, or how to land if you do don't have something to guide you.

Budgets help in three ways:

Budgets Help You Plan Ahead

Only fools go blindly through life without taking stock of the direction they are headed. Unfortunately, that is exactly what many Christians do and why their spending is often out of control.

Budgets Keep You Abreast of the Facts at All Times

Enterprises that succeed plan wisely, get strong through common sense, and profit by keeping abreast of the facts.

Budgets Help Us Stay Organized

Budgeting eliminates disorganization and keeps everything on track. No builder would try to build a house without knowing how much that house will cost. He first gets estimates and then works hard to keep the costs under control so that everything works out according to his cost sheet.

When counseling and giving advice to people as to how to manage their money, I use the following simple guidelines.

- 35 percent of income for rent or mortgage payments
- 10 percent for life-style—eating out, vacations, clothes
- 10 percent for church
- 10 percent for savings
- 35 percent for household expenses—food, fuel, utilities, and so on

Of course those numbers can be adjusted to suit individual needs and are only a method of showing how to get spending under control based on relative income. The Bible teaches in Proverbs 24:3, "Through wisdom is an house builded; and by understanding it is established."

God is not the author of confusion. In fact, because He is an orderly God, He doesn't like things messed up. Budgeting will help us keep our lives in order and will ultimately result in the wonderful blessings God has prepared for those who follow Him.

LEARNING LESSONS THE HARD WAY

I wish I could say that I had avoided those seven mistakes in my business and personal life, but I haven't. Unfortunately, I learned them the hard way—through experience. When I was a young man starting out in business, my partner and I had set our goals for the future. We were young men with dreams and little money, but we were hard workers and had a lot of talent. With some creative thinking, we built our small construction business into a fair-sized operation.

When we first started out in the foundation contracting business, all we did were the footings for the foundations. After a while, we built a unique, little business into a major operation and were doing almost 100 percent of the footing work in our town. The business eventually grew to encompass clients all over our state of Kentucky.

My partner and I began to look for ways to expand. Since we used a lot of concrete, it seemed logical for us to build a concrete plant and sell the concrete we were using. Although it took a major investment for a couple of young guys who didn't know anything about the concrete business, we plugged along pretty well. That was until truck maintenance and a zillion other complications started depleting our cash flow.

We then decided to start building entire foundations and create money to support our projects by doing the masonry work. My partner, who had never laid a concrete block or brick in his life, put a crew together and started into the masonry business. He caught on quickly and, after a couple of years, we were major contractors doing entire building foundations and servicing ourselves with concrete. Everything was going great.

Soon a concrete block plant came up for sale in our city. Since we were laying most of the concrete blocks in our area and were having a hard time getting service from the other manufacturers, we decided to buy the block plant. Although the plant was a major investment, the price we paid was nothing compared to the millions a plant like that would have normally cost.

- *When you take giant steps, you have giant risks.* • • • • • •

I remember the day we closed the loan. Alex and I stood alone in the middle of the ten-acre manufacturing plant, looking at the more than two thousand feet of railroad siding coming onto our premises and viewing the fleet of trucks and equipment used to move and store the product.

Alex turned to me and asked, "What did we just do?"

Never in our wildest dreams could we have imagined that what appeared to be such a great investment could go so sour. When you take giant steps, you have giant risks.

We knew absolutely nothing about the concrete block business. To make matters worse, we took in a partner who had money but who didn't know anything about managing a manufacturing plant either. As a result, we had to rely on other people to run the plant for us. We lost control of our circumstances, and a huge, white elephant ended up taking us down.

Alex and I both lost everything we had spent many years accumulating through hard work and self-denial. In the end, we found ourselves, not behind the desk or on the golf course, but back in the ditch starting all over to pay our debts. It wasn't fun watching the bank take everything away that we had worked so hard to accumulate. Just as Alex and I had stood there gazing at the plant we had just bought, we stood there as the auctioneer sold everything to the highest bidder to pay our debts.

But that's not the end of our story. Both of us had to sell our homes, rental properties, and everything else we had worked so hard to obtain over the years. This was not an easy, little lesson to learn; it was a major, life-changing jolt which strained a beautiful friendship. For the past few years, I have helped dozens of young people avoid the potholes into which we fell, lo, those many years ago.

I remember the day I left Kentucky to move to California: Alex stood in the parking lot of the cafe where we drank coffee every morning. I was a little sad and apprehensive, naturally, what with the prospect of leaving him and all our friends and memories behind to go to the West Coast. Alex put his hand on my shoulder and said, "Don't worry, Sherm; go on and do what God has called you to do. You have God, your family, and your health. You'll do fine." It was a moment of friendship that I wouldn't trade for all the gold in Fort Knox.

That incident was tough medicine to swallow; it set us back a few years. But it is also why I went back to school to study business management; why I am a financial adviser today; and why I can write this book. The principles in this chapter did not come from lectures in Accounting 101; I learned them in the world of trying to manage my own business—through its success and failure.

If you're smart, you will avoid the mistakes I made and keep on a straight path to prosperity.

TIP THREE:

Seven Steps to Financial Freedom

. . . .

From my experiences in dealing with people and their finances, I have learned one important lesson: The way money is used determines whether it becomes a curse or a blessing.

These verses of Scripture make clear that many sorrows come when too much emphasis is placed on money.

> But they that will be rich fall into temptation and a snare, and into many foolish and hurtful lusts, which drown men in destruction and perdition. For the love of money is the root of all evil: which while some coveted after, they have erred from the faith, and pierced themselves through with many sorrows. (1 Tim. 6:9–10)

According to the Bible, there is nothing wrong with being rich or having things. Money is neither righteous nor unrighteous; it is neither moral nor amoral. Our attitude toward money and how we use the assets God has given us most concern Him.

> Charge them that are rich in this world, that they be not highminded, nor trust in uncertain riches, but in the living God, who giveth us richly all things to enjoy; that they do good, that they be rich in good works, ready to distribute, willing to

. . . .

communicate; laying up in store for themselves a good foundation
against the time to come, that they may lay hold on eternal life.
(1 Tim. 6:17–19)

Having money is not wrong. Money used in the right way can
help you enjoy life.

I have always found it interesting that truly spiritual people often
have a lot of common sense—probably, godly wisdom—in the area
of finances and money. In 1878, Pope Leo XIII eloquently stated what
most Americans today know to be true:

> The fact that God has given the earth for the use and enjoyment of
> the whole human race can in no way be a bar to the ownership of
> private property. Men always work harder and more readily when
> they work on that which belongs to them. It is surely undeniable
> that, when a man engages in remunerative work, the impelling
> reason and motive of his work is to obtain property and thereafter
> to hold it as his very own.[1]

Pope Leo hit the nail on the head. Personal ownership and the
ability to work and earn money form the foundation of a capitalistic
society. That's why America has become the great nation it is today.

Every day in this country money is transferred from one hand to
another for the purpose of purchasing goods and for the betterment
of our citizens' life-styles. That's how our economic system works.
People go to work every day to make money to meet their needs, to
enjoy life, and to bless others. That is the American dream.

I believe most Americans want to have financial freedom and
enjoy the many blessings God has afforded us in this country. I doubt
if many of us would turn down the opportunity to be wealthy. But
there is a right and a wrong way to make your money work for you.

Here are seven steps to financial freedom that will not only increase your potential income, but will help you invest the money you
have now in ways that will benefit both you and the kingdom of God.

1. PLANT IN THE RIGHT SOIL

When I was a child, I looked for a pot of gold every time I saw
a rainbow. Digging for buried treasure in hopes of finding something

valuable fascinated me. Some adults are like that—always looking for that pot of gold at the end of the rainbow. On the beach or in a field or park, you can find them with a huge headset over their ears and a metal detector in their hands. Others play the lottery or bet on horses. Some are more ingenious and hope to make their fortune through get-rich-quick schemes promising a bright future and monetary rewards.

I read a magazine ad the other day that claimed you could make up to $2,000 a month and never leave your house. However, you had to pay $300 for the book that would tell you how to do this. The only people getting rich off that scheme are the guys selling the books.

Wealth Without Risk by Charles Givens and the sequel, *More Wealth Without Risk*, were on the best-seller list for months. Why? Because people want to get rich the easy way. These books, however, which have great titles but no substance, fail to mention how to get wealthy.

Newsweek's May 17, 1993, issue reported that the convincing Mr. Givens is not so credible after all. According to the article, Givens doles out financial advice without the proper credentials to do so. But who cares as long as Oprah, Phil Donahue, and Larry King are around to tap into his "expert" advice?

Gullible audiences are making Givens and others like him rich by buying their anemic advice on the hope that they will someday become like their mentors. It rarely happens, as the article in *Newsweek* points out. But that's not the end of the story. The fact is: Bad advice can lead to terrible consequences.

If we want to achieve financial freedom, we must follow the principles outlined in Scripture.

> Be not deceived; God is not mocked: for whatsoever a man soweth,
> that shall he also reap. For he that soweth to his flesh shall of the
> flesh reap corruption; but he that soweth to the Spirit shall of the
> Spirit reap life everlasting. And let us not be weary in well doing:
> for in due season we shall reap, if we faint not. (Gal. 6:7–9)

The Bible says that if we sow we will also reap; that's a spiritual principle that never fails. Sowing and reaping also work in the material realm. If we want our money to grow, we must plant it in the right environment and cultivate our money just as we would a crop in order for it to grow.

We've heard the saying "Rome wasn't built in a day," yet many young people want to reach their financial goals without taking the necessary steps to achieve them. The first step is knowing where to put your money to make it grow.

• *It is not God's plan for men to gain money by chance.* • • • • • • • A few years ago, when our church was struggling financially, I presented our needs to the congregation and asked them to give as much as possible to help relieve the situation. One of our young married men approached me after church that Sunday morning and said, "Pastor, I'm going to Reno, Nevada, to play the lottery. If I win, I will give the church my winnings. Do you think God will bless that?"

I remember well my answer. I said, "God's blessings do not hinge on whether you would give Him all your earnings or not. The test of His blessing hinges upon what you are doing with the dollars in your pocket right now."

It is not God's plan for us to gain money by chance. Millions and millions of lottery tickets are sold throughout the United States each year. Only on one occasion out of millions of chances have I ever seen someone praise God for the winnings—much less give a large portion of the money to their church. And even then, I wondered if God accepted the praise for doing something He condemns in Scripture.

Ephesians 4:14 teaches that we are to trust in God and His sovereignty to supply for us and avoid crafty and deceitful men. I believe Christians should stay away from slot machines and lottery tickets and trust in the providence of God for their wealth.

Deuteronomy 8:18 states that fact plainly: "But thou shalt remember the LORD thy God: for it is he that giveth thee power to get wealth."

In the parable of the talents (Matt. 25:14–30), Jesus teaches us to invest our money wisely. We need to plant our money where it will grow by sowing it in prudent, safe investments.

A woman in our town came to me one day and said, "You have to get ahold of my husband's money. If you don't get it and put it where he can't find it, we'll have nothing left for retirement."

"What is the problem?" I asked.

"My husband plays the futures and options market and has wasted $50,000 of our retirement money because he listens to these brokers who call him on the phone," she answered.

After talking with her husband about the unnecessary chances he was taking, I was able to put what money they had left away in prudent, low-risk investments. God doesn't want us to throw the money He has given us down rabbit holes or bet on race horses. Instead, He wants us to follow the principle of sowing and reaping.

Here are three points to remember about this important principle:

A. There Is a Time Lapse between Planting and Harvesting

When my son was a young boy, he planted some flowers one evening. The next morning he came into our bedroom crying.

"What's wrong?" I asked.

"The flowers didn't grow," he cried.

He couldn't understand why the seeds hadn't come up. After all, he had planted them the night before.

Like seed in the ground, it takes time for wise investments to grow before we can reap what we have sowed. In fact, it takes years of slow, steady growth before investments pay a great dividend.

B. Reaping Requires Discipline and Patience

Farmers don't go out and plow up the field every time it doesn't rain for several weeks. They wait patiently, and eventually the rains come and the crops grow. Some people give up too easily when temporary setbacks or bad times come. It takes discipline to stick it out and ride the ups and downs of the economy.

That is especially true with small business ventures. It's a known fact that it takes three to five years, in most cases, to see a profitable return on your initial capital investment in the business.

C. Harvest Is Always in Direct Proportion to Planting

I heard about a poor farm family who had several children. Although they had a few cows and four or five hogs, the family barely made it year after year.

One day the father came and told the family, "The corn from last year's crop is nearly gone, and this year's harvest won't come in for several more weeks."

The children sighed and looked at one another. Every year, it was the same old story.

"I don't know what to do," the farmer continued. "I chose the best seed available. I prepared the soil the best I knew how. I fertilized, and we had enough rain. I don't understand why we always come up short."

The mother added, "I've been very careful in preparing our meals. I measured everything just right. I haven't wasted any food. I don't overcook. I don't know what else to do."

One of their little boys was listening. Wide-eyed, he spoke up. "How much seed did you plant, Daddy?"

"Every year, I've been planting a whole bushel."

"Why don't you try planting two bushels, Daddy?"

Now there's a kid with his head screwed on right! He had more common sense than his parents. He knew that if you wanted to reap more, you had to sow more. It comes back to the old adage: To make money, you've got to spend money. Like seed planted in the soil, the more money you plant the more you harvest. Simply doubling your effort and your investment can reap big rewards.

2. LIVE WITHIN YOUR MEANS

One day a couple called to ask for my help. They told me they had no budget and didn't know how to make one. Immediately, I figured they were probably like so many others I had counseled—in credit card debt up to their ears and frustrated because they could see no way out. But I set up an appointment anyway.

To make my job as easy as possible, I required them to bring every scrap of financial evidence they could find and disclose their situation to me 100 percent. I knew from experience that it is impossible to help anyone who is lying or covering up something he or she does not want to face.

In order to bring home the point, I told the couple: "If you hold something back from your doctor, he can't find the cause of your true illness. If you don't disclose all the facts to your lawyer, he can't properly defend you in the courtroom. He'll be continuously surprised by new evidence that keeps cropping up. The same goes for your minister and financial adviser. We cannot help you if we don't know the true situation."

Convinced of my reasoning, this couple brought in every piece of information they possessed and openly disclosed all their finances. When I met with them, I was surprised to find that they had no credit cards and very little debt, yet they never had enough cash and could not pay their bills on time. As new Christians, they were also under deep conviction to tithe but hadn't been able to do so.

Further investigation revealed that they made enough money to live comfortably, but they were behind on their car payments and rent and other monthly bills. I could not understand why they couldn't meet their obligations. After talking with them for a few minutes, I concluded that they must be mismanaging their money and living beyond their means.

During the question-and-answer period about how they spend their money, I discovered that they were taking trips out of town almost every weekend and eating out every other night. Their call-in pizza bill amounted to a couple of hundred dollars per month!

This couple's financial chaos resulted from the fact that they were spending more money than they were making and had no idea where it was going. The hard part would be getting them to discipline themselves.

I worked out a budget that would make it possible for them to be totally out of debt in ten months. In addition, they could pay their tithes each week plus mission offerings and would have $4,000 in savings at the end of the ten-month period.

"How can that happen?" they asked. "We've never saved a dime in our lives!"

"Here's what I want you to do," I told them. "Set up a separate bank account in your name, but I will control the account. You will then regularly make out a check to the account, and I will deposit it and then pay your bills from the account."

They now had a budget and the means to administer it. I remember their anxiety—and excitement—about what we were going to do. Being totally out of debt, caught up on their bills, and having money in savings was more than they could imagine.

I remember the Sunday they gave their first full tithe check plus a mission offering. The expressions on their faces told me the guilt had lifted and that they were gaining a new sense of self-respect.

The solution to their financial problems, however, revolved around the fact that they were going to have to change their life-style and live within their means. It meant that, for ten months, they were going to eat out only once a month, and there would be no more Lake Tahoe vacations or hotel bills, except for emergencies. It meant pizza one night every other week and a promise to quit smoking. Today cigarettes are $2.50 a pack, which is almost half the minimum hourly wage. Cigarette prices are not relative to income, making smoking a very expensive habit—notwithstanding the fact that it will kill you.

Today that couple is living a wonderfully happy Christian life.

While I was in Germany conducting financial seminars for Christian U.S. military personnel, I told this couple's story. After my lecture that evening, a man walked up to me and said, "What you said really got to me."

"How is that?" I asked.

"I am a medical doctor, and, like the couple in your story, my wife and I have no credit card debt. We pay our bills, but we have no money left over. While you were talking, I realized where our money was going. We have been taking longer and more expensive trips back to the United States with the entire family. I make more than an adequate salary, but we are living way beyond our means."

You may think, *That is really stupid. Who would be so foolish?* You'd be surprised how many folks reading this book are wasting their money on unnecessary junk. Overspending is a habit they can't break. They are driven to purchase more than they need just to impress other people or to live a more luxurious life-style than they can afford.

3. MAINTAIN DUE DILIGENCE

In the investment world, we have a term called "due diligence." Let me explain what this means.

Before a securities firm makes any commitment concerning an investment, it will recommend to its clients that an extensive study of that investment be made by advisers working for the firm. That is done to determine if the investment is prudent for the clientele. Once that has been determined, the financial advisers or consultants working for the firm can then sell the investment to their clients.

I have been to many Due Diligence meetings where extensive presentations were made concerning particular investments. As a result, I understand the importance of knowing investments, how they work, and whether they will meet the needs of my clients. By understanding the goals of my clients, I can determine if the objectives of the investments are suited for the clients' personal needs.

If there were no due diligence procedures in the investment world, there would be chaos in the financial markets as brokers would have little means by which to judge investments. Concomitantly, the same methods should apply to our personal world of finance.

Remember, the Bible says, "Be thou diligent to know the state of thy flocks, and look well to thy herds" (Prov. 27:23). We should know the state of our flocks. In other words, we should look to our finances. Our part of due diligence is to work toward discipline.

Discipline is very important in reaching financial goals—or any other goal for that matter. Without discipline, no one can stay on target, and failure after failure will result. Being impulsive and jumping into things too quickly will surely lead to financial destruction.

No one knows that better than I do. Remember my story in the previous chapter about buying the concrete block company and trying to manage it without having the experience? I learned several lessons from that.

Don't Lose Your Head over Deals

Deals are great, but if you don't understand them, don't buy them. I am not the only person who has lost a lot of money because a deal looked good at the time.

Millions of Americans do the same thing every day when they buy a lottery ticket, when someone calls them on the phone with an investment pitch, or when they read about a new money-making scheme in a magazine article or book. The best way to hang on to your money is to stay away from deals you don't understand.

Don't Forfeit Your Discipline to Pressure Inside or Out

Sometimes an item or an offer looks so good that you feel you cannot resist. Just because something looks good doesn't mean it *is* good. In fact, something that looks too good to be true probably is.

When I was a kid and my dad would go looking for a new car, I got more excited than anybody else in the family. Of course, my choice was always the snazzy, red one with the big sticker price. I would bug my dad night and day about buying that car. "We just have to have it!" I'd say.

Because he had discipline, my father would wait until the time was right. Then, when he had the money and could afford it, he bought a car. Of course, he seldom purchased the one I had selected. Outside pressure is hard to resist, but inside pressure is the worst. You want something, and you want it right now. The pressure you put on yourself to have what you desire is sometimes unbearable. But you must resist if you cannot afford the item or do not know what you are doing. Stay disciplined and under control until all the indicators give the light to go ahead.

Don't Bet Your Financial Life on Credit Risks

We take all kinds of risks during our lifetime, but some risks are totally unnecessary and can lead to disaster. Many people have destroyed their financial futures because they impulsively justified doing a project or purchasing an expensive item. They figure, *I'll get the credit first and worry about paying for it later.*

When I was a young man in Bible college, I was considering whether I could afford to buy a new car. The pastor of the church where I was an intern told me, "Go ahead, and worry about paying for it later."

That is the definition of a credit risk. It means negotiating our future without knowing how we are going to pay for something. Remember, credit is a tool for financial growth, not a bet for the future.

Don't Plunge into Risky Ventures Without Investigating First

You should always be suspicious. The question should never be, "Where is the bottom?" but, "How deep is the water?" If you don't know how deep you're getting in, don't jump!

I wish someone had told me that before my partner and I bought the concrete block manufacturing plant. We should have gotten all the facts first, studied the ins and outs of the business, and figured out our profit and loss margins before taking the plunge.

Don't Get into Something Unless You Have a Measure of Control

What happened to my partner and me in our first major venture could also happen to you. As long as we had control, everything was fine. When we ventured into an area where we had no previous experience and had to depend on others to manage the company, we lost our control. As a result, the financial nails began coming out of the wall, and our house collapsed. It is always bad business to neglect looking after your own interests.

A pastor in the Washington, D.C., area called to ask me a very difficult question. "Should I hire a former pastor who is also my best friend to be my associate pastor?" he questioned.

I thought for a moment and then advised, "Don't do it. Although it would be great to have your best friend working with you, it is very hard to

• *Credit is a tool for financial growth, not a bet for the future.* • • • • •

manage someone who is personally close. In church work, difficult decisions have to be made, and not all of them are palatable. You may lose control of the situation. That would not make you happy and could ultimately destroy your friendship—not to mention what it would do to the church. If you don't hire him, he will still be your friend."

Don't Hurry

Inadequate due diligence will take you into insurmountable problems. Take your time. Too many major decisions are made in a couple of hours. Hurrying into decisions will cause you to be wasteful. I know that from experience. I can't tell you how many times, when money got tight, I wished I had cash that I had already spent on some foolish item.

Now, before I buy something I'm not sure about, I take a moment to ask the Lord, "Do You want me to buy this?" Then I wait twenty-four hours before I make a final decision on the purchase. Personal discipline has to be maintained for future consideration. Waiting twenty-four hours or more is good strategic management.

4. SAVE MONEY

All Christian financial advisers and counselors agree on one principle: Everyone should save money. Why? Because the Bible teaches saving.

Living like the grasshopper will catch up to you in time, which is why God's Word says:

> Go to the ant, thou sluggard; consider her ways, and be wise:
> which having no guide, overseer, or ruler, provideth her meat in the
> summer, and gathereth her food in the harvest. How long wilt thou
> sleep, O sluggard? when wilt thou arise out of thy sleep? Yet a little
> sleep, a little slumber, a little folding of the hands to sleep: so shall
> thy poverty come as one that travelleth, and thy want as an armed
> man. (Prov. 6:6–11)

Ants don't spend all their resources. Instinctively, they know they have to put aside provisions to make it from winter to spring. As a result, they are diligent in storing away what they need. They don't live paycheck to paycheck and hope everything works out all right.

These verses teach that if we spend all of our money, we are going to be in trouble at some point in time. Millions of Christian Americans, however, have not yet caught on to the fact that God wants them to save money and not spend every cent they make.

> There is treasure to be desired and oil in the dwelling of the wise;
> but a foolish man spendeth it up. (Prov. 21:20)

Almost every day, I talk with people who have been through disasters and experienced all kinds of tragedies. In almost every case, they tell me, "We could have made it through all right if we had just saved some money."

I tell my clients to use 10 percent as their guide. If a person could put away 10 percent of every dollar he earns, he would build wealth. We pay everybody else; why not pay ourselves? People who practice this principle seldom need money.

Save something even if you start with only a few dollars a week. Financial freedom depends on your ability and discipline to save money. An elderly woman who is a member of my church came to my office one morning. Although she is well-off financially, she was concerned about her children.

"They are grown," she said, "and doing all right, but they aren't very much ahead. I just can't understand it. They've been given all the advantages. My husband and I came from poor families. We had nothing when we first got married, but we started putting five to seven dollars a week out of the paycheck into a savings account."

"How much were you making back then?" I asked.

"Fifty cents an hour," she replied. "But before we knew it—within three years—the account had grown to over seven hundred dollars. We then took the seven hundred dollars and put a down payment on a house, where we still live to this day."

Of course, houses were a lot cheaper back then, and it took less money to buy one, but everything is relative. Most people today earn more than their parents did, so the same principles apply. It is still possible to build wealth today, but we must be willing to discipline ourselves to save.

Most people can't live two months without any money if they are forced into a difficult situation. To be on the safe side, every family or individual should have three to six months' income in a savings account emergency fund. I'm not talking about your retirement fund but about liquid assets—available cash—where, in case of emergency, the bills could be paid for at least that period of time. If you are job hunting and are diligently looking, you can generally find a new position within six months. Then you could begin to rebuild your savings.

My friend and associate Dr. Demas Brubacher teaches college history. In his studies of both ancient and modern cultures, he has discovered that throughout the ages, people have practiced saving by putting away small amounts on a regular basis.

When he presents this fact to his students, he finds that they are under the misconception that you have to have $15,000 or some high figure before it is actually considered savings. Dr. Brubacher suggests that they take 10 percent of every paycheck and pay themselves by putting money aside, whether it be $5 per week or $500.

Once those young people catch on to the idea, they get excited. Over the years, those who have followed Dr. Brubacher's advice have become successful. In fact, some of my investment clients today were once Dr. Brubacher's students.

. . . .

If you are twenty years old and put $100 per month into a retirement savings plan at 10 percent and do that until you are twenty-eight years old, you could then quit saving and never invest another penny. Why? Because when you are sixty-five, you will have almost $497,000 in the bank. That should make for a nice retirement!

On the other hand, if you start saving at age twenty-eight, you would have to put away $250 per month for the rest of your life to have the same amount of money you would have if you had started saving $100 per month at age twenty. That is the power of compound interest.

Forget the get-rich-quick schemes and quit chasing rainbows. Start saving now. The greatest capitalistic invention in the world is compound interest. Properly used, it will make you rich.

Most people, when they see their income tax statements, say, "You mean I actually made that much money last year? Where did it all go?" Here is a truth: You are going to make a lot of money in your lifetime. Whether it will be enough money to keep you comfortable in your later years depends on whether you can set aside a portion of it in the beginning.

In a previous chapter, we discussed Social Security and the problem of saving for retirement. That problem, however, is not exclusive to those in the ministry because Social Security by itself will not adequately meet the needs of most older Americans. Those who think their monthly government check will put them on easy street are in for a rude awakening.

Some people reach retirement age and realize they are going to have to live twenty or so more years on their meager Social Security benefits. With no money to take trips, buy extra luxuries, or maintain a good standard of living, they squeak by with the bare necessities of life. Some are even forced to take minimum-wage jobs in order to have a little extra spending money. But it doesn't have to be that way.

Start saving now, no matter what your age, and the future will begin to take care of itself.

5. INVEST WISELY

Once people have finally saved some money, they look for ways to invest it. For those who have never invested before, however, that can be a tricky business. Investing without wise counsel can lead to financial disaster.

Here are some ways you can make sure you invest wisely.

Use a Professional Financial Adviser

Some people who invest money for the first time try to do it themselves without counsel. I can understand why. The money "advisers" who write for popular magazines give their readers the idea that stockbrokers are like sleazy lawyers—they are the only ones making money. That is not true, nor is it the nature of the security business. There are crooks in every business, and the securities business is no exception. But that is no reason to go it alone.

Many new investors believe the advertisements of discount brokers that relate how a person can avoid paying commissions by doing his or her own investing. But that is probably the worst decision a new investor can make.

I know how discount brokers work. You pick your investments, they do the trades, but no one ever calls to tell you how your account is doing. No one warns you of impending trouble. When investments go to the tank because no one is watching them, you can lose a lot of money.

The argument can be made that "my broker never calls me anyway," but that is not a good reason to avoid paying someone to manage your affairs. Many investment advisers do a great job for their clients. If your broker is not meeting your needs, fire him and look for someone who will.

I can understand why people do not like to pay commissions, but the risks are not worth what little profit you *• Professional advice carries a price tag, no matter what its source. • • •* may gain. In fact, paying someone to handle your investments could be the salvation of your financial soul.

Besides, even when you buy an investment directly from a fund, you still pay a commission. In fact, it is the same commission you pay a separate broker/dealer because the fund charges everyone alike. If you buy no-load funds, you still pay fees during the life of the investment. There is no such thing as a free lunch.

Nick Murray, who is a guru in the investment world and a brilliant speaker as well as a broker, wrote an article titled, "Proof Positive: You Make a Difference." He makes this comment:

> The first of two studies, *Understanding Shareholder Redemption Decisions*, provides the statistical backup for something you and I have always known. That is, investors who buy funds using a compensated professional adviser probably do better—or at least make certain critical mistakes less often—than people who buy funds on their own.[2]

Investment magazines push the hatred of stockbrokers and tout no-load funds with fervor. Murray, however, has this to say about paying sales charges:

> Semantics aside, the unspoken, unexamined underlying journalistic hypothesis behind the "no load argument" is, of course, that investors will do equally well (or equally badly) in either type of fund, so why pay a sales charge when you don't have to?
>
> The critical fallacy here is the notion that investment returns and investor returns are the same—that the investor, unaided, will behave rationally, stay focused on the long term, and let the basic uptrend carry him to his destination.
>
> Buying an equity mutual fund turns out to be a lot like buying an airplane. In a no-load fund, the investor buys the plane. Period. He doesn't pay for, and does not get, the services of a pilot. The question therefore becomes: "Are you absolutely sure you know how to fly this plane?"
>
> When an investor buys a fund with a sales charge (or a fee, or whatever), he gets a plane and a pilot. So sit back, relax . . . the pilot will get you where you're going.[3]

Professional advice carries a price tag, no matter what its source. That's why I don't treat myself medically or defend myself in court; I hire a professional. Although legally I could doctor myself and act as my own lawyer if necessary, I won't. Why? Because it is too risky to venture into areas where I lack expertise and training. The same principle should apply to investors who consider selecting their own stocks, mutual funds, or bonds.

If you are not experienced enough to know all the ins and outs of the simple investment tips that I'm providing here, then you probably should not be buying your investments directly.

Invest in the Stock Market

Selling stocks goes back centuries. When companies needed to expand, the banks could not handle the loans required to support expansion because there was not enough money deposited in the banks. Companies then went to the public and sold interests in their businesses called stocks.

When a person bought stock in a company, he or she was promised part of the profits, if any. These were called dividends. The dividends would be paid on a regular basis as the company shared its profits. Selling shares of stock to the public brought the money into the banks and spread the risk of the business over a wide number of people. In fact, if it weren't for the stock market, few of us would have jobs because the companies we work for would be out of business or scaling back.

People often ask me, "Is playing the stock market gambling?" It can be. When I first became a broker, I quickly learned about the option market—the stock market's answer to the horse race. When a person buys an option, he does not purchase or sell the stock. Instead he buys a contract and then bets whether the stock will go up or down.

If he bets that the price will fall and then it goes up, he loses money by every dollar the stock rises in price. If he bets the stock goes up and it falls in price, he loses for every dollar the stock goes down even to zero. On the other hand, he can also gain much money if his stock rises, and the profits are limited only as to how much the stock may rise.

The stock market can also be considered gambling when a person buys a stock and doesn't know what he is doing or doesn't listen to his broker's research advice. A theory among bona fide financial advisers is: The individual investor making his own choices is wrong 90 percent of the time. It has been my experience that it's more like 95 percent, especially for first-time stock pickers who act on a tip they learned from a "barroom" broker at work.

The stock market should not be used purely for speculation—although speculating is not wrong. The stock market, however, has outperformed every other investment in total return since 1936. That's why I do not consider investing in the stock market to be a form of gambling.

Avoid Commodities, Futures, and Options Markets

More speculative and riskier than stock are the commodities, futures, and options markets. With these, the investor takes a risk that the stock will rise or fall by buying instruments called contracts. If the price of the stock falls, the investor may make money if he or she has a contract that says the investment will fall. That is called a put. If the stock rises while the owner has a "put," he or she loses all the money risked plus the amount of the stock.

The opposite is true if the person has a "call." If the stock falls, the person loses dollar for dollar as the stock declines. The only way to protect a total loss to zero is to sell the contract and take the losses.

On the other hand, there is no limit as to what the person can make if the stock continues to rise. If she or he has a call option on the stock, profits are unlimited if the stock continues to rise.

A few years ago, a client asked me if I thought American Airlines would buy out United Airlines. There had been talk of a takeover, so he bought an option (from another broker since I refuse to buy and sell options) and bet that the price of UAL would rise. He bought the option when the price of UAL was around $79. The stock rose to $240 dollars, and then he sold the stock, pocketing $161,000.

Other investors bought options when the stock was around $200 and did not sell when the stock began to fall. By gambling that the stock would rebound, they lost a great deal of money when American did not buy out United.

Most people should stay away from this kind of investing because it is too risky. I read recently that the investor loses 90 percent of the time in the options market. This type of investing, where there is little control, does verge on gambling.

Refuse to Buy Penny Stocks

Penny stocks are another form of risky stock buying. These cheap stocks are not found in any of the major exchanges—such as the New York Stock Exchange. In fact, most reputable brokerage houses do not carry penny stocks and will not allow their brokers to buy them for clients.

Penny stock brokerage houses are constantly being "busted" by the federal government for manipulating the markets on the stocks.

In addition, they have been known to sell investors stocks of companies that are poorly managed or perhaps in trouble at the time the stocks were sold. To make matters worse, the commissions can range from 8 to 150 percent, and most of the time the loser is the investor. If a slick broker calls you on the phone and wants to sell you a deal you can't refuse, be sure to refuse it.

Stay with a Well-known Brokerage House

To invest wisely you need to do business only with full-service, well-known, recognizable brokerage houses. Even then, you must be careful to choose the right broker within the company.

Since there are few born-again brokers in America, it may be hard for investors to find a Christian stockbroker. My experience with brokers across America, however, is that most of them are honest and will look after your best interests. Sure, there are a few bad apples out there, but that's true in any profession. When calling a brokerage house for the first time, ask for the manager. Tell him you want an honest broker who has no compliance problems.

What's compliance? Every brokerage house has resident lawyers who interpret the securities laws for the protection of the brokers who work for the firm. Violating those regulations can result in severe penalties, and brokers take them very seriously. That kind of regulation is called compliance because the broker is bound to comply with the rules of fair practice.

That's why you should always check with the manager of the brokerage firm where you do business to see if the broker you are dealing with has any compliance problems. That would mean he has been disciplined for an improper action in the past.

More than likely, such a question will signal to the manager that you will not be happy with a trainee type broker and will want someone with experience and integrity.

Invest in Bonds

Bonds are different from stocks. Stocks are equities, which means the shareholder has equity in the company and shares a dividend if the company has a profit and can pay one. Equity holders are paid only on the basis of a rise in the stock price or by a dividend declared by the company.

Bonds are debt securities, meaning you have a mortgage on the assets of the company. Bonds are less risky and can carry a good return. The investor is promised a certain yield, and that becomes a fixed investment, whether it be government or corporate bonds. Bondholders actually hold a piece of the mortgage on the property of the corporation.

In case of default by the company, equity holders lose their money since the price of the stock becomes worthless. Bondholders, on the other hand, can actually recover their money because the property is sold and the bondholders' portion of the security is paid by the proceeds of the sale. That makes bonds less risky than stocks.

What are junk bonds? They are bonds issued by companies that have a very high rate of return. Because of the junk bond market crash in 1987, many junk bond brokers and their firms are out of business today, and some of their principals are in jail because of illegal dealings in the bond market.

The term "junk bond" simply means the company offers a high rate of interest and the company may or may not be on slightly shaky ground. I use this rule of thumb: If the company offers 14 percent interest when the going interest rate is below 10 percent, look out! That means the company probably couldn't borrow the money from the bank and is resorting to selling bonds to raise capital. That may be a signal that the company has financial problems.

Some high yield funds, however, are by and large loaded with high yield bonds. They can produce very good returns and are liquid. In fact, there has recently been a revival in the junk bond market.

Buy When Others Are Selling; Sell When Others Are Buying

That is the investment advice of the great financial genius Sir John Templeton, founder of the successful Templeton Mutual Fund family. Also heed the words of financial expert Benjamin Graham: "Buy when most people, including experts, are pessimistic, and sell when they are actively optimistic."

Diversify Your Investments

There is safety in numbers. That adage certainly applies to the area of investments.

Early in my career I quickly learned not to listen to the pressure of wholesalers who contact brokerage houses and try to convince them to buy their funds. If you listened entirely to wholesalers, all your money would be in their particular product.

The same pressure applies when a broker wants to put most, or all, of your money into one or two investments. Why would he want to do this? Either the investment he is choosing may carry a heavier commission, or he is too lazy to properly manage the investment for his client. Don't let your broker load you up in a single area, but insist on diversification. If your broker is not diversifying, that is a good reason to find another broker.

> • *An investment portfolio should be like a baseball team: lots of diversity helps you win.* • • • • •

Diversify with stocks, bonds, cash, and mutual funds. Even some limited partnerships are good investments if they are not leveraged, have a good track record, pay cash dividends, and are not speculative, such as real estate or oil and gas leasing.

Make sure you have an investment adviser who knows how to properly position your portfolio away from the risks. That way you can take advantage of many of the swings that come in the market, allowing you to make a profit.

Resist the Temptation to Put All Your Eggs in One Basket

Whenever one or two of a client's investments are outperforming every other investment in his portfolio, he will call me and ask, "Why wasn't my other money in the portfolio put into this investment? Wouldn't I be getting more of a return if it were all in this one place that's producing such great dividends?"

Or he will make this suggestion, "I heard that Such and Such is giving super returns, let's transfer everything over there."

I quickly remind the client that even the best investments go up and down. Not even great fund managers like Louis Rukeyser or Peter Lynch can predict exactly what an investment is going to do because investments are predicated on many factors.

I explain investment management to my clients using this analogy: An investment portfolio should be like a baseball team. You have nine players. Three or four of them are superstars and are around forever.

Four or five of them need to be traded now and then. As long as you own them, the three or four superstars will perform just well enough to keep the team winning.

I advise my clients to look at the bottom line. If they have a winning portfolio and are making money, that's the telling factor. Diversification keeps your investment strategy in line. Then, in a few years, you can open up the safe and find that you have more money than you put in originally.

It is impossible for any financial adviser to pick winning investments on every call. Sometimes the investment he believes in does not perform as well as he thought it would. That's why the broker should explain to his client that security investments are riskier than bank CDs (Certificates of Deposit) and are to be treated as such. Securities can reward handsomely, but there is a measure of risk for the reward. Therefore, the losers need to be traded very quickly while the winners perform to offset the losses. Again, diversification allows that to take place.

Invest for Total Return

You should take into consideration taxes and inflation, and then make investments after the fact. Your primary concern should be to make a profit. If you do not factor in taxes and inflation, you will not know precisely what you have made.

Sometimes tax-free bonds can help with tax problems. People who do not like to pay taxes can buy a municipal bond. These bonds are issued by cities and are generally for the building of hospitals and so on. They are exempt from federal, state, and local taxes.

Municipal bonds, however, carry a much lower yield than corporate bonds. If you are in a high tax bracket, that can work to your advantage. Your equivalent yield (i.e., what you would need to earn in interest after taxes are adjusted on a taxable investment) can bring a pretty fair return on your money. Not having to pay taxes is an added bonus.

You can also buy municipal bond funds in lieu of purchasing individual municipal bonds.

Don't Neglect Your Investments

Because markets run in cycles, you can't buy an investment and then forget about it. Bull markets occur when stocks are rising in price and value, and bear markets result when stocks are slowing down and decline in price. Bull and bear markets are not permanent, however.

That's why you need to be aware of changes because they affect almost every investment. Investors who manage their own portfolios often do not understand when primary changes are taking place in the markets and how they will affect their investments.

Changes in tax laws and in the economy affect investments daily. When the government comes out with negative news on how the economy performed, the stock market reacts. If you have stock mutual funds or individual stocks, they can react by falling in price.

Changes in interest rates also affect investments. For instance, there is an inverse relationship between bond prices and interest rates. As interest rates rise, bond prices fall. As interest rates fall, bond prices rise. It is important to understand and study economic trends so you can be ready to sell or buy an investment based upon what your research and knowledge indicates may be happening in the economy.

It is also important to know what changes may take place in the long term. Presidential elections and party platforms concerning taxes, for example, will affect investments. To attain your investment goals, you must position yourself to either limit losses or increase profits by knowing what changes may be taking place in the economy.

When I take on a new client, I review his or her present portfolio. Many times, I have to report the bad news that the great investment purchased five to six years ago quit performing after the third year and proceeded to lose money. That can be a real shocker. One of my clients, who lives in Chicago, had bought an investment and held it for ten years. The investment happened to be in California real estate. Couldn't lose there. Right? Wrong.

He was almost in tears when I told him that the $20,000 he had originally invested was now worth only $1,736. Watch the markets because they are constantly changing and so should your portfolio from time to time.

Never Panic When the Market Drops

One of the big mistakes people made after the 1987 crash was cashing in their investments. You should never rush out the next day and sell everything you have.

In the investment business, we have a saying called "hand holding." That cliché came about because many investors panic whenever they see the slightest drop in the market. The financial adviser then has to explain to them why the market fell that day, why it may be down, and why he believes the investment should remain in the portfolio.

If you have a good broker, he or she will tell you when it is time to sell and time to buy. Don't trust your gut feelings alone. Although that works sometimes, it is not a good way to plan or sustain your financial future. Teamwork is the best approach, with you and your broker making investment decisions together for your best interests.

Learn from Your Mistakes

If you make a mistake, then live with it. If you are properly diversified, the mistake will have little effect.

When I first became an investment broker, my trainers told me, "Eventually, you will have an investment blow up. You're going to make mistakes. But don't panic, and don't let your clients panic."

Learn from the mistakes, and minimize losses. I have found through the years that the greater and safer investments allow you to take a little risk. The biggest mistake of all would be not investing in the first place.

Never, Ever Be Negative

This book is written to counter the philosophy of defeatism. There is no reason to think we will not have another one hundred years of prosperity in the stock market that will carry us through as it has in the last one hundred years.

Abandoning your optimistic outlook on life and sticking your head into the sand will cost you dearly in the future.

Begin Your Investment Strategy with Prayer

I believe in prayer because prayer changes things.

Although our brokerage office is not defined as a Christian organization, we operate on biblical principles. In fact, I have found that to be true among many in the investment business.

In fact, some of the points I am making—including this one on prayer—were inspired by Sir John Templeton's ideas on investing success, published in the *World Monitor* and then reprinted in many private brokerage magazines for the use of the broker/dealers only. As a Christian financial adviser, I am proud to say that I am not alone in my field.

6. PREPARE FOR THE FUTURE

No matter what happens to our government or to America's economy, you still have a future. Life will still go on until Jesus returns, and no one knows when that will be. Until then, there are several things you can do to prepare for your own personal future.

The best way to do that is to preserve what you already have. You have assets that can be used to your advantage in ways that will benefit you in the future. Here are several things you can do:

Refinance Your Home

If you own a home and your current interest rate is two percentage points or more above the lowest rate being offered today, you should refinance. That will reduce the amount of interest you will have to pay overall, and you will end up better off in the end. Take into account, however, whether that lower interest rate is attached to a fixed-rate or a variable-rate mortgage. Sometimes a slightly higher-rate loan, when fixed, can be better for you than an adjustable, which may sting you if interest rates rise.

Increase Your Liability Insurance Above Your Homeowner's Policy

You should have more liability insurance than what your homeowner's policy covers. It is usually cheap and is a good way to protect your most expensive possession.

Get Disability Insurance

People are living longer today, but they suffer serious injury more frequently. If you are under sixty-five years old, your life expectancy is going to be ninety-three years. Statistics show, however, that you have a better chance of being disabled at middle age than you have of dying. That's why disability insurance is a wise investment.

Get a Line of Credit from Your Bank

This is for emergencies only. Once you are approved, the bank will hold that line of credit for ten years. If you lose your job, you will have difficulty getting credit when you need it most. But if you already have a line of credit, you can cash in on it, if necessary.

Make Out a Will

Everyone should have a will. Don't risk putting your spouse's or your children's futures in jeopardy by not having a legal document outlining where you want your assets to go.

In addition, put the church in your will. Leaving the church 10 percent, is a good way for you to tithe on your estate.

7. GIVE TO YOUR CHURCH

The degree of your financial freedom depends upon how generous you are with God.

If you don't understand that giving is an essential part of the Christian life, read 1 Corinthians 16. That chapter talks about how to give, where to give, and who is to give. Also read and study the seventh chapter of Hebrews to learn how Abraham paid the tithe to Melchizedek the High Priest, who is a type of Christ. The tithe is the foundation for all scriptural giving, and we ought to do it because the Bible mandates it.

I know that many Christians do not tithe, and those who do are quick to forego giving whenever they experience any kind of financial difficulty. Let me give this warning: You are treading on dangerous ground when you withhold from God what rightfully belongs to Him. The advantages of tithing far outweigh any temporary financial relief you might get from using God's money to meet your own needs.

I am repeatedly asked by pastors around the country, "How often should I preach to my church on giving?"

I always answer, "Until they start doing it."

People need to be challenged in the right ways. Some pastors, however, approach the subject in a negative manner and end up beating the people over the head.

Every time I preach a sermon on giving, someone will say—not to me, of course—"How come every time I come to church, the preacher is always harping on money?" If anyone had the courage to ask me that question, I would reply, "Well, maybe you're not coming to church often enough because I don't preach on giving every Sunday. Or maybe God knows you need to hear that particular message over and over."

Don't begrudge your minister if he challenges your pocketbook. Although he may be looking at the financial condition of the church, ultimately it will be for your own financial good.

Tithing and giving affect Christians in these ways:

Giving Unleashes the Prospects of God's Blessings

When people get saved in our church, we begin to teach them to tithe and make them aware of their responsibility to give to God. In addition, new Christians need to know the blessing that can come from God through giving.

To get the point across, I talk about what God has done in my life through giving. I tell them that the wonderful blessings I'm experiencing are a direct result of my ability to honor God and worship Him through my tithes and offerings. I know, however, that new Christians cannot unleash the prospects of God's blessings unless they are taught what the Bible says about giving.

Giving Enables the Giver to Experience the Joy of Giving

I seldom take a special offering, but I vividly remember the first time I did. Our church did not need the money, but I felt impressed that we should give to God out of our abundance, put the money away, and use it for some special need in the future.

The week before, I began promoting the Special Offering Sunday as "The most unusual service you have ever attended." That particular morning, our order of service was the same as usual, and at the usual specified time I began to preach. Using the parable of the talents as my text, I noted that God commended the first two servants without differentiating between the fact that one had five talents and the other two talents. "The point is," I told the congregation, "do what is right and prudent with the talents you have."

I knew the people were thinking, *What is so unusual about this?*

Then in the middle of the message, I stopped and asked, "How many of you are puzzled as to what this service is all about and why it is so unusual?" Nearly every hand went up.

At that moment I asked our associate pastors to pass out an envelope to each person in the congregation. With puzzled looks, the people turned to one another, wondering what I was up to.

"I want you to open the envelope and take out what is inside," I instructed.

Their confusion increased as they reached in and found an uncirculated ten dollar bill, brand-new and crisp.

I asked, "How many of you have ever come to church and had the church give you money?"

No one raised a hand.

"You can do whatever you want with that ten dollars, but let me present you with a challenge. Instead of leaving here today and saying, 'Hey, the church bought me lunch,' I want you to take the money home. Then I want you to consider trusting God to see how much He can add to the ten dollars in a special offering ten weeks from today."

In the next ten weeks, I witnessed incredible things taking place as the people began to trust God for an offering. One little boy bought a small button machine at a yard sale and made Napa Valley Baptist Church buttons, using a picture of our new church building. He sold the buttons for two dollars each and gave more than $300 to the special offering.

One of our teens, who was a part-time waitress in an ice cream shop, said, "I'll give every ten-dollar tip I get to the Lord."

"How many ten-dollar tips do you usually get?" I asked.

"So far, none," she replied.

In the next ten weeks, however, she received several ten-dollar tips and was thrilled to give a substantial amount of money to the special offering.

A gentleman told me he would give all the overtime hours he received, even though he hadn't received any for more than a year. With that step of faith, he had several opportunities in the next ten weeks to work overtime. His offering was more than generous, and he could hardly contain his joy.

One of our deacons said, "If the government ships me to Saudi

Arabia to help with the clean-up operation after Desert Storm, I will give the extra money I earn to the special offering." Guess what? He went to Saudi Arabia for more than a month.

As a result, that special offering—above the normal tithes—was $47,000 that morning. For a small church, that was a miracle! But the real blessing came in the lives of those who had trusted God to increase their initial ten-dollar investment.

GIVING RAISES THE FINANCIAL PROSPERITY OF INDIVIDUALS AS THEY HONOR GOD

I wanted to raise money for our vacation Bible school and called the program "Take Stock in Our Children Sunday." That Sunday morning, I brought thirty-nine Sunday school children before the congregation. Each child held a large investment certificate on which a maturity date had been written.

My seven-month-old granddaughter, Megan Sue, held a bond certificate that stated, "I mature in the year 2015." The certificate was worth $100 for the infants and graduated down to ten dollars for the kids maturing at age twenty-one in fewer years.

I auctioned off our kids and, although we only needed $1,000 for the vacation Bible school fund, the offering was $3,500 in about five minutes. Because the people were challenged, they responded.

Sometimes people think they are the only ones giving, so they wonder why they should keep it up. It's good to provide opportunities for the entire congregation to see others putting their personal finances into the furtherance of God's kingdom.

Remember the widow's mite? Jesus said she gave more than even the rich Pharisees. No dollar given to God is ever wasted because He has a way of using the faithful to accomplish His purposes.

The best way to get people excited about giving is for them to hear the testimonies of others. There is nothing like listening to someone tell how God bailed him out of a financial crisis just in time. Most people can identify with money problems, and they need to know that God is concerned and can intervene in their finances when necessary.

As a pastor, I want people to know how to give, and I want to see them prosper. I realize, however, that it takes time for some people to fully understand why God expects them to give. Like every other pastor, I had a sermon on Malachi 3:10:

> Bring ye all the tithes into the storehouse, that there may be meat in mine house, and prove me now herewith, saith the LORD of hosts, if I will not open you the windows of heaven, and pour you out a blessing, that there shall not be room enough to receive it.

I preached that if we give to God, He will bless us abundantly.

Many times, when I have preached on the responsibility of giving, I have thought, *Boy, that should hit Mr. So-and-So right between the eyes.* Then, to my dismay, in remarks to me later, Mr. So-and-So indicates that he totally missed the point of my message.

Although I don't personally know the giving record of each of my members, I can usually tell—as can most pastors—by the reaction to my preaching, which ones tithe and which ones don't. In fact, some people have bluntly told me they don't believe that tithing is mandated in Scripture.

Several years ago, I attacked the problem of giving after studying a course in human relations during my MBA studies. I discovered that different personalities view things in different ways. Using that information, marketers target certain products and aim their advertising at specific groups of people. Although it was not a profound discovery, it certainly helped me understand how Christians look at giving.

Then I discovered that Jesus spoke about possessions in 38 percent of His parables. If He spent that much time relating to possessions and what to do with them, I decided He must have had a reason.

One day I correlated the personalities that marketers target to sell their products and related them to the teachings of Jesus concerning possessions in the Bible. I discovered that He had a message to fit each different personality type in order to achieve a response. That's probably why Jesus used so many different parables.

Every person has one of five personalities, and each looks at the world of finance and giving in completely different ways.

Have you noticed that Kmart and Wal-Mart are sometimes located in the same town and often on the same street near each other? Doesn't that seem odd since they both sell the same products at the same discount prices?

People are fickle, however, and will choose one store over the other for different reasons. No one knows why, but certain people shop at Kmart because they prefer the big red K. Others admire Sam Walton and, therefore, go to Wal-Mart. Marketing specialists have yet to figure out this phenomenon, but they know it takes place.

The same factors affect how we view money and why we give or don't give to the church. In my dealings with people in this area, I have found that Christians basically fall into one of five different types when it comes to giving and tithing. See where you fit.

Hoarders

These are people who like to save and budget money. Because of this unique personality trait, it takes a lot of time to convince them to part with their money for the Lord's work. In addition, hoarders want to make sure the church doesn't spend too much money. That's why they are usually the ones who protest when it comes to spending out of the church budget for special projects. This type of person seldom gives to special offerings.

Money Monks

These rather austere and astute people believe the church should be run like a monastery. The money monks like to know everything to the minutest detail before they turn loose of a dime. That's why they usually want to serve on committees. If they don't, they won't give to the project or will hold up its progress.

Money Avoiders

These people abdicate their responsibilities in giving and let everybody else take care of them. It's not that they don't have money. They do—they just don't want to give it up.

One pastor calls this group the UFOs—not Unidentified Flying Objects but Unidentified Freeloading Onlookers. To defend their position, the money avoiders can usually come up with several reasons why the Bible does not teach tithing.

Money Amassers

These are givers who have amassed money for themselves. Before you can get them to give, however, they will insist on being in control. Money amassers will not let their money go until you have appointed them to a committee and, most preferably, as chairman of the committee. Because they do not want the church to waste money, they insist on controlling how the money is spent.

Spenders

This is the largest group in the church. These are the merciful people who come to church and leave the worship service heavy-hearted without giving anything. They have no money to give because they have spent it all.

Spenders are teachable, however, and will respond to the financial principles taught in God's Word. When they do get their finances straightened out, they will fully support the church. Whenever they are challenged to give, they will respond over and beyond what is necessary. As a result, God continuously blesses and prospers them.

WHY GOD GIVES US MONEY

During your lifetime, you will earn an enormous amount of money. If you had all of that money at one time, you would be very wealthy. But most people don't get it all at once. Instead, God doles it out to us over a period of time. Why? I believe He wants to see how we will manage what He does give us. Whether or not it is enough depends on how responsible we are in using it.

Those who spend their money wisely are given more. Remember, Jesus said:

He that is faithful in that which is least is faithful also in much: and he that is unjust in the least is unjust also in much. If therefore ye have not been faithful in the unrighteous mammon, who will commit to your trust the true riches? And if ye have not been faithful in that which is another man's, who shall give you that which is your own? No servant can serve two masters: for either he will hate the one, and love the other; or else he will hold to the one, and despise the other. Ye cannot serve God and mammon. (Luke 16:10–13)

God owns all your money. Your paycheck, the money in your bank account, even that cash you have buried in the backyard or stuck under your mattress does not belong to you.

God Himself has said, "The silver is mine, and the gold is mine, saith the LORD of Hosts" (Hag. 2:8). All the silver and gold still to be mined does not belong to the earth, it belongs to the Lord. All the money in your IRA and retirement account and all the investments in your portfolio do not belong to you—they belong to the Lord.

God commanded us never to forget that fact when He said, "But thou shalt remember the LORD thy God: for it is he that giveth thee power to get wealth, that he may establish his covenant which he sware unto thy fathers, as it is this day" (Deut. 8:18). If we are blessed of the Lord financially, it is only because God has allowed us to prosper. It's not something that our grand intelligence or our great personalities and character have garnished.

The apostle Paul made this fact clear when he wrote, "For who maketh thee to differ from another? and what hast thou that thou didst not receive? now if thou didst receive it, why dost thou glory, as if thou hadst not received it?" (1 Cor. 4:7).

Some Americans flaunt their wealth as if by some great achievement they had amassed it by themselves. The Bible teaches just the opposite—that if we have obtained wealth or have received any blessing, it has come from Him. Who are we to think we have achieved anything on our own?

There is, however, an important factor that determines financial success. This verse from Proverbs makes it clear: "In all labour there is profit: but the talk of the lips tendeth only to penury" (14:23). What is the Bible saying here? That God has ordained a little four-letter word, and He expects us all to do it. It is called "work."

Many people in America are trying to figure out how to make it in life by devising schemes so they won't have to work. They don't realize that

*• **What if God called you to go somewhere and serve Him? Could you go?** • •*

God ordained work when our great-great-grandfather, Adam, rebelled in the garden. "God sent him forth from the garden of Eden, to till the ground" (Gen. 3:23) by the sweat of his face. Work is a result of the curse that affects our lives on this earth. Like it or not, we must go to work.

In today's economy, if we have a job, we should be thankful, much less think that we deserve to live a life of luxurious leisure. We only deserve what God has blessed us with to use and enjoy.

That brings me to one of the main reasons why I wrote this

book. I'm tired of seeing Christians squander their money, live in desperation, and forfeit giving to the furtherance of God's kingdom.

The purpose of teaching these financial principles is not so you can own a new Cadillac but so that your finances will be managed according to God's Word. As a result, your household will be blessed, and you can then bring the increases of God's blessings to Him.

Many Christians today live with financial difficulty and the guilt it brings because they cannot fulfill God's calling on their life. What if God called you to go somewhere and serve Him? Could you go? Some Christians turn God down because they have foolishly wasted their goods, and they can't respond.

Maybe you are thinking, *But God is not calling me to go to Africa or Brazil or anywhere else for that matter.* God is still calling. He calls every time there is a mission offering and you don't give or can't give. He calls you every week to bring your tithes and offerings to the storehouse and give so His work can prosper.

Where is the storehouse? I believe it is the local church where you attend—and hopefully, are a member. God uses the local church to accomplish His purpose of taking the gospel to a lost and dying world. Your greatest blessings will come—not from financial prosperity—but from the eternal rewards of seeing souls saved as a result of your giving.

God uses material things to accomplish His purposes on this earth, but they don't just fall out of the sky or happen by accident. The money invested in the kingdom of God comes from dedicated, committed Christians who are willing to do what God calls them to do.

Jesus said, "For where your treasure is, there will your heart be also" (Matt. 6:21). If your treasure is in the bank, then your heart will eventually become as dark and cold as a metal vault. But if you really love God, you'll surrender your life to Him and commit yourself and your resources to furthering His kingdom. Then, your heart will be full to overflowing with joy and peace and contentment—things money will never buy.

NOTES

. . . .

Myth 1: The End Is Near!

1. Larry Burkett, *The Coming Economic Earthquake* (Chicago: Moody Press, 1991), 205.
2. Edgar Whisenant, *88 Reasons Why the Second Advent Could Be in '88* (Nashville: World Bible Society, 1988).
3. Burkett, *Economic Earthquake*, 88.
4. Ibid., 8.
5. Ibid., 94.
6. Ibid., 122.
7. Larry Burkett, *Investing for the Future* (Wheaton, Ill.: Victor Books, 1992), 20–21.
8. Ibid., 20.
9. Ibid.
10. Ibid.
11. Burkett, *Economic Earthquake*, 8.
12. Ibid., 212.
13. Ibid., 222.
14. Burkett, *Investing for the Future*, 80–81.
15. William Glasgall, "Mega Bit Finance, Mega Trouble?" *Business Week*, 26 April 1993, 14.
16. Ibid.
17. Ibid.
18. Ibid.
19. Harry E. Figgie, *Bankruptcy 1995* (Boston: Little, Brown & Co., 1992), 1.
20. Ibid., 3.
21. Ibid., 84–85.
22. *The Economist*, 17 July 1993.
23. Burkett, *Economic Earthquake*, 71.
24. Burkett, *Investing for the Future*, 21.

. . . .

Myth 2: America Is Going Down the Tubes!

1. Robert Conquest, "Jefferson Lecture in the Humanities, 1993," *National Review*, 7 June 1993, 28.
2. Cited in Clarence B. Carson, *Basic Economics* (Wadley, Ala.: Textbook Committee, 1988), 97.
3. Ibid., 98.
4. Ibid.
5. Carson, *Basic Economics*, 101.
6. Walter Williams, "U.S. Thrives in Idea Marketplace," *Greensburg Tribune Review*, 14 July 1993.
7. Ibid.
8. Ibid.
9. Michael Prowse, "Is America in Decline?" *Harvard Business Review*, July-Aug. 1992, 41.
10. Ibid., 42.
11. Harry S. Dent, Jr., *The Great Boom Ahead: Your Comprehensive Guide to Personal and Business Profit in the New Era of Prosperity* (New York: Hyperion, 1993), 107–8.
12. Williams, "U.S. Thrives in Idea Marketplace."
13. Laurence Hecht and Peter Morici, "World View: Managing Risks In Mexico," *Harvard Business Review*, July-Aug. 1993, 32.
14. Ibid.
15. Dent, *The Great Boom*, 198.
16. Wesley J. Smith, "The Face-Off: Clinton and Small Business," *Home Office Computing*, Aug. 1993, 42.
17. Ibid.
18. Ibid.
19. R. Lee Sullivan, *Forbes*, 2 Aug. 1993.

Myth 3: The Deficit Is Killing Us!

1. Robert Eisner, "Sense and Nonsense about Budget Deficits," *Harvard Business Review*, May-June 1993, 99.
2. Ibid., 103.
3. Ibid.
4. Laurence J. Kotlikoff, "From Deficit Delusion to Generational Accounting," *Harvard Business Review*, May-June 1993, 104–5.
5. Stephen Moore, "Clinton's Dismal Scientists," *National Review*, 15 March 1993, 32–29.